Taste of Home

A TASTE OF HOME/READER'S DIGEST BOOK

Vice President/Executive Editor, Books: Heidi Reuter Lloyd
Project Editor: Julie Schnittka
Senior Editor, Retail Books: Jennifer Olski
Content Production Supervisor: Julie Wagner
Associate Layout Designer: Kathleen Bump
Cover Design: Courtney Lentz
Proofreaders: Linne Bruskewitz, Jean Duerst
Editorial Assistant: Barb Czysz
Recipe Testing and Editing: Taste of Home Test Kitchen
Food Photography: Reiman Photo Studio

Senior Vice President/Editor in Chief: Catherine Cassidy
Chief Marketing Officer: Lisa Karpinski
President, Consumer Marketing: Dawn Zier
President, Food & Entertaining: Suzanne M. Grimes
President and Chief Executive Officer: Mary G. Berner

International Standard Book Number (10): 0-89821-699-0
International Standard Book Number (13): 978-0-89821-699-8
Library of Congress Control Number: 2008921814

For other *Taste of Home* books and products, visit **www.tasteofhome.com.**
For more Reader's Digest products and information, visit
www.rd.com (in the United States) or **www.rd.ca** (in Canada).

PRINTED IN CHINA
3 5 7 9 10 8 6 4 2

halloween
party favorites

Getting into a spooky spirit on October 31 will be a snap if you turn to this devilishly good collection featuring three creepy cookbooks in one.

In *Halloween Food & Fun*, *Spirited Shindigs* and *Bewitching Bashes*, we've scared up 294 ghoulish goodies guaranteed to frighten away your fears of hosting a haunting Halloween bash.

You won't need hocus-pocus to concoct these simple-to-fix foods because they've all been tested and approved by the Taste of Home Kitchen Staff.

Mummy Man Cheese Spread, Scarecrow Veggie Pizza, Serpent Tongue Potatoes and Magic Potion Punch will jump start your eye-popping party.

For a fiendish feast, turn to Bat Wing Soup, Jack-o'-Lantern Burgers, Spooky Monster Sandwiches, Slimy Red Goop Salad and Pumpkin Stew.

Little goblins will do tricks for treats like Scaredy-Cat Cupcakes, Halloween Caramel Apples, Pretzel Pumpkin Grahams and Quick Ghost Cookies.

Other to-die-for desserts include Haunted House Cake, Great Pumpkin Brownie, Spiderweb Cheesecake, Mousse-Filled Witches' Hats and Pumpkin Trifle.

Your eerie event will come together like magic when you rely on our spooky-but-easy party ideas, creepy crafts and clever costumes.

It's all here in *Halloween Food & Fun*, *Spirited Shindigs* and *Bewitching Bashes*. So turn the page and "enter"...if you dare!

Halloween Food & Fun

CONTENTS · Halloween Food & Fun

Haunting Halloween Buffets

Recipes

Projects

Wiggly Pumpkins

(Pictured at far right)

Pumpkin-shaped cookie cutters form these festive finger snacks. My grandkids love them!
— Frances Poste, Wall, South Dakota

    2 packages (6 ounces *each*) orange gelatin
2-1/2 cups boiling water
    1 cup cold milk
    1 package (3.4 ounces) instant vanilla
        pudding mix
Candy corn
Black licorice *and/or* gumdrops

Dissolve gelatin in water; set aside for 30 minutes. Whisk milk and pudding mix until smooth, about 1 minute. Pour into gelatin; whisk until blended.

Pour into 13-in. x 9-in. x 2-in. pan coated with cooking spray. Chill until set. Cut into circles or use a pumpkin-shaped cookie cutter. Just before serving, add the candy eyes and mouths. **Yield:** 14-16 servings.

Halloween Layer Cake

(Pictured at far right)

There's nothing "scary" about this chocolaty cake. I make it every Halloween for my husband and our three children. — Karen Wirth, Tavistock, Ontario

    1 cup butter, softened
    2 cups sugar
    4 eggs
    3 cups all-purpose flour
    1 tablespoon baking powder
1/2 teaspoon salt
    1 cup milk
1/4 cup baking cocoa
1/4 cup water
1/2 teaspoon vanilla extract
1/2 teaspoon orange extract
    1 tablespoon grated orange peel
  10 drops yellow food coloring
    6 drops red food coloring
FROSTING:
    3 packages (3 ounces *each*) cream cheese,
        softened
5-3/4 cups confectioners' sugar
    2 tablespoons milk
    8 drops yellow food coloring
    6 drops red food coloring
GLAZE:
    3 squares (1 ounce *each*) semisweet chocolate
1/3 cup heavy whipping cream
Candy corn

In a mixing bowl, cream butter and sugar until light and fluffy. Add eggs, one at a time, beating well after each. Combine flour, baking powder and salt; add alternately with milk to creamed mixture. Mix well.

In another bowl, combine the cocoa, water and vanilla; stir in 2 cups cake batter. Pour into a greased and floured 9-in. round baking pan. Add the orange extract, peel and food coloring to the remaining batter. Pour into two greased and floured 9-in. round baking pans. Bake at 350° for 30 minutes or until a toothpick inserted near the center comes out clean. Cool in pans for 10 minutes before removing to wire racks to cool completely.

In a mixing bowl, beat all frosting ingredients until smooth. Place one orange cake layer on a cake plate; spread with 1/2 cup frosting. Top with chocolate layer; spread with 1/2 cup frosting. Top with second orange layer. Frost the sides and top of cake.

Microwave chocolate and cream on high 1-1/2 minutes or until melted, stirring once. Stir until smooth; let cool minutes. Slowly pour over cake, letting glaze drizzle down sides. Garnish with candy. **Yield:** 12-16 servings.

Quick Ghost Cookies

(Pictured at right)

It's a snap to dress up store-bought peanut butter cookies for Halloween parties. These yummy treats are a real hit. — Denise Smith, Lusk, Wyoming

    1 pound white candy coating, cut into chunks
    1 package (1 pound) Nutter Butter peanut
        butter cookies
Mini semisweet chocolate chips

In top of double boiler over simmering water, melt candy coating, stirring occasionally. Dip cookies into coating, covering completely. Set on waxed paper to cool.

Brush ends with a pastry brush dipped in coating where fingers touched cookies. While coating is still warm, place two chips on each cookie for eyes. **Yield:** about 3 dozen.

Quick Ghost Cookies
Halloween Layer Cake
Wiggly Pumpkins
Cream Puff Monsters (p. 8)

Frankenstein Salads

(Pictured below and on page 10)

Kids of all ages will love these fruity Frankenstein faces made from rectangles of jiggly green gelatin resting on bright purple kale. Our Test Kitchen staff added bean sprout hair, jelly bean eyes and a nose, mini marshmallow bolts and a sour cream smile to give this monster some playful personality.

> **2 packages (6 ounces *each*) lime gelatin**
> **2-1/2 cups boiling water**
> **3/4 cup canned bean sprouts**
> **12 orange jelly beans**
> **6 red jelly beans**
> **3 tablespoons sour cream**
> **12 miniature marshmallows**
> **Purple kale, optional**

In a bowl, dissolve gelatin in water. Pour into an 8-in. square pan coated with cooking spray. Refrigerate for 4 hours or until firm.

Cut into six rectangles; place each on a plate. Decorate with bean sprouts for hair, orange jelly beans for eyes and a red jelly bean for nose.

Fill a small plastic bag with sour cream; cut a small hole in the corner of the bag. Pipe a jagged smile on face. Place marshmallows on side of head for bolts. Garnish plates with kale if desired. **Yield:** 6 servings.

Cream Puff Monsters

(Pictured on page 7)

Cute-as-can-be are these "costumed" cream puffs. Their fun, freaky faces are limited only by your imagination. —Susan Seymour, Valatie, New York

> **3/4 cup plus 2 tablespoons all-purpose flour**
> **2 tablespoons sugar**
> **2 tablespoons baking cocoa**
> **1 cup water**
> **1/2 cup butter**
> **4 eggs**
> **1 package (3.9 ounces) instant chocolate pudding mix**
> **2 cups cold milk**
> **Yellow, red, blue and green food coloring**
> **1 can (16 ounces) vanilla frosting**
> **Sprinkles, small candies and slivered almonds**

Combine flour, sugar and cocoa; set aside. In a saucepan over medium heat, bring water and butter to a boil; reduce heat to low. Add flour mixture all at once; stir until a smooth ball forms. Remove from the heat; let stand 5 minutes. Add eggs, one at a time, beating well after each. Beat until smooth.

Cover baking sheets with foil; grease foil. Drop batter by tablespoonfuls at least 2 in. apart onto baking sheets. Bake at 400° for 25-30 minutes or until lightly browned. Lift foil and transfer to a wire rack. Immediately cut a slit in each puff to allow steam to escape; cool.

Beat pudding mix and milk according to package directions; chill. When puffs are cool, split and remove soft dough from inside. Spoon pudding into puffs; replace tops. Following food coloring package directions, combine red and yellow to make orange, and red and blue to make purple. Divide frosting among three microwave-safe bowls; tint with orange, purple and green food coloring. Microwave frosting until thin (not runny).

Spoon one or more colors onto puffs. Add sprinkles and candy for eyes; use almonds for teeth or whiskers. Chill. **Yield:** 2 dozen.

Sweet Spooks Treat Jar

(Pictured below)

his cute favor is easy to create with a toddler's food jar. My daughter and I both hit on the idea one day when he was munching on some candy corn. Painted so that the treats inside look like happy figures, the handmade vor always gets smiles at Halloween parties.
—Angie Yeager, Mahaffey, Pennsylvania

laterials Needed:

atterns at bottom right; junior-size baby food jar; nough candy corn to fill jar; air-dry enamel paints—Ul- a White and Ultra Black (Angie used Delta Air-Dry rmEnamel paints); surface cleaner and conditioner for r-dry enamel paints; clear satin glaze for air-dry namel paints; clear gloss glaze (optional); paintbrush- —No. 0 round and large flat; toothpick; 5-inch square Halloween print fabric; natural raffia.

nished Size:

ecorated treat jar is about 3-1/2 inches high x 2-1/4 ches wide.

irections:

horoughly wash the baby food jar and lid in warm apy water. When completely dry, fill with candy rn, packing tightly.

Add lid and gently shake jar. If candies shift position, en jar, add more candy corn and replace lid. Repeat needed until candies don't move.

Following the manufacturer's instructions, prepare jar ith surface cleaner and conditioner for air-dry enam- paints.

Paint the glass with a basecoat of clear satin glaze. t dry.

Look for candy pieces that can be seen in full view om the outside of the jar. Following the instructions elow, paint faces on the jar so they appear to be on ese candy pieces.

To paint the faces, use the tip of a paintbrush handle dab on two Ultra White dots for each set of eyes. When dry, use a toothpick to dab a tiny Ultra Black dot in each eye, changing the position on each face as shown on face pat- terns or as desired. Use the No. 0 round brush and Ultra Black to paint each mouth as shown on the face pat-

FACE PATTERNS

terns or as desired. When dry, add another coat if need- ed. Let dry.

Add a topcoat of either clear satin glaze or clear gloss glaze. Let dry.

Center the Halloween print fabric square, right side up, on top of the lid. Tie raffia around the rim of the jar to hold fabric in place and make a bow.

Frankenstein Salads (p. 8)
Bat Wing Soup
Great Pumpkin Sandwiches
Black Cat Cupcakes (p. 12)

Turn Bread into Bat Wings

To make bat wings to float in Bat Wing Soup (pictured at left), remove the crusts from the bread. Flatten the bread with a rolling pin. Using a kitchen shears and referring to the diagram at right, cut each slice in half diagonally, cutting wavy lines to resemble bat wings.

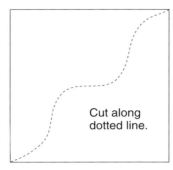

Cut along dotted line.

Bat Wing Soup

(Pictured at left)

Convenient stewed tomatoes are the base for this spooky soup that gets extra richness from whipping cream. Our home economists garnished it with toasty bat wings (see directions above).

- **4 garlic cloves, peeled**
- **2 tablespoons vegetable oil**
- **4 cans (14-1/2 ounces *each*) stewed tomatoes**
- **1/2 cup heavy whipping cream**
- **6 slices bread, crusts removed**
- **2 tablespoons butter, softened**
- **2 teaspoons Italian seasoning**

In a saucepan, saute garlic in oil until tender. In a blender or food processor, process garlic and tomatoes in batches until smooth. Return all to the pan; bring to a boil. Reduce heat to low. Add cream and heat through.

Follow the directions above to cut bat wings from slices of bread. Place on an ungreased baking sheet. Spread with butter; sprinkle with Italian seasoning. Bake at 400° for 5-8 minutes or until golden brown, turning once. Add two wings to each bowl of soup. Serve immediately. **Yield:** 6 servings.

Great Pumpkin Sandwiches

(Pictured at far left)

Visited by the Great Pumpkin? Your guests might think so when you serve these cheesy sandwiches our Test Kitchen created. A celery stick with leaves makes them look like fresh-picked pumpkins.

- **3 cups (12 ounces) shredded cheddar cheese**
- **3/4 cup butter, softened**
- **3 eggs**
- **1/2 teaspoon garlic salt**
- **1/2 teaspoon onion salt**
- **9 flour tortillas (6 inches)**
- **Paprika**
- **3 celery sticks with leaves, optional**

In a food processor, blend cheese and butter. Add the eggs, garlic salt and onion salt; process for 1 minute or until creamy. Spread 1/2 cupful on each tortilla. Stack three tortillas, cheese side up, for each sandwich; sprinkle with paprika. Place on an ungreased baking sheet.

Bake at 400° for 10-15 minutes or until golden and bubbly. If desired, add the celery to resemble a pumpkin stem. Cut sandwiches into halves to serve. **Yield:** 6 servings.

Halloween Fun Fact

Halloween is the third largest party day of the year in the U.S., behind New Year's Eve and Super Bowl Sunday.

(Source: Hallmark Cards)

Black Cat Cupcakes

(Pictured above and on page 10)

If a black cat crosses your path, we hope it's one of these cute chocolaty creations from our Test Kitchen. This time-saving recipe relies on a boxed cake mix, prepared frosting and simple decorations.

  1 package (18-1/4 ounces) chocolate cake mix
  1 can (16 ounces) dark chocolate frosting
  12 chocolate cream–filled sandwich cookies, quartered
  48 yellow jelly beans
  24 black jelly beans
  24 pieces black rope licorice

Prepare and bake cake according to package directions for cupcakes, using paper-lined muffin cups. Cool for 10 minutes; remove from pans to wire racks to cool completely. Frost tops of cupcakes. Insert two cookie pieces into each for ears. Add yellow jelly beans for eyes and a black jelly bean for nose. Cut each piece of licorice into

thirds, then in half; place three halves on each side of nose for whiskers. **Yield:** 2 dozen.

Jack-o'-Lantern Burgers

(Pictured below and on page 15)

Cut these faces close to the center of the cheese slice because the cheese spreads out when it melts.
—*Vicki Schlechter, Davis, California*

  1 envelope onion soup mix
  1/4 cup ketchup
  2 tablespoons brown sugar
  2 teaspoons prepared horseradish
  2 teaspoons chili powder
  2-1/2 pounds ground beef
  10 slices process American cheese
  10 hamburger buns, split

In a bowl, combine soup mix, ketchup, brown sugar, horseradish and chili powder. Add beef; mix well. Shape into 10 patties. Grill, broil or pan-fry until the meat is no longer pink.

Cut eyes, nose and mouth out of each cheese slice to create a jack-o'-lantern. Place cheese on burgers; cook until cheese is slightly melted, about 1 minute. Serve on buns. **Yield:** 10 servings.

No-Sew Fabric Pumpkins

(Pictured below)

These quick-to-craft pumpkins ripen easily...and last a lifetime! Instead of carving real pumpkins, I decided to try something different. First, I wrapped quilt batting around tissue paper and covered it with fabric. Then I wound twine around a folded brown sack for a stem. The pumpkins are fun to make for young and old alike.

—Marjorie Goodman, State Center, Iowa

Materials Needed for Each:
8-inch square of 100% cotton or cotton-blend fabric—fall novelty print, orange check or orange solid; 8-inch x 5-inch piece of brown paper grocery bag; roll of tissue paper; polyester quilt batting; 3-ply jute string; artificial fall leaf or green ivy spray; 18 inches of green, gold or orange 20-gauge craft wire (optional); glue gun and glue stick; wire cutters; scissors.

Finished Size:
The pumpkins measure 5 to 6 inches wide x 8 to 9 inches high.

Directions for Each:
Wrap roll of tissue paper with enough polyester quilt batting to make a pumpkin shape, leaving one end of the cardboard roll uncovered.

Place fabric square wrong side up on a flat surface. Center batting-covered roll on top of fabric square with uncovered end of roll facing up.

Bring the corners of the fabric up to center of the roll. Stuff the fabric into uncovered end of roll, covering batting and maintaining the pumpkin shape as shown in the photo above.

Fold the 8-inch x 5-inch piece of brown paper grocery bag in half, making a 4-inch x 5-inch rectangle. Starting at one short end, roll paper rectangle to make a 4-inch-long stem about 1 inch in diameter. Glue stem as needed to hold.

Wrap jute string around stem as shown in photo. Trim excess and glue ends to hold.

Insert one end of stem into opening on top of pumpkin. Glue to hold.

Use wire cutters to trim stem from fall leaf or ivy spray. Glue leaves or ivy around the base of the stem as shown in the photo.

Wrap center of craft wire around base of stem and coil ends for tendrils if desired.

Broccoli Boo Salad

(Pictured at far right)

This refreshing salad is a colorful accompaniment and can be made a day ahead. For a startling garnish, I place a plastic spider (available at craft stores) in the center of each serving. If your guests are young, you may prefer to use plastic spiders to decorate the table rather than as a spooky surprise on the salad.
—Vicki Schlechter, Davis, California

> 1 cup mayonnaise
> 1/4 cup sugar
> 2 tablespoons white vinegar
> 8 cups broccoli florets
> 1 can (11 ounces) mandarin oranges, drained
> 1/2 cup chopped red onion
> 6 to 8 bacon strips, cooked and crumbled
> 1/2 cup raisins

In a small bowl, whisk mayonnaise, sugar and vinegar. Cover and refrigerate for at least 2 hours. In a large bowl, combine broccoli, oranges, onion, bacon and raisins. Add dressing and toss to coat. Cover and refrigerate for 1 hour. **Yield:** 10-12 servings.

Graveyard Cake

(Pictured at far right)

With its "cemetery" topping, this eye-catching cake is a hit! Cookie tombstones and whipped-topping ghosts set an eerie mood atop the haunted holiday dessert. To complete the ghoulish graveyard, I add plenty of pumpkin-shaped candies and gummy worms. —*Vicki Schlechter, Davis, California*

> 2 cups all-purpose flour
> 2 cups sugar
> 1 teaspoon baking soda
> 1/2 teaspoon salt
> 1 cup butter
> 1 cup water
> 1/4 cup baking cocoa
> 1/2 cup sour cream
> 2 eggs
> **FROSTING:**
> 1/4 cup butter

> 3 tablespoons milk
> 2 tablespoons baking cocoa
> 2 cups confectioners' sugar
> 1/2 teaspoon vanilla extract
> 18 cream-filled chocolate sandwich cookies
> **Green and brown decorator's icing *or* gel**
> 9 cream-filled oval vanilla sandwich cookies
> 1 cup whipped topping
> **Pumpkin candies and gummy worms, optional**

In a mixing bowl, combine flour, sugar, baking soda and salt; set aside. In a saucepan, combine butter, water and cocoa; bring to a boil over medium heat. Add to flour mixture; beat well. Beat in sour cream and eggs. Pour into a greased 13-in. x 9-in. x 2-in. baking pan. Bake at 350° for 35-38 minutes or until a toothpick inserted near the center comes out clean. Cool on a wire rack for 5 minutes.

Meanwhile, for frosting, in a saucepan, combine butter, milk and cocoa; bring to a boil. Remove from the heat; stir in sugar and vanilla. Pour over warm cake. Crumble chocolate cookies; sprinkle over frosting while still warm. Cool completely.

For tombstones, use icing to decorate vanilla cookies with words or faces; place on cake. For ghosts, make mounds of whipped topping; use icing to add eyes and mouths as desired. Refrigerate for at least 1 hour. Just before serving, add pumpkins and gummy worms if desired. **Yield:** 16 servings.

Wormy Orange Punch

(Pictured at right)

This chilling thirst-quencher doesn't appear creepy at all...until I drape gummy worms over the side of the bowl. It's a simple way to make this frothy beverage festive for October events. I also drop a worm into each guest's cup, which never fails to get grins.
—Vicki Schlechter, Davis, California

> 1 gallon orange sherbet, softened
> 1 quart pineapple juice, chilled
> 1 liter lemon-lime soda, chilled
> **Gummy worms**

Combine sherbet and pineapple juice in a punch bowl; stir well. Add soda; stir until sherbet is almost dissolved. Decorate bowl with gummy worms. Serve immediately. **Yield:** 20 (1-cup) servings.

Jack-o'-Lantern Burgers (p. 12)
Wormy Orange Punch
Graveyard Cake
Broccoli Boo Salad

Creepy Cupcakes
Halloween Punch
Spooky Cream Puffs

Trick or Treat
Something Sweet

Halloween Punch

(Pictured at left)

...ting right into October fun is this suitably orange-...lored sipper. —Sue Ross, Casa Grande, Arizona

1 can (46 ounces) pineapple juice, *divided*
1 package (3 ounces) orange gelatin
1 carton (64 ounces) orange juice
1 liter ginger ale, chilled
1 quart orange sherbet

...a saucepan, bring 1 cup of pineapple juice to a boil. ...r in gelatin until dissolved. Cool; transfer to a large ...tcher or container. Add orange juice and remaining ...neapple juice. Chill. Just before serving, pour into a ...nch bowl; add ginger ale and mix well. Top with ...ops of sherbet. **Yield:** 20-24 servings.

Creepy Cupcakes

(Pictured at left)

...om our Test Kitchen staff, these cute spiders on cob-...ebs will "catch" attention fast!

1 package (18-1/4 ounces) devil's food
   cake mix
1/4 cup butter, softened
1 package (3 ounces) cream cheese, softened
3 cups confectioners' sugar
2 tablespoons plus 1 teaspoon milk, *divided*
1/2 teaspoon vanilla extract
...d and yellow liquid food coloring *or* orange paste
   food coloring
1 tablespoon baking cocoa
...und pastry tip #3
9 chocolate kisses
9 semisweet chocolate chips
...ack shoestring licorice, cut into 3/4-inch pieces
18 white nonpareils

...epare cake mix according to package directions. Fill ...eased jumbo muffin cups with 1/2 cup batter. Bake at ...0° for 25-30 minutes or until a toothpick comes out ...ean. Cool for 5 minutes before removing from pans to ...re racks to cool completely. Cut a thin slice off the top ...each cupcake.

...In a mixing bowl, cream butter, cream cheese, con-...ctioners' sugar, 2 tablespoons milk and vanilla; mix ...ell. Remove 1 cup; tint orange and frost cupcakes. To

the remaining frosting, add baking cocoa and remaining milk. Cut a small hole in the corner of a pastry or plastic bag; insert round tip. Fill with chocolate frosting. Pipe a web on each cupcake; set remaining frosting aside.

For spider, insert chocolate kiss, point side down, near edge of cupcake. For head, insert chocolate chip, point side down, next to kiss. For legs, place four licorice pieces on each side of kiss. For eyes, pipe two small circles of chocolate frosting on chocolate chip; insert nonpareils. **Yield:** 9 cupcakes.

Spooky Cream Puffs

(Pictured at far left)

Boo! These goblins from our home economists are sure to spark smiles at Halloween events.

1 cup water
1/2 cup butter
1 teaspoon sugar
1/4 teaspoon salt
1 cup all-purpose flour
4 eggs
1 package (3 ounces) cream cheese, softened
1/3 cup peanut butter
1 tablespoon confectioners' sugar
1/4 cup strawberry jam
2 cups whipped topping
Additional confectioners' sugar
18 semisweet chocolate chips *or* **miniature**
   M&M's

In a large saucepan, bring water, butter, sugar and salt to a boil. Add flour all at once and stir until a smooth ball forms. Remove from the heat; let stand for 5 minutes. Add eggs, one at a time, beating well after each addition. Continue beating until mixture is smooth and shiny.

Drop by 1/3 cupfuls onto ungreased baking sheets; spread into 4-in. x 3-in. ovals. Using a knife coated with cooking spray, shape four triangles on one short side of each. Bake at 400° for 30-35 minutes or until golden brown. Remove to wire racks to cool.

Meanwhile, in a bowl, beat the cream cheese, peanut butter and confectioners' sugar until smooth. Add jam; mix well. Fold in whipped topping; set aside 1 tablespoon. Split cream puffs in half; remove dough from the inside. Fill with cream mixture and replace tops. Dust with confectioners' sugar. For eyes, place two small dots of filling on each ghost; top with chocolate chips. **Yield:** 9 cream puffs.

Barbecued Pork Sandwiches

(Pictured at far right)

Spirits will rise with every bite of these sandwiches! Family and friends always ask me to bring these to parties and other get-togethers.
—Mrs. Jerome Privitera, Geneva, Ohio

   3 medium onions, chopped
   4 cups ketchup
   2 cups water
   2 tablespoons Worcestershire sauce
   1-1/2 teaspoons white vinegar
   2-1/2 teaspoons pepper
   1 teaspoon salt
   1 teaspoon *each* paprika and chili powder
   1/2 teaspoon cayenne pepper
   1 boneless pork shoulder roast (3-1/2 to 4 pounds)
   12 to 16 sandwich buns

In a bowl, combine onions, ketchup, water, Worcestershire sauce, vinegar and seasonings. Place pork in a large roasting pan or Dutch oven; pour sauce over pork. Cover and bake at 325° for 6 hours.

Remove roast and cool for 20 minutes; shred with a fork. Return to sauce in pan and heat through. Fill buns using a slotted spoon. **Yield:** 12-16 servings.

Potato Wedges

(Pictured above far right)

These spuds are sure to root up fun at your spooky affair. Our Test Kitchen staff came up with these wedges to flavor Halloween gatherings. But the well-seasoned potatoes are so tasty and easy to prepare, you'll want to make them for other celebrations and even suppers during the week.

   2 tablespoons vegetable oil
   1/4 cup Italian-seasoned bread crumbs
   2 tablespoons grated Parmesan cheese
   1 teaspoon Italian seasoning
   1/2 teaspoon paprika
   1/2 teaspoon garlic salt

   4 medium unpeeled potatoes (about 1-1/2 pounds)

Spread oil over the bottom of a 13-in. x 9-in. x 2-in. baking pan. Combine the next five ingredients in a large plastic bag. Cut each potato lengthwise into eight wedges. Place half of the potatoes in the bag; shake well to coat. Place in a single layer in pan. Repeat with remaining potatoes. Bake, uncovered, at 350° for 40-45 minutes or until tender, turning once after 25 minutes. **Yield:** 6-8 servings.

Lemon Cider

(Pictured at right)

With a quick wave of your kitchen "wand," you can conjure up a beverage that's ripe with apple and citrus flavor. I got the idea from my sister, who operates an apple orchard with her husband. She's a wizard when it comes to creating new fruit recipes.
—Annette Engelbert, Bruce Crossing, Michigan

   1 gallon apple cider
   1 can (12 ounces) frozen lemonade concentrate, thawed
   1 lemon, thinly sliced *or* cinnamon sticks

In a punch bowl, combine cider and lemonade; mix well. Float lemon slices on top. Or, to serve warm, heat cider and lemonade; garnish individual servings with cinnamon stick. **Yield:** 4-1/2 quarts.

Mice Creams

(Pictured above right)

Mice can be nice—at least when they're as charming as these critters! Kids of all ages enjoy seeing—and eating—these creature treats. They're usually the first dessert to disappear at Halloween parties.
—Marilyn Dunlap, Fresno, California

   1 pint vanilla ice cream
   1 package (6-count) single-serve graham cracker crusts
   12 chocolate-covered mint cookies

Lemon Cider
Barbecued Pork Sandwiches
Spider Tartlets
Mice Creams
Potato Wedges

3 chocolate twigs, halved *or* 6 pieces (3 inches
   each) black shoestring licorice
18 brown M&M's
2 teaspoons chocolate sprinkles

Place one round scoop of ice cream into each crust. Tuck
in cookies for ears and twigs or licorice for tail into
the cream. Press M&M's in place for eyes and nose.
Place chocolate sprinkles around nose for whiskers.
Yield: 6 servings.

Spider Tartlets

(Pictured above)

These creepy crawlers will spin plenty of excitement
into your October events. For extra fun, just make
the pudding ahead of time, then let your party guests
decorate their own spooky spiders.
—*Lorna Schledorn, West Columbia, South Carolina*

1 package (3.9 ounces) instant chocolate
   pudding mix
2 cups cold milk
1 package (6-count) single-serve graham
   cracker crusts
1/2 cup finely crushed chocolate sandwich
   cookies
48 pieces (3-1/2 inches *each*) red *or* black
   shoestring licorice
12 red *or* green M&M's

Prepare pudding with milk according to package directions. Spoon into crusts; sprinkle with cookie crumbs.
Push licorice into pudding to form legs, eight per spider
(the bent pieces work best). Press M&M's in place for
eyes. Refrigerate until serving. **Yield:** 6 servings.

Orange Witches' Brew Punch

(Pictured at far right)

This slushy punch requires no ice ring to keep it cold. It's not too sweet, so it appeals to everyone. Use this refreshing beverage for any celebration.
—Susan Johnson, Lyons, Kansas

    1 package (6 ounces) orange gelatin
    1/2 to 1 cup sugar
    2 cups boiling water
    1 can (46 ounces) apricot nectar
    1 can (46 ounces) pineapple juice
    3/4 cup lemon juice
    4 liters ginger ale, chilled

In a large bowl, dissolve gelatin and sugar in water. Stir in the apricot nectar, pineapple juice and lemon juice. Freeze in two 2-qt. freezer containers. Remove from the freezer 2-3 hours before serving.

Place contents of one container in a punch bowl; mash with potato masher. Stir in 2 liters of ginger ale just before serving. Repeat. **Yield:** about 8 quarts.

Bewitching Ice Cream Cones

(Pictured at far right)

Both young and old members of my family request these frozen treats every Halloween. Shaped like whimsical witches with ice cream cone "hats," they've been a fun tradition around here for many years.
—Edie DeSpain, Logan, Utah

    8 chocolate sugar ice cream cones
    1 tube chocolate decorating gel
    8 thin round chocolate wafers (2-1/4-inch
       diameter)
    1 quart pistachio, mint *or* ice cream of your
       choice
Black shoestring licorice
    16 semisweet chocolate chips
    8 pieces candy corn
Red decorating gel

Coat the edge of ice cream cones with decorating g[...] press chocolate wafer against gel to make brim of h[...] Set aside.

Drop eight scoops of ice cream onto a waxed pape[...] lined baking sheet. Cut licorice into strips for hair; pre[...] into ice cream. Add chocolate chips for eyes and can[...] corn for noses. Pipe red gel for mouths. Flatten scoo[...] slightly to hold hats in place; position hats on top [...] heads. Freeze ice cream for at least 2 hours or until ha[...] are set. Wrap each in plastic wrap after solidly froze[...] **Yield:** 8 servings.

Frightening Fingers

(Pictured at right)

These creepy-but-yummy cookies have becom[...] somewhat famous at the school our children atten[...] One year, I made more than 150 of these finge[...] shaped treats for their classroom Halloween partie[...]
—Natalie Hyde, Cambridge, Ontar[...]

    1 cup butter, softened
    1 cup confectioners' sugar
    1 egg
    1 teaspoon vanilla extract
    1 teaspoon almond extract
    2-3/4 cups all-purpose flour
    1 teaspoon baking powder
    1 teaspoon salt
Red decorating gel
    1/2 cup sliced almonds

In a mixing bowl, cream butter and sugar. Beat in the eg[...] and extracts. Combine the flour, baking powder and sal[...] gradually add to the creamed mixture. Divide dough in[...] to fourths. Cover and refrigerate for 30 minutes or un[...] til easy to handle.

Working with one piece of dough at a time, roll th[...] pieces into 1-in. balls. Shape the balls into 3-in. x 1/2-in[...] fingers. Using the flat tip of a table knife, make an in[...] dentation on one end of each finger for the fingernai[...] With a knife, make three slashes in the middle of eac[...] finger for the knuckle. Place 2 in. apart on lightly grease[...] baking sheets.

Bake at 325° for 20-25 minutes or until lightl[...] browned. Cool for 3 minutes. Squeeze a small amount o[...] red gel on nail bed; press a sliced almond over gel fo[...] nail, allowing gel to ooze around nail. Remove to wir[...] racks to cool. **Yield:** about 5 dozen cookies.

Orange Witches' Brew Punch
Frightening Fingers
Bewitching Ice Cream Cones
Black Cat Cookies (p. 23)
Marshmallow Ghosts (p. 23)

Candy Corn Clay Pot

(Pictured below and on page 21)

Want a centerpiece for a children's Halloween party? Create one that will give the youngsters "paws." Ju[...]
paint a clean clay pot like our home economists did, then fill it with candy and Black Cat Cookies (recipe at righ[...]
The kids can dip into this clever container for snacks. Or use the whole display as a door prize.

Materials Needed:
New 6-inch clay pot; paper towels; water basin; palette or foam plate; ruler; pencil; two wide flat rubber bands; foam brush; acrylic craft paints—white, yellow and orange; craft knife; candy corn; Black Cat Cookies (recipe at far right).

Finished Size:
Unfilled clay pot is 6 inches wide.

Directions:
Keep paper towels and a basin of water handy to clean brush. When painting, place dabs of each paint color onto palette or foam plate as needed. Let paint dry after each application.

Using ruler and pencil, measure and lightly mark a line around clay pot, positioning the line 2 inches from the top rim of pot. In the same way, mark a line 1-1[...] inches from bottom of pot. Center a rubber band ov[...] each marked line (see photo 1 below).

With foam brush and white paint, basecoat the bo[...] tom and top sections of pot, taking care not to allow t[...] paint to puddle along the edges of rubber bands (s[...] photo 2 below). In same way, basecoat inside the rim[...]

Add an additional coat of white paint to the po[...] bottom section only. Paint the pot's outer top sectio[...] and inside of rim yellow (see photo 3 below).

When paint is completely dry, use craft knife to sco[...] paint along painted edges of the rubber bands to brea[...] any paint seal that may have formed.

Position edge of bottom rubber band along the whi[...] painted edge and position edge of top rubber bar[...] along yellow painted edge to use as guides. Paint ce[...] ter section of pot orange (see photo 4 below). Let dr[...]

Remove rubber bands the same as before. Line p[...] with plastic wrap. Fill with candy and cookies.

Black Cat Cookies

(Pictured below left and on page 21)

...ur children look forward to helping me bake these ...ute cat cookies each year. They've become experts at ...aking the faces with candy corn and Red-Hots.
—Kathy Stock, Levasy, Missouri

- 1 cup butter, softened
- 2 cups sugar
- 2 eggs
- 3 teaspoons vanilla extract
- 3 cups all-purpose flour
- 1 cup baking cocoa
- 1/2 teaspoon baking powder
- 1/2 teaspoon baking soda
- 1/2 teaspoon salt
- 24 wooden craft *or* Popsicle sticks
- 48 pieces candy corn
- 24 red-hot candies

...a mixing bowl, cream butter and sugar. Beat in eggs ...d vanilla. Combine the flour, cocoa, baking powder, ...aking soda and salt; gradually add to the creamed mix-...re. Roll dough into 1-1/2-in. balls. Place 3 in. apart ...n lightly greased baking sheets. Insert a wooden stick ...to each cookie. Flatten with a glass dipped in sugar. ...nch top of cookie to form ears. For whiskers, press a ...rk twice into each cookie.

Bake at 350° for 10-12 minutes or until cookies are ...t. Remove from the oven; immediately press on candy ...orn for eyes and red-hot candies for noses. Remove to ...ire racks to cool. **Yield:** 2 dozen.

Marshmallow Ghosts

(Pictured on page 21)

...ids of all ages can help prepare these easy-to-...ake treats. With just three ingredients that I often ...eep on hand, they can be put together at a moment's ...otice. —Nancy Foust, Stoneboro, Pennsylvania

- 12 ounces white candy coating
- ...-1/2 cups miniature marshmallows
- ...hocolate decorating gel *or* assorted candies

...a microwave, melt candy coating; stir until smooth. ...ool slightly. Stir in marshmallows until coated. Drop by heaping tablespoonfuls onto waxed paper; smooth and flatten into ghost shapes. Decorate with gel or candies for eyes. Cool completely. Store in an airtight container. **Yield:** about 15 servings.

Monster Munchies

(Pictured on page 24)

Magically transform squash or pumpkin seeds into this spellbinding snack from our Test Kitchen using ranch salad dressing mix.

- 1 cup seeds from freshly cut squash *or* pumpkin, washed and dried
- 2 tablespoons vegetable oil
- 1 to 2 tablespoons ranch salad dressing mix

In a skillet, saute seeds in oil for 5 minutes or until light-ly browned. Using a slotted spoon, transfer seeds to an ungreased 15-in. x 10-in. x 1-in. baking pan.

Sprinkle with salad dressing mix; stir to coat. Spread in a single layer. Bake at 325° for 10-15 minutes or un-til crisp. Store in an airtight container for up to 3 weeks. **Yield:** 1 cup.

Boo Beverage

(Pictured on page 24)

Silly spooks formed with whipped topping garnish glasses of this smooth drink made with sherbet, or-ange juice and bananas, created by our Test Kitchen home economists.

- 2 cups orange juice
- 2 cups milk
- 2 pints orange sherbet
- 4 medium ripe bananas
- 2 cups whipped topping
- 18 miniature chocolate chips

In four batches, process the orange juice, milk, sherbet and bananas in a blender until smooth. Pour into glass-es. Cut a hole in the corner of a pastry or plastic bag; fill with whipped topping. Pipe a ghost shape on top of each beverage. Position chocolate chips for eyes. **Yield:** 9 servings.

Boo Beverage (p. 23)
Monster Munchies (p. 23)
Bewitching Chili
Cauldron Bread Bowls
Candy Corn Cookies

Bewitching Chili

(Pictured at left)

...round beef, red and green peppers, garlic and cumin ...ve great flavor to this hearty homespun chili.
—Anne Mitchell, Lynchburg, Ohio

- ...-1/2 pounds ground beef
- 1/2 cup chopped sweet red pepper
- 1/2 cup chopped green pepper
- 1 medium onion, chopped
- 1 garlic clove, minced
- 1 can (32 ounces) tomato juice
- 1 can (15-1/2 ounces) hot chili beans, undrained
- 1 can (14-1/2 ounces) diced tomatoes, undrained
- 1 can (10-1/2 ounces) condensed beef broth, undiluted
- 1 can (6 ounces) tomato paste
- 2 tablespoons chili powder
- ...-1/2 teaspoons ground cumin
- 1 teaspoon salt
- 1 teaspoon sugar
- 1/4 teaspoon pepper

...ur cream

...a Dutch oven, cook beef, peppers, onion and garlic ...ver medium heat until meat is no longer pink; drain. Stir ...tomato juice, beans, tomatoes, broth, tomato paste ...nd seasonings; bring to a boil.

Reduce heat; cover and simmer for 15 minutes. Serve ...Cauldron Bread Bowls (recipe below) if desired. Gar-...sh with sour cream. **Yield:** 8-10 servings.

Cauldron Bread Bowls

(Pictured at left)

...ur home economists used quick-rise yeast to pre-...are these make-ahead rolls. Hollow them out and fill ...em with Bewitching Chili (recipe above) or the dip ...f your choice for veggies or chips.

- 4 to 5 cups all-purpose flour
- 1 cup rye flour
- 3 teaspoons quick-rise yeast
- 3 teaspoons salt
- 2 teaspoons baking cocoa
- 2 cups water

- 1/3 cup molasses
- 1/4 cup vegetable oil

In a mixing bowl, combine 4 cups all-purpose flour, rye flour, yeast, salt and cocoa. Heat water, molasses and oil to 120°-130°. Add to dry ingredients; beat until smooth. Stir in enough remaining all-purpose flour to form a soft dough.

Turn onto a floured surface; knead until smooth and elastic, about 6-8 minutes. Cover and let rest for 10 minutes. Divide dough into eight portions; shape each into a ball. Place on greased baking sheets. Cover and let rise in a warm place until doubled, about 20 minutes.

Bake at 375° for 20 minutes or until golden brown. Cut the top fourth off each roll; carefully hollow out bottom, leaving a 1/4-in. shell (discard removed bread or save for another use). Fill each bowl with about 1/2 cup chili. Serve bread tops on the side if desired. **Yield:** 8 bread bowls.

Candy Corn Cookies

(Pictured at far left)

Get a head start on these buttery cookies from our Test Kitchen by shaping and chilling the dough ahead of time. When you're ready, just slice and bake the tri-color treats.

- 1-1/2 cups butter, softened
- 1-1/2 cups sugar
- 1/2 teaspoon vanilla extract
- 3 cups all-purpose flour
- 1 teaspoon baking soda
- 1/2 teaspoon salt

Yellow and orange paste food coloring

In a mixing bowl, cream butter and sugar. Beat in vanilla. Combine flour, baking soda and salt; gradually add to creamed mixture. Divide dough in half. Tint one portion yellow. Divide remaining dough into two-third and one-third portions. Tint the larger portion orange; leave smaller portion white.

Shape each portion of dough into two 8-in. logs. Flatten top and push sides in at a slight angle. Place orange logs on yellow logs; push the sides in at a slight angle. Top with white logs; form a rounded top. Wrap in plastic wrap. Chill for 4 hours or until firm.

Unwrap and cut into 1/4-in. slices. Place 2 in. apart on ungreased baking sheets. Bake at 350° for 10-12 minutes or until set. Remove to wire racks to cool. **Yield:** about 5 dozen.

Bewitching
Breads,
Soups + Salads

Recipes

Projects

sticks. Sprinkle half with sesame seeds and half with poppy seeds. Bake at 350° for 16-22 minutes or until golden brown. Remove to wire racks. **Yield:** 32 breadsticks.

Butternut Boats

(Pictured below)

My daughter, Jane, and I share recipes all the time. This thick and creamy soup, we both agree, is a real treat! To make it extra fun, use the squash shells as serving bowls and add sour cream "cobwebs."
—Evelyn Bentley, Ames, Iowa

    3 small butternut squash (about 1-1/2
       pounds *each*)
    4 large leeks (white portion only), sliced
    1 teaspoon dried thyme
    5 tablespoons butter
    3 cups chicken broth
1-1/4 teaspoons salt
  1/2 teaspoon pepper
  1/2 cup sour cream
Chopped chives *or* parsley

Cut squash in half; remove and discard seeds. Place with cut side down in a greased 13-in. x 9-in. x 2-in. baking pan. Add 1/4 in. of water to pan. Cover and bake at 375° for 40 minutes or until tender. Scoop out pulp, leaving about a 1/4-in. shell. Set shells and pulp aside.

In a large saucepan, saute leeks and thyme in butter until tender. Add pulp, broth, salt and pepper; simmer for

Soft Onion Breadsticks

(Pictured above)

These golden, chewy breads flavored with chopped onion have homemade taste that can't be beat.
—Maryellen Hays, Wolcottville, Indiana

  3/4 cup chopped onion
    1 tablespoon vegetable oil
2-1/4 teaspoons active dry yeast
  1/2 cup warm water (110° to 115°)
  1/2 cup warm milk (110° to 115°)
    2 eggs
  1/4 cup butter, softened
    1 tablespoon sugar
1-1/2 teaspoons salt
3-1/2 to 4 cups all-purpose flour
    2 tablespoons cold water
    2 tablespoons sesame seeds
    1 tablespoon poppy seeds

In a skillet, saute onion in oil until tender; cool. In a mixing bowl, dissolve yeast in warm water. Add milk, 1 egg, butter, sugar, salt and 1 cup flour. Beat on medium speed for 2 minutes. Stir in onion and enough remaining flour to form a soft dough. Turn onto a floured surface; knead until smooth and elastic, 6-8 minutes. Place in a greased bowl; turn once to grease top. Cover and let rise in a warm place until doubled, about 1 hour.

Punch dough down. Let stand for 10 minutes. Turn onto a lightly floured surface; divide into 32 pieces. Shape each piece into an 8-in. rope. Place ropes 2 in. apart on greased baking sheets. Cover and let rise for 15 minutes.

Beat cold water and remaining egg; brush over bread-

3 large potatoes, peeled and cut into 1-inch cubes
4 medium carrots, sliced
1 large green pepper, cut into 1/2-inch pieces
4 garlic cloves, minced
1 medium onion, chopped
2 teaspoons salt
1/2 teaspoon pepper
2 tablespoons instant beef bouillon granules
1 can (14-1/2 ounces) diced tomatoes
1 pumpkin (10 to 12 pounds)

In a Dutch oven, brown meat in 2 tablespoons oil. Add water, potatoes, carrots, green pepper, garlic, onion, salt and pepper. Cover and simmer for 2 hours. Stir in bouillon and tomatoes.

Wash pumpkin; cut a 6- to 8-in. circle around top stem. Remove top and set aside; discard seeds and loose fibers from inside. Place pumpkin in a shallow sturdy baking pan. Spoon stew into pumpkin and replace the top. Brush outside of pumpkin with remaining oil.

Bake at 325° for 2 hours or just until the pumpkin is tender (do not overbake). Serve stew from pumpkin, scooping out a little pumpkin with each serving. **Yield:** 8-10 servings.

0 minutes. Remove from the heat; cool slightly. Puree a blender; return to pan and heat through. Spoon in- squash shells.

Place sour cream in a heavy-duty resealable plastic ag; cut a small hole in corner of bag. Pipe a coil of sour ream over squash filling. Beginning at the center, use a oothpick to draw right angles across piped lines about /2 in. apart. Sprinkle with chives. **Yield:** 6 servings.

Pumpkin Stew

(Pictured above)

orepare this special stew when we have pumpkins in he garden. The stew is cooked and served in the umpkin shell. —Donna Mosher, Augusta, Montana

2 pounds beef stew meat, cut into 1-inch cubes
3 tablespoons vegetable oil, *divided*
1 cup water

Festive Fruit Salad

As colorful as the leaves on the autumn trees, this fruit salad disappears fast down to the very last spoonful. —Julianne Johnson, Grove City, Minnesota

1 can (20 ounces) pineapple chunks
1/2 cup sugar
3 tablespoons all-purpose flour
1 egg, lightly beaten
2 cans (11 ounces *each*) mandarin oranges, drained
1 can (20 ounces) pears, drained and chopped
3 kiwifruit, peeled and sliced
2 large unpeeled apples, chopped
1 cup pecan halves

Drain pineapple, reserving juice. Set pineapple aside. Pour juice into a small saucepan; add sugar and flour. Bring to a boil. Quickly stir in egg; cook until thickened. Remove from the heat; cool. Refrigerate.

In a large bowl, combine the pineapple, oranges, pears, kiwi, apples and pecans. Pour dressing over and blend well. Cover and chill for 1 hour. **Yield:** 12-16 servings.

10 minutes. Combine filling ingredients; set aside. Ro[ll]
dough into a 24-in. x 8-in. rectangle. Spread filling t[o]
within 1/2 in. of edges. Fold rectangle in half lengthwis[e];
cut widthwise into 24 pieces. Pinch seams to seal. Twi[st]
each piece three times.

Place 2 in. apart on greased baking sheets; pinch end[s.]
Bake at 350° for 15-20 minutes or until lightly browne[d.]
Remove from pans to wire racks to cool. Combine icin[g]
ingredients; drizzle over twists. **Yield:** 2 dozen.

Editor's Note: If your bread machine has a time[r]
delay feature, we recommend you do not use it for th[is]
recipe. Reduced-fat or generic brands of peanut butte[r]
are not recommended for this recipe.

Peanut Butter Twists

(Pictured above)

I use my bread machine to make these crowd-pleas-
ing treats that have a peanut butter filling and icing.
—Renea De Kam, George, Iowa

    3/4 cup water (70° to 80°)
    1/3 cup butter, softened
      1 egg
    1/4 cup nonfat dry milk powder
    1/3 cup sugar
    3/4 teaspoon salt
      3 cups bread flour
 2-1/4 teaspoons active dry yeast
FILLING:
    3/4 cup creamy peanut butter
    1/4 cup butter, softened
    1/3 cup confectioners' sugar
ICING:
 1-1/2 cups confectioners' sugar
      2 tablespoons creamy peanut butter
      5 to 7 tablespoons warm water

In bread machine pan, place the first eight ingredients in
order suggested by manufacturer. Select dough setting
(check dough after 5 minutes of mixing; add 1 to 2 tablespoons of water or flour if needed).

When cycle is completed, turn dough onto a lightly
floured surface. Punch down; cover and let stand for

Turkey Noodle Soup

(Pictured below)

We enjoy this chunky soup year-round. It's terrif[ic]
served with hot bread on cool autumn days an[d]
with a green salad in warmer weather.
—Elaine Bickford, Las Vegas, Nevad[a]

      2 cans (14-1/2 ounces *each*) chicken broth
      3 cups water
 1-3/4 cups sliced carrots
    1/2 cup chopped onion
      2 celery ribs, sliced
      1 package (12 ounces) frozen egg noodles
      3 cups chopped cooked turkey

1 package (10 ounces) frozen peas
2 envelopes chicken gravy mix
1/2 cup cold water

In a large saucepan, bring the broth, water, carrots, onion and celery to a boil. Reduce heat; cover and simmer for 5-6 minutes or until vegetables are crisp-tender. Add the noodles. Simmer, uncovered, for 20 minutes or until noodles are tender.

Stir in turkey and peas. Combine gravy mixes and cold water until smooth; stir into the soup. Bring to a boil; cook and stir for 2 minutes or until thickened. **Yield:** 7 servings.

Glass Bowl Salad

(Pictured at right)

The crisp veggies, creamy dressing and crumbled bacon in this layered salad assure there are no leftovers.
—Anne Heinonen, Howell, Michigan

1 medium head iceberg lettuce, shredded
1/2 cup chopped celery
1 cup shredded carrots
1 package (10 ounces) frozen peas, thawed
5 green onions, sliced
1 medium green pepper, chopped
1 cup mayonnaise
2/3 cup sour cream
6 bacon strips, cooked and crumbled

In a 3-qt. clear glass serving bowl, layer the first six ingredients in order given. Combine mayonnaise and sour cream until smooth; spread evenly over salad. Cover and chill overnight. Sprinkle with bacon just before serving. **Yield:** 8-10 servings.

Chocolate Cookie Muffins

These mouth-watering muffins have crushed cream-filled chocolate cookies in the batter and topping. They're a double treat—like eating muffins and cookies at the same time. No one can resist them!
—Jan Blue, Cuyahoga Falls, Ohio

1-3/4 cups all-purpose flour
1/4 cup sugar
3 teaspoons baking powder
1/3 cup cold butter
1 egg
1 cup milk
16 cream-filled chocolate sandwich cookies, coarsely chopped
TOPPING:
3 tablespoons all-purpose flour
3 tablespoons sugar
5 cream-filled chocolate sandwich cookies, finely crushed
2 tablespoons cold butter
1 cup vanilla chips
1 tablespoon shortening

In a large bowl, combine flour, sugar and baking powder. Cut in butter until mixture resembles coarse crumbs. Beat egg and milk; stir into dry ingredients just until moistened. Fold in chopped cookies. Fill greased muffin cups two-thirds full. For topping, combine the flour, sugar and crushed cookies. Cut in the butter until crumbly; sprinkle about 1 tablespoon over each muffin.

Bake at 400° for 16-18 minutes or until a toothpick comes out clean. Cool for 5 minutes before removing from pan to a wire rack. In a heavy saucepan over low heat, melt vanilla chips and shortening until smooth. Drizzle over cooled muffins. **Yield:** 1 dozen.

Beaded Pumpkin Earrings

(Pictured at right)

To give my wardrobe fall flair, I created jack-o'-lantern jewelry using orange and green seed beads. The earrings are a snap to assemble, even if you've never worked with beads before. I like to wear these pumpkins for festive occasions throughout the autumn season. —Cynthia Busko, Essex, Ontario

Materials Needed:
Beading thread; No. 12 beading needle; one shallow, rimmed container for each bead color; scissors; gem glue or clear nail polish; transparent glass seed beads or 10/0 glass rocaille beads—4 green and 24 orange; two gold earring wires.

Forming earring

Finished Size:
Excluding the ear wire, each earring is about 1/2 inch high x 1/4 inch wide.

Directions:
Place the green seed beads and orange seed beads into separate shallow, rimmed containers.

Cut two 5-inch lengths of beading thread. Thread the needle with one length. String two green beads on to the center of the length of thread, then add 12 orange beads.

Form a pumpkin shape by bringing the needle back through the two green beads as shown in the figure at left. Pull the needle until thread is taut and the green "stem" is centered above the orange beads.

Tie both ends of the thread to the loop of an earring wire. Dot knot with gem glue or clear nail polish. When dry, trim thread ends and dot knot again with gem glue or nail polish. Let dry.

Use the remaining thread piece to make the second earring the same as before.

Favorite Apple Salad

A friend gave us this refreshing recipe, which immediately became a family favorite. I prepare this crisp, colorful dish in place of an ordinary green salad for both quick meals and special occasions.
—Sharon Bielmyer, Holtwood, Pennsylvania

   1 can (20 ounces) unsweetened pineapple chunks
1/4 cup butter
1/4 cup sugar
   1 tablespoon lemon juice
   2 tablespoons cornstarch
   2 tablespoons cold water
   1 cup mayonnaise
   8 cups chopped tart apples
   2 cups green grapes

Halloween Fun Fact

If all the candy corn produced for Halloween (20 million pounds) were laid end-to-end, it could circle the moon twice with some left over.

(Source: National Confectioners Association)

   2 teaspoons poppy seeds
3/4 cup chopped pecans, toasted

Drain pineapple, reserving juice; set the pineapple aside. Place juice in a saucepan; add butter, sugar and lemon juice. Bring to a boil. Combine the cornstarch and cold water until smooth; add to the saucepan, stirring constantly. Return to a boil; cook and stir for 2 min-

es. Chill. Stir in mayonnaise.

In a large bowl, combine pineapple, apples, grapes, ppy seeds and cooked dressing. Fold in the pecans just fore serving. **Yield:** 14 servings.

Eyeball Soup

(Pictured above)

family has fun serving this creamy soup to unsuscting guests. We tell them the name of the soup, en watch their reaction when they stir up an onion eball." The recipe is also convenient for parties cause you can make it a day ahead.

—Aleta Clegg, Pleasant Grove, Utah

1/4 cup butter
1/4 cup all-purpose flour
  1 teaspoon salt
1/2 to 1 teaspoon coarsely ground pepper
  5 cups milk
  1 can (46 ounces) V8 juice *or* 4 cans (11-1/2 ounces *each*) picante V8 juice
  1 cup frozen pearl *or* small whole onions, thawed

In a large saucepan, melt butter. Stir in the flour, salt and pepper until blended. Gradually whisk in milk. Bring to a boil; cook and stir for 1-2 minutes or until thickened. In another saucepan, bring V8 to a boil. Reduce heat; gradually whisk in white sauce. Add onions; heat through. **Yield:** 10 servings (about 2-3/4 quarts).

Editor's Note: If a smoother soup is desired, cool and puree in batches in a blender before adding the onions.

Cheeseburger Mini Muffins

(Pictured below)

I invented these cute little muffins so I could enjoy the flavor of cheeseburgers without resorting to fast food. I often freeze a batch and reheat however many I need. —Teresa Kraus, Cortez, Colorado

     1/2 pound ground beef
       1 small onion, finely chopped
 2-1/2 cups all-purpose flour
       1 tablespoon sugar
       2 teaspoons baking powder
       1 teaspoon salt
     3/4 cup ketchup
     3/4 cup milk
     1/2 cup butter, melted
       2 eggs
       1 teaspoon prepared mustard
       2 cups (8 ounces) shredded cheddar cheese

In a skillet, cook beef and onion over medium heat until meat is no longer pink; drain. In a bowl, combine the flour, sugar, baking powder and salt. In another bowl, combine the ketchup, milk, butter, eggs and mustard; stir into the dry ingredients just until moistened. Fold in the beef mixture and cheese. Fill greased miniature muf-

fin cups three-fourths full.

Bake at 425° for 15-18 minutes or until a toothpic comes out clean. Cool for 5 minutes before removin from pans to wire racks. Refrigerate leftovers. **Yield:** dozen.

Editor's Note: Muffins may be baked in regular-siz muffin cups for 20-25 minutes; recipe makes 2 dozen.

Spiced Peach Salad

(Pictured above)

This refreshing salad is my most requested recipe. touch of cinnamon makes it taste like fresh peach pi My father-in-law is an especially big fan of this fruit treat. —Karen Hamilton, Ludington, Michiga

     1/2 cup sugar
       3 tablespoons white vinegar
       2 cups water
       1 tablespoon whole cloves
       4 cinnamon sticks
       1 package (6 ounces) peach gelatin
       1 can (29 ounces) peach halves

In a medium saucepan, combine sugar, vinegar and wa ter. Tie cloves and cinnamon in a cheesecloth bag place in the saucepan. Bring to a boil. Reduce hea

mmer, uncovered, for 10 minutes. Remove from the
eat and discard spice bag. Add peach gelatin; stir until
ssolved.

Drain peaches, reserving syrup; set peaches aside. Add
ater to syrup to equal 2 cups. Add to gelatin mixture;
ir well. Chill until slightly thickened. Thinly slice peach-
; add to gelatin. Pour into a 2-qt. glass bowl; chill un-
firm. **Yield:** 8-10 servings.

Editor's Note: If desired, 1/2 teaspoon ground cinna-
on and 1/4 teaspoon ground cloves may be substitut-
for the whole spices; combine with the gelatin before
ding to sugar mixture.

Chocolate Chip Pumpkin Bread

(Pictured below)

*touch of cinnamon helps blend the chocolate and
umpkin flavors you'll find in this tender bread.*
—Lora Stanley, Bennington, Kansas

      3 cups all-purpose flour
      2 teaspoons ground cinnamon
      1 teaspoon salt
      1 teaspoon baking soda
      4 eggs
      2 cups sugar
      2 cups canned pumpkin
  1-1/4 cups vegetable oil
  1-1/2 cups semisweet chocolate chips

In a large bowl, combine the flour, cinnamon, salt and
baking soda. In another bowl, beat the eggs, sugar,
pumpkin and oil. Stir into the dry ingredients just until
moistened. Fold in the chocolate chips. Pour into two
greased 8-in. x 4-in. x 2-in. loaf pans.

Bake at 350° for 60-70 minutes or until a toothpick
inserted near the center comes out clean. Cool for 10
minutes before removing from pans to wire racks. **Yield:**
2 loaves.

Pumpkin Soup

*While it looks elegant, this creamy autumn soup is
easy to make. My husband was skeptical at first, but
after one bowl, he asked for second helpings!*
—Elizabeth Montgomery, Taylorville, Illinois

  1/2 cup finely chopped onion
    2 tablespoons butter
    1 tablespoon all-purpose flour
    2 cans (14-1/2 ounces *each*) chicken broth
    1 can (15 ounces) solid-pack pumpkin
    1 teaspoon brown sugar
  1/4 teaspoon salt
  1/8 teaspoon pepper
  1/8 teaspoon ground nutmeg
    1 cup heavy whipping cream

In a large saucepan, saute onion
in butter until tender. Remove
from the heat; stir in flour until
smooth. Gradually stir in broth,
pumpkin, brown sugar, salt,
pepper and nutmeg; bring to
a boil. Reduce heat and simmer for 5 minutes. Add the
cream; cook for 2
minutes or until
heated through.
Yield: 6 servings.

Place peas, lentils and beans in a Dutch oven; ad
enough water to cover. Bring to a boil; boil for 2 min
utes. Remove from the heat; let stand for 1 hour.

Drain and discard liquid. Add 2 qts. water and season
ings; bring to a boil. Reduce heat; cover and simmer f
1-1/2 to 2 hours or until beans are just tender. Stir
tomatoes; increase heat to medium. Cook, uncovered, f
15-30 minutes. Discard bay leaves. **Yield:** 14 servings (
1/2 quarts).

Ribbon Pumpkin Bread

*When I serve this pretty pumpkin bread, the first thir
people notice is the tempting ribbon of cream chee.
inside.* —Beth Ask, Ulster, Pennsylvan

> **6 ounces cream cheese, softened**
> **1/4 cup sugar**
> **1 tablespoon all-purpose flour**
> **2 egg whites**
> **BATTER:**
> **1 cup pumpkin**
> **1/2 cup unsweetened applesauce**
> **1 egg**
> **2 egg whites**
> **1 tablespoon vegetable oil**
> **1-2/3 cups all-purpose flour**
> **1-1/4 cups sugar**
> **1 teaspoon baking soda**
> **1/2 teaspoon salt**
> **1/2 teaspoon ground cinnamon**
> **1/2 teaspoon ground cloves**
> **1/3 cup chopped walnuts**

For filling, combine the cream cheese, sugar, flour an
egg whites in a bowl; set aside. In a mixing bowl, be
the pumpkin, applesauce, egg, egg whites and oil. Com
bine the flour, sugar, baking soda, salt, cinnamon an
cloves; add to pumpkin mixture. Stir in walnuts.

Divide half of the batter between two 8-in. x 4-in.

Lucky Bean Soup

(Pictured above)

*This recipe is from a bean soup gift pack I developed
as a fund-raiser for our church. A big bowlful is
wonderful with breadsticks or a green salad.*
—Doris Cox, South Orange, New Jersey

> **1/4 cup *each* dry yellow split peas, lentils, black
> beans, great northern beans, pinto beans,
> baby lima beans and kidney beans**
> **1/2 cup *each* dry green split peas, black-eyed
> peas and navy beans**
> **2 quarts water**
> **1/3 cup dried minced onion**
> **1 tablespoon salt**
> **1 teaspoon dried thyme**
> **1 teaspoon dried rosemary, crushed**
> **1 teaspoon garlic powder**
> **1/2 teaspoon celery seed**
> **1/2 teaspoon dried basil**
> **1/4 to 1/2 teaspoon crushed red pepper flakes**
> **2 bay leaves**
> **1 can (28 ounces) crushed tomatoes**

apples and walnuts. Transfer to a 2-qt. serving bowl. Cover and refrigerate overnight. **Yield:** 12 servings.

Pizza Soup

(Pictured below)

I like to serve this family favorite with garlic bread, and I'll sometimes use pieces of bacon or salami instead of the pepperoni (just like a pizza!).
—Janet Beldman, London, Ontario

> **1 pound ground beef**
> **1 small onion, chopped**
> **1 cup sliced fresh mushrooms**
> **1 medium green pepper, cut into strips**
> **1 can (28 ounces) diced tomatoes, undrained**
> **1 cup beef broth**
> **1 cup sliced pepperoni**
> **1 teaspoon dried basil**
Shredded mozzarella cheese

In a large saucepan, cook the beef, onion, mushrooms and green pepper over medium heat until the meat is no longer pink and the vegetables are almost tender; drain. Stir in the tomatoes, broth, pepperoni and basil. Cook until heated through.

Ladle into ovenproof bowls; top with cheese. Broil or microwave until cheese melts and is bubbly. **Yield:** 4-6 servings (6 cups).

2-in. loaf pans coated with cooking spray. Spread each with filling; top with remaining batter. Bake at 350° for 40-45 minutes or until a toothpick inserted near the center comes out clean. Cool for 10 minutes before removing from pans to wire racks to cool completely. Store in the refrigerator. **Yield:** 2 loaves.

Apple Cider Salad

(Pictured above)

This cool, refreshing salad with crunchy nuts and apples makes me think of my mother. Mom prepared it each year when apples were plentiful.
—Jeannette Mack, Rushville, New York

> **2 envelopes unflavored gelatin**
> **3-3/4 cups apple cider,** *divided*
> **3 tablespoons lemon juice**
> **3 tablespoons sugar**
> **1/2 teaspoon salt**
> **3-1/2 to 4 cups chopped peeled apples**
> **1 cup chopped walnuts**

In a small saucepan, sprinkle gelatin over 1/4 cup of cider; let stand for 2 minutes. Add lemon juice, sugar, salt and remaining cider. Cook and stir over medium heat until sugar and gelatin are dissolved. Cover and refrigerate until slightly thickened, about 2-1/2 hours. Fold in

Dress Up Fun

Want creative ideas for Halloween costumes? These clever getups are bound to inspire your own frightfully fun attire.

COSTUMES, STAT! Coordinating costumes were a perfect fit for Jenna and Jared Stiek of Marshall, Missouri. Their mother, Judy, doctored these up with toy stethoscopes.

NICE MICE. Kelli and brother Bret Palmer of Cypress, California were up to their ears in fun thanks to the outfits Mom Bobbi made. "Mickey and Minnie are their favorite characters," Bobbi says.

BRIGHT IDEA. Her daughter's request for a rainbow costume stumped Joanne Budney of Lafayette, Indiana. "Then I found fabric left over from a flag I'd made," she says. "I used wire to shape an arc."

LITTLE GREEN MEN came to Cedar Park, Texas as twin brothers Camden (left) and Cole Greinke. Wendy Greinke added alien eyes, ears and antennae to purchased felt hats, then dressed her sons in bodysuits.

HAVING A FIELD DAY. In Richland, Indiana, Wendy Taylor outfitted her son as a farmer, complete with a cardboard tractor. "Zane was so happy with that costume that he wore it 2 years in a row," she shares.

SNACK SIZE. To produce a popcorn look for Krystal Decker, Mom Robin of Chicago, Illinois cut and painted a cardboard box. "I added real popcorn for extra fun," she says.

LIVING DOLL. When Betty Hellebrand of Satellite Beach, Florida made a wig and sewed a dress for a rag doll costume, her granddaughter was sitting pretty.

WASH 'N' WEAR. Creating a laundry outfit proved to be good clean fun for Sandy Rollinger of Apollo, Pennsylvania. She cut out the bottom of a basket so her cousin, Tara, could fit inside, then added clothes and detergent.

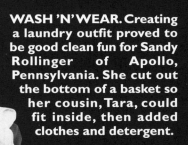

WIZARD Lori Rader of McComb, Ohio created Oz outfits from fabrics and dryer vents for her children (left to right) Emily, Ashley, Bruce and Max.

Cookie + Bar Boo-nanza

Recipes

Projects

Pumpkin Cheesecake Bars

(Pictured at right)

A special autumn dessert, these spicy bars have a gingery cookie crust and candied pecans on top. They perfectly complement the pumpkin filling.
—Marcie Matthews, Santa Rosa, California

- 2 cups crushed windmill cookies (about 12 cookies)
- 1/2 cup butter, melted
- 4 packages (8 ounces *each*) cream cheese, softened
- 1-1/4 cups sugar
- 1 cup canned pumpkin
- 1/4 cup heavy whipping cream
- 3 tablespoons all-purpose flour
- 1/2 teaspoon *each* ground nutmeg, ginger, cinnamon and cloves
- 1/4 teaspoon salt
- 1/4 teaspoon vanilla extract
- 4 eggs
- 2 egg yolks

TOPPING:
- 1/2 cup sugar
- 1 cup pecan halves
- 2 cups heavy whipping cream
- 1/2 cup confectioners' sugar
- 1/4 teaspoon vanilla extract

Combine cookie crumbs and butter; press into a greased 13-in. x 9-in. x 2-in. baking dish. Bake at 325° for 8-10 minutes or until set. Cool on a wire rack.

In a large mixing bowl, beat cream cheese and sugar until smooth. Beat in the pumpkin, cream, flour, spices, salt and vanilla. Add the eggs and yolks; beat on low speed just until combined. Pour over prepared crust. Bake at 325° for 35-40 minutes or until center is almost set. Cool on a wire rack for 1 hour. Refrigerate for 3 hours or until chilled.

Sprinkle sugar into a large nonstick skillet. Without stirring, heat over medium-low until sugar is melted. Stir in pecans. Transfer to a piece of greased foil; cool. Break pecans into pieces.

In a small mixing bowl, beat cream until it begins to thicken. Add confectioners' sugar and vanilla; beat until stiff peaks form. Spread over chilled cheesecake. Sprinkle with sugared pecans. Cut into bars. Refrigerate leftovers. **Yield:** 2 to 2-1/2 dozen.

Editor's Note: This recipe was tested with Archway windmill cookies.

Apple Pie Bars

(Pictured below right)

These delicious bars, with their flaky crust and fruit filling, are my favorite way to serve apple pie to a crowd. —Janet English, Pittsburgh, Pennsylvania

- 4 cups all-purpose flour
- 1 teaspoon salt
- 1 teaspoon baking powder
- 1 cup shortening
- 4 egg yolks
- 2 tablespoons lemon juice
- 8 to 10 tablespoons cold water

FILLING:
- 7 cups finely chopped peeled apples
- 2 cups sugar
- 1/4 cup all-purpose flour
- 2 teaspoons ground cinnamon
- Dash ground nutmeg

GLAZE:
- 1 cup confectioners' sugar
- 1 tablespoon milk
- 1 tablespoon lemon juice

In a bowl, combine first three ingredients. Cut in shortening until mixture resembles coarse crumbs. In a bowl, whisk egg yolks, lemon juice and water; gradually add to flour mixture, tossing with a fork until dough forms a ll. Divide in half. Chill 30 minutes.

Roll out one portion of dough between two large eets of waxed paper into a 17-in. x 12-in. rectangle. ansfer to an ungreased 15-in. x 10-in. x 1-in. baking n. Press pastry onto bottom and up sides of pan; trim stry even with top edge.

In a bowl, toss the apples, sugar, flour, cinnamon d nutmeg; spread over crust. Roll out remaining pas- y to fit top of pan; place over filling. Trim edges; ush edges between pastry with water or milk; pinch to al. Cut slits in top.

Bake at 375° for 45-50 minutes or until golden own. Cool on a wire rack. Combine glaze ingredients; izzle over bars before cutting. **Yield:** about 2 dozen.

Chocolaty Double Crunchers

(Pictured at right)

acked with oats, cornflakes and coconut, these ispy cookies are a "regular" at our house.
—Cheryl Johnson, Upper Marlboro, Maryland

1/2 cup butter, softened
1/2 cup sugar

1/2 cup packed brown sugar
  1 egg
1/2 teaspoon vanilla extract
  1 cup all-purpose flour
1/2 teaspoon baking soda
1/4 teaspoon salt
  1 cup quick-cooking oats
  1 cup crushed cornflakes
1/2 cup flaked coconut
FILLING:
  2 packages (3 ounces *each*) cream cheese, softened
1-1/2 cups confectioners' sugar
  2 cups (12 ounces) semisweet chocolate chips, melted

In a mixing bowl, cream butter and sugars. Add egg and vanilla; mix well. Combine flour, baking soda and salt; add to creamed mixture and mix well. Add oats, cornflakes and coconut.

Shape into 1-in. balls and place 2 in. apart on greased baking sheets. Flatten with a glass dipped lightly in flour. Bake at 350° for 8-10 minutes or until lightly browned. Remove to wire racks to cool.

For filling, beat cream cheese and sugar until smooth. Add chocolate; mix well. Spread about 1 tablespoon on half of cookies and top each with another cookie. Store in refrigerator. **Yield:** about 2 dozen.

Painted Pumpkin Luminaries

(Pictured below)

In my kitchen, empty tin cans pile up fast. This craft idea got its start while I was shopping. I saw a can with design punched in it, and I thought I could do the same. The pumpkin luminaries look just as nice indoors o the windowsill as they do outside lining our walkway.
—Margaret Hanson-Maddox, Montpelier, Indian

Materials Needed:

Patterns below; tracing paper; pencil; ruler; graphit transfer paper; stylus or dry ballpoint pen; clean dr cans in desired sizes (see finished size); hammer and na or drill with fine drill bit; orange spray paint; acrylic craf paints—mauve, yellow, red, white, black and orange palette or foam plate; water basin; paper towels; paint brushes—No. I liner and Nos. 4 and 8 flat; fine-line per manent black marker (optional); gloss spray finish; I4 inches of 16- or 19-gauge black craft wire; needle-nos pliers.

Finished Size:

Small luminary is 2-3/4 inches wide x 4 inches high medium luminary is 4 inches wide x 6 inches high and large luminary is 6 inches wide x 6-3/4 inches high.

Directions:

Punch holes in can with hammer and nail or drill holes (1-1/4 inch es apart for small can, 1-1/2 inch es apart for medium and 2 inch es apart for large). Spray-paint can sides orange. Let dry.

Trace patterns at left onto tracing paper. Use graphite paper under pattern of choice to trans fer pattern onto side of can us ing stylus or dry ballpoint pen.

With transferred face in front, add holes on opposite sides of can for handle, 1/4 inch from up per edge.

Place a small amount of white paint on palette or plate. Using whichever brush bests fits the area, paint the eyes and teeth white. When dry, add a second coat if needed. Let dry.

In same way, paint the tongue and cheeks mauve, the pupils black and the noses orange, yel-

FACE PATTERNS

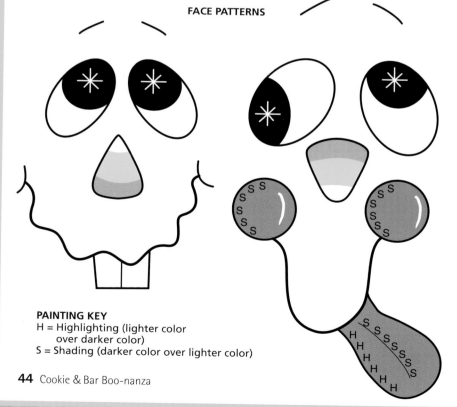

PAINTING KEY
H = Highlighting (lighter color
    over darker color)
S = Shading (darker color over lighter color)

ow and white.

Dip No. 8 brush in clean water. Remove excess water by touching brush to paper towel until shine disappears. Gently touch one corner of brush into red paint. Blend by wiping brush back and forth on a clean area of palette or plate until the color gradually fades from red on one side to clear on opposite side. Paint shading on cheeks, positioning the loaded side of brush against outer edge where shown on pattern.

In the same way, shade tongue with red and highlight tongue with white.

Use black paint or marker to outline and add mouth and eyebrows. Add white comma strokes to cheeks and stars to eyes.

When paint is thoroughly dry, apply two coats of gloss finish, allowing drying time between coats.

For handle, insert ends of wire through holes at top of can. Use pliers to twist wire around itself above can.

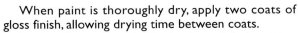

Halloween Fun Fact

Jack-o'-lanterns get their name from the Irish legend about "Stingy Jack," a ghost who carries a carved-out turnip with a burning coal inside.

Dark Chocolate Mocha Brownies

(Pictured at right)

Dark chocolate is a favorite around our house, so these frosted brownies are a hit. I came up with this treat by reworking a recipe I've used for a long time.
—Linda McCoy, Oostburg, Wisconsin

> 2 cups packed brown sugar
> 1 cup butter, melted
> 3 eggs
> 1 tablespoon instant coffee granules
> 2 teaspoons vanilla extract
> 1 cup all-purpose flour
> 1 cup baking cocoa
> 1/2 teaspoon baking powder
> 1/2 teaspoon salt
> 6 ounces bittersweet chocolate, coarsely chopped

FROSTING:
> 1/4 cup butter, melted
> 3 tablespoons sour cream
> 2 teaspoons vanilla extract
> 2-3/4 to 3 cups confectioners' sugar
> 2 ounces grated bittersweet chocolate

In a mixing bowl, combine brown sugar and butter. Beat in eggs, one at a time. Add coffee granules and

vanilla; mix well. Combine the flour, cocoa, baking powder and salt; add to sugar mixture and mix well. Stir in chocolate. Spread into a greased 13-in. x 9-in. x 2-in. baking pan. Bake at 350° for 25-30 minutes or until a toothpick inserted near the center comes out clean. Cool on a wire rack.

For frosting, combine butter, sour cream and vanilla; mix well. Gradually stir in sugar until frosting is smooth and reaches desired consistency. Frost brownies. Sprinkle with grated chocolate. **Yield:** 5 dozen.

Pumpkin Drop Cookies

(Pictured above)

With just a hint of pumpkin flavor and a buttery cinnamon frosting, these cake-like drop cookies are a special autumn treat and always a hit.
—Denise Smith, Lusk, Wyoming

    1/2 cup butter-flavored shortening
    3 cups sugar
    1 can (15 ounces) solid-pack pumpkin
    2 eggs
    1/2 cup milk
    6 cups all-purpose flour
    2 teaspoons baking soda
    2 teaspoons ground cinnamon
    1 teaspoon salt
    1 teaspoon ground allspice
    1/2 teaspoon ground cloves
CINNAMON FROSTING:
    1/2 cup butter, softened
    2-1/2 cups confectioners' sugar
    2 tablespoons milk
    1 teaspoon ground cinnamon
    1 teaspoon vanilla extract

In a large mixing bowl, cream the shortening and sugar. Beat in the pumpkin, eggs and milk. Combine the flour, baking soda, cinnamon, salt, allspice and cloves; gradually add to the creamed mixture. Drop by tablespoonfuls 2 in. apart onto greased baking sheets. Bake at 375° for 10-13 minutes or until lightly browned. Remove

to wire racks to cool completely.

In a small mixing bowl, combine the frosting ingredients; beat until smooth. Frost cookies. Store in the refrigerator. **Yield:** 11 dozen.

S'more Sandwich Cookies

(Pictured below)

Capture the taste of campfire s'mores in your kitchen! These cookies combine all the ingredients of the fireside favorite.   —Abby Metzger, Larchwood, Iowa

    3/4 cup butter, softened
    1/2 cup sugar
    1/2 cup packed brown sugar
    1 egg
    2 tablespoons milk
    1 teaspoon vanilla extract
1-1/4 cups all-purpose flour
1-1/4 cups graham cracker crumbs (about 20
        squares)
    1/2 teaspoon baking soda
    1/4 teaspoon salt
    1/8 teaspoon ground cinnamon
    2 cups (12 ounces) semisweet chocolate chips
    24 to 28 large marshmallows

In a mixing bowl, cream butter and sugars. Beat in egg, milk and vanilla. Combine the flour, graham cracker

...mbs, baking soda, salt and cinnamon; gradually add ...creamed mixture. Stir in chocolate chips.

...Drop by tablespoonfuls 2 in. apart onto ungreased ...king sheets. Bake at 375° for 8-10 minutes or until ...lden brown. Remove to wire racks to cool.

...Place four cookies bottom side up on a microwave-...e plate; top each with a marshmallow. Microwave, un-...vered, on high for 16-20 seconds or until marshmal-...ws begin to puff (do not overcook). Top each with ...other cookie. Repeat. **Yield:** about 2 dozen.

Blond Toffee Brownies

...e first time I prepared these thin chewy brownies, ...y family said they were the best they've ever tast-...A fresh-baked batch never lasts very long.
—*Mary Williams, Lancaster, California*

1/2 cup butter, softened
   1 cup sugar
1/2 cup packed brown sugar
   2 eggs
   1 teaspoon vanilla extract
...-1/2 cups all-purpose flour
   2 teaspoons baking powder
1/4 teaspoon salt
   **1 cup English toffee bits *or* almond brickle
     chips**

...a mixing bowl, cream butter and sugars. Add eggs, one ...a time, beating well after each addition. Beat in vanil-...Combine the flour, baking powder and salt; gradual-...add to creamed mixture. Stir in toffee bits.

...Spread evenly into a greased 13-in. x 9-in. x 2-in. ...king pan. Bake at 350° for 35-40 minutes or until a ...othpick inserted near the center comes out clean. Cool ...a wire rack. Cut into bars. **Yield:** 1-1/2 dozen.

Witch Hat Treats

(Pictured above right)

...re's a fun twist on ordinary marshmallow cereal ...ats. I cut them into witch hat shapes, then deco-...te them with frosting, licorice and jimmies. They add ...the festive feeling around Halloween.
—*Nancy Foust, Stoneboro, Pennsylvania*

   3 tablespoons butter
   1 package (10 ounces) large marshmallows
1/2 cup peanut butter
   6 cups crisp rice cereal
1-1/2 cups milk chocolate chips
   1 teaspoon shortening
Orange frosting
Chocolate jimmies
Black rope licorice

In a large microwave-safe bowl, melt butter on high for about 45 seconds. Add marshmallows; stir to coat. Microwave on high for 45 seconds; stir. Microwave 45 seconds longer or until smooth. Stir in peanut butter. Immediately add cereal; stir gently until coated. Press into a greased 13-in. x 9-in. x 2-in. baking pan.

In a small microwave-safe bowl, heat chocolate chips and shortening on 70% power for 1 minute. Heat in 10- to 20-second intervals until melted; stir until smooth. Spread over cereal mixture. Cool completely.

Cut into 2-1/2-in. x 2-in. triangles with a thin base on bottom of triangle for hat brim. Decorate with frosting, jimmies for the buckle and licorice for the brim. **Yield:** 2 dozen.

Editor's Note: This recipe was tested in an 850-watt microwave.

Frosted Pumpkin Cranberry Bars

(Pictured below)

With dried cranberries inside and a brown butter frosting, these mildly spiced bars are doubly delightful. —Barbara Nowakowski, Mesa, Arizona

1-1/2 cups all-purpose flour
1-1/4 cups sugar
   2 teaspoons baking powder
   2 teaspoons ground cinnamon
   1 teaspoon baking soda
1/2 teaspoon ground ginger
   3 eggs
   1 can (15 ounces) solid-pack pumpkin
3/4 cup butter, melted
3/4 cup chopped dried cranberries
BROWN BUTTER FROSTING:
1/2 cup butter
   4 cups confectioners' sugar
   1 teaspoon vanilla extract
   4 to 6 tablespoons milk

In a bowl, combine the first six ingredients. In another bowl, whisk the eggs, pumpkin and butter; stir into dry ingredients until well combined. Stir in the chopped cranberries. Spread into a greased 15-in. x 10-in. x 1-in. baking pan. Bake at 350° for 20-25 minutes or until a toothpick inserted near the center comes out clean. Cool on a wire rack.

For frosting, heat the butter in a saucepan over medium heat until golden brown, about 7 minutes. Remove

from the heat; cool for 5 minutes. Stir in confectione[r's] sugar, vanilla and enough milk to achieve spreading co[n]sistency. Spread over bars before cutting. **Yield:** abo[ut] 4 dozen.

Pumpkin Chip Cookies

(Pictured above)

These soft, golden cookies disappear quickly fro[m] dessert trays. The pumpkin and cinnamon flavors p[air] wonderfully with the chocolate chips.
—Tami Burroughs, Salem, Oreg[on]

1-1/2 cups butter, softened
   2 cups packed brown sugar
   1 cup sugar
   1 can (15 ounces) solid-pack pumpkin
   1 egg
   1 teaspoon vanilla extract
   4 cups all-purpose flour
   2 cups quick-cooking oats
   2 teaspoons baking soda
   2 teaspoons ground cinnamon
   1 teaspoon salt
   2 cups (12 ounces) semisweet chocolate chip[s]

a large mixing bowl, cream butter and sugars. Beat
the pumpkin, egg and vanilla. Combine the flour, oats,
king soda, cinnamon and salt; gradually add to
amed mixture. Stir in chocolate chips. Drop by ta-
spoonfuls 2 in. apart onto ungreased baking sheets.
ke at 350° for 10-12 minutes or until lightly browned.
move to wire racks to cool. **Yield:** 10 dozen.

Frosted Peanut Butter Fingers

(Pictured below)

*rst discovered these quick crowd-pleasers when I
elled the tempting aroma of a batch a neighbor
s baking.* —Leah Gallington, Corona, California

  1 cup butter, softened
-1/2 cups packed brown sugar
  1 cup sugar
-1/2 cups creamy peanut butter, *divided*
  1 egg
-1/2 teaspoons vanilla extract
-1/2 cups quick-cooking oats
  2 cups all-purpose flour
  1 teaspoon baking soda
1/2 teaspoon salt
OCOLATE FROSTING:
  6 tablespoons butter, softened

  4 cups confectioners' sugar
1/2 cup baking cocoa
  1 teaspoon vanilla extract
  6 to 8 tablespoons milk

In a mixing bowl, cream butter and sugars. Add 1 cup
peanut butter, egg and vanilla; mix well. Combine oats,
flour, baking soda and salt; add to the creamed mixture. Spread into a greased 15-in. x 10-in. x 1-in. baking pan.

  Bake at 350° for 13-17 minutes or until golden
brown. Cool slightly on a wire rack, about 12 minutes.
Spread with remaining peanut butter. Cool completely.

  In a mixing bowl, combine the butter, confectioners'
sugar, cocoa, vanilla and enough milk to achieve spreading consistency. Spoon over peanut butter layer, then
spread. Cut into bars. **Yield:** about 3 dozen.

  Editor's Note: Reduced-fat or generic brands of
peanut butter are not recommended for this recipe.

Macadamia Chip Cookies

*If you like cookies with a crunch, you'll love these
golden treats.* —Dorothy Kollmeyer, Dupo, Illinois

   1 cup butter, softened
  3/4 cup packed brown sugar
  1/4 cup sugar
   2 eggs
   1 teaspoon vanilla extract
2-1/4 cups all-purpose flour
   1 package (3.4 ounces) instant vanilla
     pudding mix
   1 teaspoon baking soda
  1/4 teaspoon salt
   1 package (10 to 12 ounces) vanilla *or*
     white chips
   2 jars (3-1/4 ounces *each*) macadamia nuts,
     chopped
  1/2 cup finely crushed peanut brittle

In a mixing bowl, cream butter and sugars until smooth.
Add eggs, one at a time, beating well after each addition. Beat in vanilla. Combine the flour, dry pudding mix,
baking soda and salt; gradually add to creamed mixture
and mix well. Stir in chips, nuts and peanut brittle.

  Drop by rounded tablespoonfuls 2 in. apart onto
greased baking sheets. Bake at 375° for 10-12 minutes
or until golden brown. Remove to wire racks to cool.
Yield: 5-1/2 dozen.

Jumbo Jack-o'-Lantern Cookies

(Pictured above)

Every Halloween, I'd bake a batch of these cookies for my kids and let them decorate their own.
—Marlene Kuiper, Oostburg, Wisconsin

        1 cup butter, softened
        1 cup sugar
        1 cup packed brown sugar
        1 egg
        1 teaspoon vanilla extract
        2 cups all-purpose flour
        1 cup quick-cooking oats
        1 teaspoon baking soda
        1 teaspoon ground cinnamon
    1/2 teaspoon salt
        1 cup canned pumpkin
        1 cup (6 ounces) semisweet chocolate chips
Orange and green decorating icing *or* vanilla frosting and orange and green gel food coloring

In a large mixing bowl, cream the butter and sugars; add the egg and vanilla. Combine the flour, oats, baking soda, cinnamon and salt; add to the creamed mixture alternately with pumpkin. Stir in the chocolate chips.

Drop by 1/4 cupfuls onto ungreased baking sheets. Spread into 3-1/2-in. pumpkin shapes. Drop 1/2 teaspoon of dough at the top of each for stem. Bake at 350° for 15-18 minutes or until edges are golden brown. Cool for 1 minute before removing to wire racks to cool completely. Create jack-o'-lantern faces on cookies with decorating icing or tinted frosting. **Yield:** 1-1/2 dozen.

Peanut Mallow Bars

(Pictured below)

When you taste the mix of salty and sweet ingredients in these chewy bars, you won't be able to stop at just one! They combine salted peanuts and caramel topping with marshmallow creme and brown sugar.
—Claudia Ruiss, Massapequa, New York

        1 cup chopped salted peanuts
    3/4 cup all-purpose flour
    3/4 cup quick-cooking oats
    2/3 cup packed brown sugar
    1/2 teaspoon salt
    1/2 teaspoon baking soda
        1 egg, lightly beaten
    1/3 cup cold butter
TOPPING:
        1 jar (7 ounces) marshmallow creme
    2/3 cup caramel ice cream topping
    1-3/4 cups salted peanuts

In a bowl, combine the first six ingredients; stir in the egg. Cut in butter until crumbly. Press into a greased 13-in. x 9-in. x 2-in. baking pan. Bake at 350° for 8-10 minutes or until lightly browned.

Spoon marshmallow creme over hot crust; carefully spread evenly. Drizzle with the caramel topping; sprinkle with peanuts. Bake for 15-20 minutes or until lightly browned. Cool on a wire rack. Cut into bars. **Yield:** 3 dozen.

Ghost Papier-Mache Gourd

(Pictured below)

This good-natured goblin has a garden-grown air about him. But instead of creating him from a real gourd, I used a purchased papier-mache version that'll last for many Halloweens to come. You can conjure up this ghostly guy in a flash, too, with basic craft supplies.
—Paula Del Favero, Deerfield Beach, Florida

Materials Needed:
One 9-1/2-inch-high x 6-3/4-inch-wide crooked-neck papier-mache gourd with stem; pencil; ruler; palette or foam plate; water basin; paper towels; acrylic craft paints—black, pink and white; 1-inch foam brush; 1/2-inch stencil brush; black fine-line permanent marker; tacky craft glue; scissors; two 10mm oval glue-on wiggle eyes; 3/8-inch wooden screwhole button; No. 1 liner paintbrush; 18-inch circle of white nylon netting; orange chenille stem.

Finished Size:
Ghost is about 9-1/2 inches high x 7 inches wide.

Directions:
Keep paper towels and a basin of water handy to clean paintbrushes. When painting, place dabs of each paint color onto palette or foam plate as needed. Add coats of paint as needed for complete coverage, letting paint dry after each application.

Using foam brush, paint the entire papier-mache gourd and stem white.

Using liner brush, paint the wooden screwhole button black for nose.

Turn gourd so the stem points toward the left-hand side. To mark the center of each cheek, measure about 2-1/4 inches up from bottom of gourd and lightly pencil-in two dots about 2-1/4 inches apart.

Dip stencil brush into pink paint, then remove most of the paint on paper towel. With an up-and-down motion, paint a 3/4-inch circle centered over each marked dot for the cheeks.

Dip the end of liner handle into white paint and dab a dot onto the center of each cheek.

Lightly pencil-in a squiggly smile for the mouth. Trace over drawn mouth with black marker.

Glue flat side of nose to center of face between cheeks.

Glue the eyes 1/8 inch apart just above the nose. Using black paint and liner, paint a crescent-shaped eyelid on upper portion of each wiggle eye. Let dry.

Place the gourd in the center of the nylon netting circle and hand-gather the netting around the base of the narrow end of the gourd. Wrap the orange chenille stem tightly around gathered netting and twist ends together to secure.

Wrap ends of chenille stem around pencil to coil. Remove pencil and gently stretch the coils to a 1-1/2-inch length. Trim netting to about 2-3/4 inches from chenille tie if needed.

Owl Cookies

(Pictured above)

These chocolaty cookies with cashew beaks are a real hoot for Halloween...and they taste as good as they look. —Liz Clemons, Sumter, South Carolina

    3/4 cup butter, softened
      1 cup packed brown sugar
      1 egg
      1 teaspoon vanilla extract
2-1/2 cups all-purpose flour
      2 teaspoons baking powder
      1/4 teaspoon salt
      1 square (1 ounce) unsweetened chocolate,
        melted
      1/4 teaspoon baking soda
Orange and yellow M&M's
Whole cashews

In a mixing bowl, cream butter and brown sugar. Add egg and vanilla; mix well. Combine flour, baking powder and salt; add to creamed mixture. Remove two-thirds of the dough; roll into an 8-in. square on waxed paper and set aside.

Combine chocolate and baking soda until thoroughly blended; beat into remaining dough. Shape into an 8-in.-long roll; place on edge of white dough. Wrap white dough around roll and pinch seam together. Wrap in waxed paper; chill for at least 2 hours. Cut in 1/4-in. slices.

To form owl's face, place two slices side by side or lightly greased baking sheet. Pinch dough at the top circles to form ears. Place M&M's in the center of ea circle for eyes. Place a cashew in the center of the fa for the beak. Bake at 350° for 9-11 minutes or un edges are lightly browned. Cool for 2 minutes befo removing to a wire rack. **Yield:** about 1-1/2 dozen.

Honey Chip Granola Bar

Not too sweet, these bars boast marshmallows a peanut butter. —RosAnna Troyer, Millersburg, Ol

      1/4 cup butter
      1/4 cup vegetable oil
1-1/2 pounds miniature marshmallows
      1/4 cup honey
      1/4 cup peanut butter
      5 cups old-fashioned oats
4-1/2 cups crisp rice cereal
      1 cup graham cracker crumbs
        (about 16 squares)
      1 cup flaked coconut
      1 cup crushed peanuts
      1/2 cup miniature chocolate chips

a large saucepan, combine the butter, oil and marsh-mallows. Cook and stir over low heat until mixture is melted and smooth. Remove from the heat; stir in honey and peanut butter. Combine the oats, cereal, cracker crumbs, coconut and peanuts. Add to the marshmallow mixture; mix well.

Press into a greased 15-in. x 10-in. x 1-in. pan. Cool for 10-15 minutes. Sprinkle with chips and gently press into top. Cool completely. Cut into bars. **Yield:** about 4 dozen.

Editor's Note: Reduced-fat or generic brands of peanut butter are not recommended for this recipe.

Strawberry Jam Bars

(Pictured below)

For a change of pace, you can give these scrumptious bars your own twist by replacing the strawberry jam with the fruit jam or preserves of your choice.
—Karen Mead, Pittsburgh, Pennsylvania

1/2 cup butter, softened
1/2 cup packed brown sugar
1 egg
1 package (18-1/4 ounces) white cake mix
1 cup finely crushed cornflakes
1 cup strawberry jam *or* preserves

In a mixing bowl, cream butter and brown sugar until smooth. Add egg; mix well. Gradually add dry cake mix and cornflakes. Set aside 1-1/2 cups for topping. Press remaining dough into a greased 13-in. x 9-in. x 2-in. baking pan.

Carefully spread jam over crust. Sprinkle with reserved dough; gently press down. Bake at 350° for 30 minutes or until golden brown. Cool completely on a wire rack. Cut into bars. **Yield:** 2 dozen.

Peanut Butter Squares

As a child, I spent a lot of time in the kitchen with my mom and grandmother making treats like this.
—Rachel Keller, Roanoke, Virginia

3/4 cup cold butter, cubed
2 squares (1 ounce *each*) semisweet chocolate
1-1/2 cups graham cracker crumbs (about 24 squares)
1 cup flaked coconut
1/2 cup chopped salted peanuts
1/4 cup toasted wheat germ
FILLING:
2 packages (8 ounces *each*) cream cheese, softened
3/4 cup sugar
2/3 cup chunky peanut butter
1 teaspoon vanilla extract
TOPPING:
4 squares (1 ounce *each*) semisweet chocolate
1/4 cup butter

In a microwave-safe bowl, heat cubed butter and chocolate on high for 1 minute; stir. Microwave 30-60 seconds longer or until melted; stir until smooth. Stir in cracker crumbs, coconut, peanuts and wheat germ. Press into a greased 13-in. x 9-in. x 2-in. pan. Cover; refrigerate for at least 30 minutes.

In a mixing bowl, combine filling ingredients; mix well. Spread over crust. Cover; refrigerate at least 30 minutes. In a microwave-safe bowl, heat chocolate and butter on high 45 seconds; stir. Microwave 30 seconds longer or until melted; stir until smooth. Pour over filling. Cover; refrigerate at least 30 minutes or until topping is set. Cut into squares. Refrigerate leftovers. **Yield:** 4 dozen.

Editor's Note: This recipe was tested in an 850-watt microwave.

Harvest Sugar Cookies

(Pictured at right)

Rich buttery cookies like these never last long. I got this recipe from a friend years ago and have made it many times since. —Lynn Burgess, Rolla, Missouri

> 3/4 cup butter, softened
> 1 cup sugar
> 2 eggs
> 1 teaspoon vanilla extract
> 2-3/4 cups all-purpose flour
> 1 teaspoon baking powder
> 1/2 teaspoon salt
> **Frosting *or* additional sugar, optional**

In a mixing bowl, cream butter and sugar. Add eggs and vanilla; beat until light and fluffy. Combine flour, baking powder and salt; gradually add to creamed mixture and mix well. Chill for 1 hour or until firm.

On a lightly floured surface, roll dough to 1/4-in. thickness. Cut with desired pumpkin, leaf or other cookie cutters. Using a floured spatula, place cookies on greased baking sheets. Sprinkle with sugar if desired (or frost baked cookies after they have cooled). Bake at 375° for 8-10 minutes or until lightly browned. Cool on wire racks. **Yield:** 6-7 dozen (2-1/2-inch cookies).

Editor's Note: For a richer color, tint frosting with food coloring paste.

Orange Cheesecake Bars

These creamy layered bars are so simple to make, you'll want to indulge in them year-round.
—Connie Faulkner, Moxee, Washington

> 2 cups crushed vanilla wafers (about 40)
> 1/4 cup butter, melted
> 3 packages (8 ounces *each*) cream cheese, softened
> 1 can (14 ounces) sweetened condensed milk
> 3 eggs
> 2 teaspoons vanilla extract
> 2 tablespoons orange juice concentrate
> 1 teaspoon grated orange peel
> 1 teaspoon orange extract
> 5 drops yellow food coloring
> 3 drops red food coloring

In a bowl, combine wafer crumbs and butter. Press in a greased 13-in. x 9-in. x 2-in. baking pan. In a mixi bowl, beat cream cheese until smooth. Add milk, eg and vanilla; beat just until combined. Pour half ov crust. Add orange juice concentrate, orange peel, extra and food coloring to remaining cream cheese mixtu beat until combined. Pour over first layer.

Bake at 325° for 45-50 minutes or until center is most set. Cool on a wire rack. Refrigerate for at leas hours before cutting. **Yield:** 3 dozen.

M+M Oat Bars

These irresistible bars are the perfect way to sweet any gathering. Use fall-color M&M's for Hallowe parties. —Renee Schwebach, Dumont, Minneso

> 1/2 cup butter, softened
> 1 cup packed brown sugar
> 1 egg
> 1 teaspoon vanilla extract
> 1-1/4 cups all-purpose flour

1/2 teaspoon baking soda
1/2 teaspoon salt
2 cups quick-cooking oats
1 package (14 ounces) caramels
3 tablespoons water
1 cup miniature semisweet chocolate chips
1 cup chopped walnuts
1 cup plain M&M's
3 ounces white candy coating

In a mixing bowl, cream butter and brown sugar. Beat in egg and vanilla. Combine flour, baking soda and salt; add to the creamed mixture. Stir in oats. Press into a greased 15-in. x 10-in. x 1-in. baking pan. Bake at 350° for 10-15 minutes or until golden brown. Cool on a wire rack.

In a microwave-safe bowl, melt caramels and water. Spread over crust. Sprinkle with chips, nuts and M&M's. Gently press into caramel mixture. Melt candy coating; drizzle over top. Cut into bars. **Yield:** 6 dozen.

Monster Chip Cookies

I share these jumbo chocolate chip cookies with the "monsters" who ring my doorbell every Halloween.
—Judy Mabrey, Myrtle Beach, South Carolina

1 cup shortening
1/2 cup butter, softened
1-1/3 cups sugar
1 cup packed brown sugar
4 eggs
3 teaspoons vanilla extract
1 teaspoon lemon juice
3 cups all-purpose flour
1/2 cup quick-cooking oats
2 teaspoons baking soda
1-1/2 teaspoons salt
1 teaspoon ground cinnamon
4 cups (24 ounces) semisweet chocolate chips
2 cups chopped nuts

In a mixing bowl, cream shortening, butter and sugars until light and fluffy, about 5 minutes. Add eggs, one at a time, beating well after each. Add vanilla and lemon juice. Combine the dry ingredients; add to creamed mixture and mix well. Stir in chips and nuts. Refrigerate 8 hours or overnight.

Drop by 1/4 cupfuls 3 in. apart onto lightly greased baking sheets. Bake at 350° for 14-16 minutes or until lightly browned and center is set. Cool for 2 minutes before removing to wire racks. **Yield:** about 3 dozen.

Halloween Cat Cookies

(Pictured below)

Trick-or-treaters of all ages will gobble up these festive feline goodies conjured up by our Test Kitchen home economists.

1 tube (18 ounces) refrigerated chocolate chip cookie dough
54 pieces candy corn
1 can (16 ounces) chocolate frosting
Red shoestring licorice, cut into 1-3/8-inch pieces
9 thin chocolate wafers (2-1/4-inch diameter), quartered

Bake cookies according to package directions. Cool on wire racks. Cut off yellow tips from 18 pieces of candy corn (discard orange and white portion or save for another use). Frost cookies with chocolate frosting.

Immediately decorate with two whole candy corns for eyes, a yellow candy corn tip for nose, six licorice pieces for whiskers and two wafer quarters for ears. **Yield:** 1-1/2 dozen.

Spirited Snacks + Sweets

Recipes

Project

Crispy Kiss Squares

(Pictured at right)

White or milk chocolate kisses add the final touch to these sweet treats. —Chris Budd, Lewiston, Idaho

 6 cups Cocoa Puffs
 1/4 cup butter
 40 large marshmallows
 1 package (11-1/2 ounces) milk chocolate chips
 24 striped chocolate kisses

Place cereal in a large bowl; set aside. In a microwave-safe bowl, combine the butter and marshmallows. Microwave, uncovered, on high for 3 minutes; stir. Continue cooking until smooth, stirring every minute. Add chocolate chips and stir until melted.

Pour over cereal; stir until well-coated. Spread evenly in a greased 13-in. x 9-in. x 2-in. pan. Arrange kisses in rows over the top. Cool before cutting. **Yield:** 2 dozen.

Editor's Note: This recipe was tested in an 850-watt microwave.

Halloween Snack Mix
Crispy Kiss Squares

Halloween Snack Mix

(Pictured above right)

Here's a simple snack mix I created on the spur of the moment. It's easy to toss together for a Halloween party. —Barbara Roberts, Middleton, Wisconsin

 6 cups caramel corn
 2 cups salted cashews *or* peanuts
 1-1/2 cups candy corn
 1/3 cup raisins

In a large bowl, combine the caramel corn, cashews, candy corn and raisins; mix well. Store in an airtight container. **Yield:** about 2 quarts.

Halloween Fun Fact

The first recorded Halloween celebration in the U.S. took place in Anoka, Minnesota in 1921.
(Source: U.S. Census Bureau)

Chili Cheddar Pinwheels

These baked Southwestern bites, made with crescent roll dough, will steal the show at your next get-together. —Mary Dorchester, Midland, Texas

 1 package (8 ounces) cream cheese, softened
 1 cup (4 ounces) shredded cheddar cheese
 1 can (4 ounces) chopped green chilies, drained
 2 tablespoons picante sauce
 1/2 teaspoon chili powder
 1/4 teaspoon garlic salt
 1/4 teaspoon onion powder
 2 tubes (8 ounces *each*) refrigerated crescent rolls
Additional chili powder, optional

In a mixing bowl, beat cream cheese. Add the cheddar cheese, chilies, picante sauce, chili powder, garlic salt and onion powder. Separate each tube of crescent roll dough into four rectangles; press perforations to seal. Spread about 1/4 cup cheese mixture over each rectangle. Roll up jelly-roll style, starting with a short side. Wrap in plastic wrap and chill for at least 1 hour.

Cut each roll into eight slices; place on ungreased

king sheets. Sprinkle with additional chili powder if
sired. Bake at 350° for 10-12 minutes or until golden
own. **Yield:** 64 appetizers.

Mini Hamburgers

's guaranteed—these snack sandwiches will disap-
ar fast! —Judy Lewis, Sterling Heights, Michigan

- **1/2 cup chopped onion**
- **1 tablespoon butter**
- **1 pound lean ground beef**
- **1 egg, beaten**

- **1/4 teaspoon seasoned salt**
- **1/4 teaspoon rubbed sage**
- **1/4 teaspoon salt**
- **1/8 teaspoon pepper**
- **40 mini rolls, split**
- **8 ounces process American cheese slices, cut into 1-1/2-inch squares, optional**
- **40 dill pickle slices, optional**

In a skillet, saute onion in butter. Transfer to a bowl; add meat, egg and seasonings. Spread over bottom halves of the rolls; replace tops. Place on baking sheets; cover with foil. Bake at 350° for 20 minutes.

If desired, place a cheese square and pickle on each hamburger; replace tops and foil and return to the oven for 5 minutes. **Yield:** 40 appetizers.

Halloween Votive Holder

(Pictured below right)

sparked a festive Halloween look in my home by painting a plain wooden holder for
a votive candle. —Barbara Matthiessen, Port Orchard, Washington

Materials Needed:
2-3/4-inch square wooden votive candle holder with a glass candle cup; fine sandpaper; tack cloth; water basin; paper towels; palette or foam plate; 1-inch foam brush; small flat paintbrush; acrylic craft paints—black, yellow, gold, orange and white; 1-inch stencil brush; stencil of small stars of different sizes; acrylic sealer; white votive candle.

Finished Size:
Votive candle holder measures 2-3/4 inches square.

Directions:
Keep paper towels and a basin of water handy to clean paintbrushes. When painting, place dabs of each paint color onto palette or foam plate as needed. Add coats of paint as needed for complete coverage, letting paint dry after each application.

Remove glass cup from candle holder and set aside. Sand candle holder and wipe clean with tack cloth. Using foam brush, paint exterior of candle holder black.

Hold star stencil firmly against candle holder. Using

stencil brush and gold paint, stencil a star onto candle holder using an up-and-down motion. Repeat, stenciling gold stars where desired.

Using flat paintbrush, paint white candy corn shapes on the candle holder where desired. When dry, paint wide end of each candy corn orange. Paint center section of each candy corn yellow.

Dip the end of small brush handle into white paint and dab a dot onto candle holder where desired. Continue adding dots as desired in the same way.

Apply two coats of sealer following sealer manufacturer's instructions. Let dry.

Replace glass cup in candle holder and place candle in cup.

Popcorn Balls
Walnut Chicken Spread
Chocolate Coconut Bars

Chocolate Coconut Bars

(Pictured above)

With nuts, chocolate and a creamy cheesecake-like layer, these treats taste like homemade candy bars.
—Carolyn Kyzer, Alexander, Arkansas

> 1 tube (8 ounces) refrigerated crescent rolls
> 1 package (8 ounces) cream cheese, softened
> 1/3 cup confectioners' sugar
> 1 egg
> 3/4 cup flaked coconut
> 1 cup (6 ounces) semisweet chocolate chips
> 1/4 cup chopped nuts

Unroll crescent roll dough into one long rectangle on an ungreased baking sheet; seal seams and perforations. Roll out into a 13-in. x 9-in. rectangle, building up dough around edges. In a small mixing bowl, beat the cream cheese, confectioners' sugar and egg until smooth; stir in coconut. Spread over crust.

Bake at 375° for 10-15 minutes or until cream cheese mixture is set. Immediately sprinkle with chips. Let stand for 5 minutes; spread melted chips over the top. Sprin-

kle with nuts. Cool completely before cutting. **Yiel** 2-1/2 dozen.

Popcorn Balls

(Pictured above)

These sweet chewy snacks are made from one of ou state's most popular crops—popcorn! This version ho a tempting caramel color and nice flavor.
—Edna Hoffman, Hebron, Indian

> 2 quarts popped popcorn
> 1 cup packed brown sugar
> 1/3 cup water
> 1/3 cup dark corn syrup
> 1/4 cup butter
> 1/2 teaspoon salt
> 1 teaspoon vanilla extract

Place popcorn in a large bowl; set aside. In a heav saucepan, combine brown sugar, water, corn syru butter and salt. Bring to a boil over medium heat, stir

constantly. Continue cooking, without stirring, until a candy thermometer reads 270° (soft-crack stage).
Remove from the heat; stir in vanilla. Pour over
popcorn; stir until evenly coated. When cool enough to
handle, quickly shape into balls. **Yield:** 6 servings.

Editor's Note: We recommend that you test your
candy thermometer before each use by bringing water
to a boil; the thermometer should read 212°. Adjust your
recipe temperature up or down based on your test.

Walnut Chicken Spread

(Pictured at left)

*We love this mild combination of chicken, crunchy
nuts, onion and celery. It's perfect with crackers or in
a sandwich.* —Joan Whelan, Green Valley, Arizona

  1-3/4 cups finely chopped cooked chicken
      1 cup finely chopped walnuts
     2/3 cup mayonnaise
      1 celery rib, finely chopped
      1 small onion, finely chopped
      1 teaspoon salt
     1/2 teaspoon garlic powder
Assorted crackers

In a bowl, combine the chicken, walnuts, mayonnaise,
celery, onion, salt and garlic powder. Serve with crackers. Refrigerate any leftovers. **Yield:** 2-1/2 cups.

Cheddar Potato Strips

*This easy dish wins compliments every time I serve it
to family and guests. Fresh parsley adds flavor and
looks nice sprinkled over the melted cheddar cheese.*
—Lucinda Walker, Somerset, Pennsylvania

    3 large potatoes, cut into 1/2-inch strips
  1/2 cup milk
     1 tablespoon butter
Salt and pepper to taste
  1/2 cup shredded cheddar cheese
     1 tablespoon minced fresh parsley

In a greased 13-in. x 9-in. x 2-in. baking dish, arrange
potatoes in a single layer. Pour milk over potatoes. Dot
with butter; sprinkle with salt and pepper. Cover and
bake at 425° for 30 minutes or until the potatoes are
tender. Sprinkle with cheese and parsley. Bake, uncovered, 5 minutes longer or until cheese is melted. **Yield:**
4 servings.

Hot Macadamia Spread

(Pictured below)

*Whenever guests sample this rich spread, they can't
quite put their finger on the zippy ingredient—horseradish. It keeps them coming back for more.*
       —Naomi Francis, Waukesha, Wisconsin

    1 package (8 ounces) cream cheese, softened
    2 tablespoons milk
  1/2 cup sour cream
    2 teaspoons prepared horseradish
  1/4 cup finely chopped green pepper
    1 green onion, chopped
  1/2 teaspoon garlic salt
  1/4 teaspoon pepper
  **1/2 cup chopped macadamia nuts *or* blanched
      almonds**
    2 teaspoons butter
Assorted crackers

In a mixing bowl, beat cream cheese and milk until
smooth. Stir in sour cream, horseradish, green pepper,
onion, garlic salt and pepper. Spoon into an ungreased
shallow 2-cup baking dish; set aside.

In a skillet, saute the nuts in butter for 3-4 minutes
or until lightly browned. Sprinkle over the cream cheese
mixture. Bake, uncovered, at 350° for 20 minutes. Serve
with crackers. **Yield:** 6-8 servings.

Crunchy Italian Mix

We love this savory mix when we get the munchies in the evening. I started out fixing it for the friends in our bridge group, and now I often make it for my family, too. —Sharon Evans, Rockwell, Iowa

    1/2 cup butter
      1 tablespoon Worcestershire sauce
      1 teaspoon Italian seasoning
    1/2 teaspoon garlic powder
      5 cups Crispix cereal
      2 cups Cheerios cereal
  2-1/2 cups mini pretzels
      1 can (10 ounces) mixed nuts
    1/4 cup grated Parmesan cheese

In a saucepan or microwave-safe bowl, heat the first four ingredients until butter is melted; mix well. In a large bowl, combine the cereals, pretzels, nuts and Parmesan cheese. Drizzle with butter mixture and mix well. Place in an ungreased 15-in. x 10-in. x 1-in. baking pan. Bake, uncovered, at 250° for 45 minutes, stirring every 15 minutes. **Yield:** 10 cups.

Baked Potato Skins

(Pictured below)

Both crisp and satisfying, this tasty snack also makes a great side dish when you're serving a main course of beef or seafood. —Trish Perrin, Keizer, Oregon

      4 large baking potatoes, baked
      3 tablespoons vegetable oil
      1 tablespoon grated Parmesan cheese
    1/2 teaspoon salt
    1/4 teaspoon garlic powder
    1/4 teaspoon paprika
    1/8 teaspoon pepper
      8 bacon strips, cooked and crumbled
  1-1/2 cups (6 ounces) shredded cheddar cheese
    1/2 cup sour cream
      4 green onions, sliced

Cut potatoes in half lengthwise; scoop out pulp, leaving a 1/4-in. shell (save pulp for another use). Place potato skins on a greased baking sheet. Combine oil, Parmesan cheese, salt, garlic powder, paprika and pepper; brush over both sides of skins.

Bake at 475° for 7 minutes; turn. Bake until crisp, about 7 minutes more. Sprinkle bacon and cheddar cheese inside skins. Bake 2 minutes longer or until the cheese is melted. Top with sour cream and onions. Serve immediately. **Yield:** 8 servings.

Haunting Hot Chocolate

I serve mugs of this quick-to-fix hot cocoa outside when the kids in our neighborhood go trick-or-treating for Halloween. It's a nice change of pace from candy. —Suzanne Cleveland, Lyons, Georgia

      1 cup nonfat dry milk powder
      5 tablespoons sugar
      3 tablespoons baking cocoa
    1/8 to 1/4 teaspoon ground cinnamon
Dash salt
      3 cups boiling water

In a saucepan, combine the milk powder, sugar, cocoa, cinnamon and salt. Add boiling water; stir until milk powder is dissolved. **Yield:** 5 servings.

Taco Pumpkin Seeds

Here's a spicy idea from the Taste of Home Test Kitchen—toast seeds from a freshly cut pumpkin in taco seasoning and a bit of garlic salt. The unusual combination packs a tasty punch!

Chocolate Spiders
Mini Corn Dogs

1-2/3 cups all-purpose flour
1/3 cup cornmeal
3 teaspoons baking powder
1 teaspoon salt
3 tablespoons cold butter
1 tablespoon shortening
1 egg
3/4 cup milk
24 miniature hot dogs
HONEY MUSTARD SAUCE:
1/3 cup honey
1/3 cup prepared mustard
1 tablespoon molasses

In a large bowl, combine the first four ingredients. Cut in butter and shortening until mixture resembles coarse crumbs. Beat egg and milk; stir into dry ingredients until a soft dough forms.

Turn onto a lightly floured surface; knead 6-8 times or until smooth. Roll out to 1/4-in. thickness. Cut with a 2-1/4-in. biscuit cutter. Fold each dough circle over a hot dog and press edges to seal (dough will be sticky). Place on greased baking sheets.

Bake at 450° for 10-12 minutes or until golden brown. Combine sauce ingredients in a small bowl; mix well. Serve with the corn dogs. **Yield:** 2 dozen.

1 cup seeds from freshly cut pumpkin, washed
and dried
2 tablespoons vegetable oil
1 to 2 tablespoons taco seasoning
1/4 to 1/2 teaspoon garlic salt

a skillet, saute pumpkin seeds in oil for 5 minutes or
ntil lightly browned. Using a slotted spoon, transfer
eds to an ungreased 15-in. x 10-in. x 1-in. baking
n. Sprinkle with taco seasoning and garlic salt; stir to
at. Spread into a single layer.

Bake at 325° for 15-20 minutes or until crisp. Remove
paper towels to cool completely. Store in an airtight
ntainer for up to 3 weeks. **Yield:** 1 cup.

Mini Corn Dogs

(Pictured above)

*or fun flavor, try this snack of cornmeal dough
round mini hot dogs with a tangy dipping sauce.*
       —Geralyn Harrington, Floral Park, New York

Chocolate Spiders

(Pictured above left)

*Turn your kitchen into a "web site" by making these
candy crawlers.   —Sandi Pichon, Slidell, Louisiana*

8 squares (1 ounce *each*) semisweet chocolate
2 cups miniature marshmallows
Black *or* red shoestring licorice
24 small round candy-coated milk
chocolate balls (such as Hersheys *or* Sixlets)

In a microwave-safe bowl, heat chocolate for 2 minutes at 50% power, stirring after 1 minute. Stir until melted; let stand for 5 minutes. Stir in marshmallows. Drop by tablespoonfuls onto a waxed paper-lined baking sheet.

Cut licorice into 2-in. pieces; press eight pieces into each mound for legs. Press two chocolate balls into each for eyes. Refrigerate until firm, about 20 minutes. **Yield:** 2 dozen.

Editor's Note: This recipe was tested in an 850-watt microwave.

Caramel Apple Bites

(Pictured below)

This recipe is one everyone enjoys. I bake cookies that have an apple filling, then dip them into caramel and nuts. —Darlene Markel, Sublimity, Oregon

FILLING:
- 1/3 cup chopped unpeeled apple
- 1/3 cup evaporated milk
- 1/3 cup sugar
- 1/3 cup chopped walnuts

DOUGH:
- 1/2 cup butter, softened
- 1/4 cup confectioners' sugar
- 1/4 cup packed brown sugar
- 1 egg
- 1 teaspoon vanilla extract
- 1/4 teaspoon salt
- 2 cups all-purpose flour

TOPPING:
- 1 package (14 ounces) caramels
- 2/3 cup evaporated milk

Green toothpicks
- 1 cup chopped walnuts

In a small saucepan, combine filling ingredients. Cook and stir over medium heat until thickened; set aside to cool. In a mixing bowl, cream butter and sugars. Add egg, vanilla and salt; beat well. Add flour; mix well.

Shape dough into 1-in. balls. Flatten and place 1/4 teaspoon filling in center of each. Fold dough over filling and reshape into balls. Place 1 in. apart on greased baking sheets. Bake at 350° for 12-15 minutes or until lightly browned. Remove to wire racks to cool.

In a saucepan over low heat, cook caramels and evaporated milk, stirring occasionally, until caramels are melted. Insert a toothpick into each cookie and dip int caramel topping until completely coated. Dip bottoms cookies into nuts. Place on wire racks to set. **Yield:** abou 3 dozen.

Creamy Sourdough Snack

(Pictured at right)

Hearty and impressive-looking, this bread dip was big hit at my mom's 50th birthday party and othe get-togethers. —Darelyn Payes, Hayward, Californ

- 1-1/2 cups (12 ounces) sour cream
- 2 packages (3 ounces *each*) cream cheese
- 1/2 cup chopped green onions
- 1 teaspoon Worcestershire sauce
- 2 cups (8 ounces) shredded sharp cheddar cheese
- 1-1/2 cups cubed fully cooked ham
- 1 round loaf (1 pound) sourdough bread

Chopped fresh parsley, optional

In a saucepan, combine sour cream, cream cheese, onior and Worcestershire sauce; cook and stir over low hea until blended. Add cheese and ham; cook and stir unt cheese is melted and ham is heated through.

Cut off top of loaf; carefully hollow out top an bottom, leaving a 1/2-in. shell. Cut bread into cube Pour dip into shell; sprinkle with parsley if desire Serve with bread cubes. **Yield:** 3-1/2 cups.

Goblin Chewies

(Pictured above right)

These light, crispy cookies are packed with fun ir gredients like candy orange slices—just right for Ha loween. —Bernice Morris, Marshfield, Missou

- 1 cup shortening
- 1 cup packed brown sugar
- 1 cup sugar
- 2 eggs
- 1 teaspoon vanilla extract
- 2 cups all-purpose flour

Creamy Soudough Snack
Caramel Peanut Butter Dip
Goblin Chewies

1 teaspoon baking soda
1/2 teaspoon baking powder
1/2 teaspoon salt
1-1/2 cups old-fashioned oats
1 cup crisp rice cereal
1 cup diced candy orange slices
1 cup (6 ounces) semisweet chocolate chips
   or raisins
Additional raisins *or* chocolate chips and candy
   orange slices

In a mixing bowl, cream shortening and sugars. Add eggs
and vanilla; mix well. Combine the flour, baking soda,
baking powder and salt; add to creamed mixture. Stir in
oats, cereal, orange slices and chips or raisins.

Drop by tablespoonfuls 2 in. apart onto greased
baking sheets. Flatten slightly with a fork. Decorate with
raisin or chocolate chip eyes and orange slice mouths.
Bake at 350° for 10-14 minutes. Cool on wire racks.
Yield: about 6 dozen.

Editor's Note: Orange slices cut easier if microwaved
for 5 seconds on high and cut with a sharp knife or
kitchen scissors.

Caramel Peanut Butter Dip

(*Pictured above*)

*When crisp autumn apples are available, I whip up
this quick delicious dip. Add nuts to give it crunch.*
—Sandra McKenzie, Braham, Minnesota

30 caramels
1 to 2 tablespoons water
1/4 cup plus 2 tablespoons creamy peanut butter
1/4 cup finely crushed peanuts, optional
Sliced apples

In a microwave-safe bowl, microwave the caramels and
water on high for 1 minute; stir. Microwave 1 minute
more or until smooth. Add peanut butter and mix well;
microwave for 30 seconds or until smooth. Stir in
peanuts if desired. Serve warm with apples. **Yield:** 1 cup.

Editor's Note: This recipe was tested in a 700-watt
microwave.

Sweet 'n' Spicy Halloween Munch

(Pictured at left and below left)

Kids of all ages find the combination of salted peanuts and candy in this festive finger food irresistible. With just three ingredients, it comes together in a snap. —Shana Reiley, Theresa, New York

- **1 pound spiced gumdrops**
- **1 pound candy corn**
- **1 can (16 ounces) salted peanuts**

In a bowl, combine the gumdrops, candy corn and peanuts. Store in an airtight container. **Yield:** 2 quarts.

Pecan-Date Cheese Ball

This lightly sweet cheese ball is nice to have on hand when we crave something creamy...and it's always a hit at parties. —Sue Broyles, Cherokee, Texas

- **1 teaspoon ground mustard**
- **1 teaspoon water**
- **2 packages (8 ounces *each*) cream cheese, softened**
- **1/4 cup mayonnaise**
- **1/4 teaspoon ground nutmeg**
- **2 cups (8 ounces) shredded cheddar cheese**
- **1 cup chopped dates**
- **1 cup chopped pecans**
Crackers

In a small bowl, dissolve the mustard in water; let stand for 10 minutes. In a mixing bowl, beat cream cheese and mayonnaise until smooth. Add nutmeg and mustard mixture. Stir in cheese and dates. Chill for 15 minutes. Shape into a ball; roll in pecans. Chill. Serve with crackers. **Yield:** 3-1/2 cups (4-inch ball).

Fried Cinnamon Strips

I first made these crispy strips for a special family night at our church. Most of them were snapped up before dinner! —Nancy Johnson, Laverne, Oklahoma

- **1 cup sugar**
- **1 teaspoon ground cinnamon**

Snack Mix Serving Tip

INSTEAD of simply setting out bowls of Sweet 'n' Spicy Halloween Munch (recipe above right), place individual servings in edible containers like waffle cones and set them in a bowl filled with candy corn (as shown below). This way, guests will be able to munch as they mingle.

Or, instead of using waffle cones, make paper cones (like those in the photo above).

Take heavy-duty paper (we used origami paper) and roll it to make a cone shape. Secure with tape and fill with snack mix.

1/4 teaspoon ground nutmeg
10 flour tortillas (8 inches)
Cooking oil

In a large resealable plastic bag, combine sugar, cinnamon and nutmeg; set aside. Cut tortillas into 3-in. x 2-in. strips. Heat 1 in. of oil in a skillet or electric fry pan to 375°; fry 4-5 strips at a time for 30 seconds on each side or until golden brown. Drain on paper towels.

While still warm, place strips in bag with sugar mixture; shake gently to coat. Serve immediately or store in an airtight container. **Yield:** 5 dozen.

Pronto Mini Pizzas

(Pictured below)

These quick pizzas on pita bread crusts are a great snack anytime. I also serve them as a light meal on busy days. —Debbi Smith, Crossett, Arkansas

    1 pound ground beef *or* turkey
    1 cup sliced fresh mushrooms
  1/2 cup chopped green pepper
  1/2 cup chopped onion
    2 garlic cloves, minced
    1 can (8 ounces) tomato sauce
    1 teaspoon fennel seed
  1/2 teaspoon salt
  1/2 teaspoon dried oregano
    4 pita breads
    1 cup (4 ounces) shredded mozzarella cheese

In a skillet over medium heat, cook meat, mushrooms, green pepper, onion and garlic until meat is no longer pink and vegetables are tender; drain. Stir in tomato sauce, fennel, salt and oregano. Simmer for 1-2 minutes.

Meanwhile, warm pitas in the microwave. Top each with meat mixture; sprinkle with cheese. Microwave or broil until cheese is melted. Cut into quarters. **Yield:** 4 servings.

Marbled Orange Fudge

(Pictured above)

This soft, colorful fudge is guaranteed to get smiles. It has the familiar taste of frozen Creamsicles.
—Diane Wampler, Morristown, Tennessee

1-1/2 teaspoons plus 3/4 cup butter, *divided*
    3 cups sugar
  3/4 cup heavy whipping cream
    1 package (10 to 12 ounces) vanilla *or* white chips
    1 jar (7 ounces) marshmallow creme
    3 teaspoons orange extract
   12 drops yellow food coloring
    5 drops red food coloring

Grease a 13-in. x 9-in. x 2-in. pan with 1-1/2 teaspoons butter. In a heavy saucepan, combine the sugar, cream and remaining butter. Cook and stir over low heat until sugar is dissolved. Bring to a boil; cook and stir for 4 minutes. Remove from the heat; stir in chips and marshmallow creme until smooth. Remove 1 cup and set aside.

Add orange extract and food colorings to remaining mixture; stir until blended. Pour into prepared pan. Drop the reserved marshmallow mixture by tablespoonfuls over top; cut through mixture with a knife to swirl. Cover and refrigerate until set. Cut into squares. **Yield:** about 2-1/2 pounds.

Ghostly
Good
Desserts

Recipes

Projects

Pumpkin Cake Roll

(Pictured below)

Roll out this well-rounded dessert—and get set to harvest plenty of compliments! It earns me raves whenever I serve it. —June Mullins, Livonia, Missouri

> 3 eggs
> 1 cup sugar
> 2/3 cup canned pumpkin
> 3/4 cup biscuit/baking mix
> 2 teaspoons ground cinnamon
> 1 teaspoon pumpkin pie spice
> 1/2 teaspoon ground nutmeg
> 1 cup chopped nuts
> Confectioners' sugar
> FILLING:
> 2 packages (3 ounces *each*) cream cheese, softened
> 1/4 cup butter, softened
> 1 cup confectioners' sugar
> 1 teaspoon vanilla extract

In a mixing bowl, beat eggs. Gradually add sugar. Stir in pumpkin; mix well. Combine the biscuit mix, cinnamon, pie spice and nutmeg; add to egg mixture and mix well. Line a 15-in. x 10-in. x 1-in. pan with waxed paper; grease and flour the paper. Spread batter evenly in pan. Sprinkle with nuts.

Bake at 375° for 13-15 minutes or until a toothpick inserted near the center comes out clean. Cool for 10 minutes. Turn cake onto a linen towel dusted with confectioners' sugar. Remove paper; roll up cake in towel, starting with a short side. Cool on a wire rack.

For filling, in a mixing bowl, beat cream cheese, butter, sugar and vanilla until smooth. Unroll cake. Spread filling over cake to within 1 in. of edges. Gently roll up; place seam side down on a platter. Refrigerate until serving. **Yield:** 10 servings.

Caramel Apple Cupcakes

(Pictured above)

Bring these fun cupcakes to a bake sale and watch how quickly they disappear—if your family doesn't eat them first! —Diane Halferty, Corpus Christi, Texas

> 1 package (18-1/4 ounces) spice *or* carrot cake mix
> 2 cups chopped peeled tart apples
> 20 caramels
> 3 tablespoons milk
> 1 cup finely chopped pecans, toasted
> 12 Popsicle sticks

Prepare cake batter according to the package directions; fold in the apples. Fill 12 greased or paper-lined jumbo muffin cups three-fourths full. Bake at 350° for 20 minutes or until a toothpick comes out clean. Cool for

10 minutes before removing from pans to wire racks to cool completely.

In a saucepan, cook the caramels and milk over low heat until smooth. Spread over cupcakes. Sprinkle with pecans. Insert a wooden stick into the center of each cupcake. **Yield:** 1 dozen.

Chocolate Cream Cake

(Pictured below)

Whenever I take this moist chocolate cake with butter cream filling to a function, I'm asked for the recipe.
—Marge Dellert, Shepherd, Michigan

    1 package (18-1/4 ounces) devil's food
      cake mix
  1/2 cup butter, softened
  1/2 cup shortening
1-1/4 cups sugar
  3/4 cup milk
    1 teaspoon vanilla extract
GLAZE:
    1 cup sugar
  1/3 cup baking cocoa
    3 tablespoons cornstarch
    1 cup water
    3 tablespoons butter, cubed
    1 teaspoon vanilla extract

Prepare and bake cake according to package directions, using a greased and floured 13-in. x 9-in. x 2-in. baking pan. Cool for 10 minutes before inverting onto a wire rack. Cool completely.

For filling, in a mixing bowl, cream the butter, shortening and sugar until light and fluffy. In a small saucepan, heat milk to 140°; add to the creamed mixture. Beat until sugar is dissolved. Stir in vanilla. Split cake into two horizontal layers; spread filling over bottom cake layer. Top with remaining cake layer.

In a saucepan, combine sugar, cocoa, cornstarch and water until smooth. Bring to a boil over medium heat, stirring constantly. Cook and stir for 1-2 minutes or until thickened.

Remove from the heat; stir in butter and vanilla until glaze is smooth. Cool to lukewarm. Spread over top of the cake. Let stand until set. Refrigerate leftovers. **Yield:** 16-20 servings.

Creamy Orange Fluff

I got this yummy recipe from a friend but came up with my own tasty topping. Creamy, fruity and refreshing, this treat is simple to make ahead of time and cuts nicely into squares for ease in serving.
—Nancy Callis, Woodinville, Washington

    1 package (6 ounces) orange gelatin
2-1/2 cups boiling water
    2 cans (11 ounces *each*) mandarin oranges,
      drained
    1 can (8 ounces) crushed pineapple, undrained
    1 can (6 ounces) frozen orange juice
      concentrate, thawed
TOPPING:
    1 package (8 ounces) cream cheese, softened
    1 cup cold milk
    1 package (3.4 ounces) instant vanilla
      pudding mix

In a bowl, dissolve the orange gelatin in boiling water. Stir in the mandarin oranges, pineapple and orange juice concentrate. Coat a 13-in. x 9-in. x 2-in. dish with cooking spray; add the gelatin mixture. Refrigerate until firm.

In a mixing bowl, beat the cream cheese until light. Gradually add the milk and pudding mix; beat until smooth. Spread over orange layer. Chill until firm. **Yield:** 12-16 servings.

Tropical Carrot Cake

My great-aunt gave me this recipe. To add festive color, garnish each piece with a sprinkling of shredded carrots. —Victoria Teeter-Casey, Enterprise, Oregon

 3 eggs
 3/4 cup vegetable oil
 3/4 cup buttermilk
 2 cups all-purpose flour
 2 cups sugar
 2 teaspoons baking soda
 2 teaspoons ground cinnamon
 1/2 teaspoon salt
 2 teaspoons vanilla extract
 2 cups finely shredded carrots
 1 cup raisins
 1 can (8 ounces) crushed pineapple, undrained
 1 cup chopped walnuts
 1 cup flaked coconut
FROSTING:
 1 package (8 ounces) cream cheese, softened
 4 to 4-1/2 cups confectioners' sugar
 1 to 2 tablespoons heavy whipping cream
 1 teaspoon vanilla extract

In a large mixing bowl, beat eggs, oil and buttermilk. Combine flour, sugar, baking soda, cinnamon and salt; add to egg mixture and mix well. Stir in vanilla, carrots, raisins, pineapple, walnuts and coconut; mix well. Pour into a greased 13-in. x 9-in. x 2-in. baking pan.

Bake at 350° for 45-50 minutes or until a toothpick inserted in center comes out clean. Cool. For frosting, beat all the ingredients in a large mixing bowl until smooth. Frost the cake. Store in the refrigerator. **Yield:** 12-16 servings.

Chocolate Mousse Pumpkin Pie

This fluffy delight combines pumpkin with two kinds of chocolate. —Kathy Peters, Omaha, Nebraska

 1 cup canned pumpkin
 2 cups miniature marshmallows
 1/2 cup milk chocolate chips
 1/2 cup miniature semisweet chocolate chips
 1 carton (12 ounces) frozen whipped topping, thawed

 1 graham cracker crust (9 inches)
Additional miniature semisweet chocolate chips, optional

In a large microwave-safe bowl, combine the pumpkin, marshmallows and chips. Microwave, uncovered, on high for 1-1/2 minutes; stir. Microwave 30-45 seconds longer or until marshmallows are melted and mixture is smooth, stirring every 15 seconds. Cool to room temperature, stirring several times.

Set aside about 1 tablespoon of whipped topping. Fold remaining topping into pumpkin mixture. Spoon into crust. Garnish with the reserved topping and miniature chips if desired. Refrigerate for at least 2 hours before slicing. **Yield:** 6-8 servings.

Editor's Note: This recipe was tested in an 850-watt microwave.

Apple Crisp Pizza

(Pictured below)

While visiting a Wisconsin apple orchard bakery, I tried an apple pizza. At home, I created my own version of that treat. —Nancy Preussner, Delhi, Iowa

Pastry for a single-crust pie
 2/3 cup sugar

3 tablespoons all-purpose flour
1 teaspoon ground cinnamon
4 medium tart apples, peeled and cut into
   1/2-inch slices
TOPPING:
   1/2 cup all-purpose flour
   1/3 cup packed brown sugar
   1/3 cup old-fashioned rolled oats
     1 teaspoon ground cinnamon
   1/4 cup butter, softened
   1/4 to 1/2 cup caramel ice cream topping *or*
     caramel apple dip
Vanilla ice cream, optional

Roll pastry to fit a 12-in. pizza pan; fold under or flute the edges. Combine sugar, flour and cinnamon in a bowl. Add apples and toss. Arrange the apples in a single layer in a circular pattern to completely cover pastry. Combine the first five topping ingredients; sprinkle over apples.

Bake at 350° for 35-40 minutes or until apples are tender. Remove from the oven and immediately drizzle with caramel topping or dip. Serve warm with ice cream if desired. **Yield:** 12 servings.

Great Pumpkin Dessert

(Pictured above)

This treat is an effortless alternative to pumpkin pie.
   —Linda Guyot, Fountain Valley, California

     1 can (15 ounces) solid-pack pumpkin
     1 can (12 ounces) evaporated milk
     3 eggs
     1 cup sugar
     4 teaspoons pumpkin pie spice
     1 package (18-1/4 ounces) yellow cake mix
   3/4 cup butter, melted
1-1/2 cups chopped walnuts
Vanilla ice cream *or* whipped cream

In a mixing bowl, combine the first five ingredients. Transfer to a greased 13-in. x 9-in. x 2-in. baking pan. Sprinkle with dry cake mix and drizzle with butter. Top with walnuts. Bake at 350° for 1 hour or until a knife inserted near the center comes out clean. Serve with ice cream or whipped cream. **Yield:** 12-16 servings.

Peanut Butter Candy Pie

It takes only a couple of ingredients and a few minutes to create two of these crispy colorful "pizzas."
   —Laura Mahaffey, Annapolis, Maryland

   1/4 cup butter
     4 cups miniature marshmallows
     6 cups crisp rice cereal
    50 milk chocolate kisses *or* 1-1/3 cups milk
       chocolate chips
   1/2 cup flaked coconut
     2 cups Reese's Pieces

In a microwave-safe bowl, heat the butter and marshmallows on high for 1 minute; stir until marshmallows are melted. Add the cereal; mix well. Press onto the bottom and up the sides of two greased 9-in. pie plates.

In a microwave or heavy saucepan, melt chocolate kisses; stir until smooth. Spread over prepared crusts. Sprinkle with coconut and candy pieces; press down lightly. Let stand until chocolate is set. Cut into slices. **Yield:** 2 pies (8 slices each).

Editor's Note: This recipe was tested in an 850-watt microwave.

Halloween Fun Fact

The average amount of candy each American consumed in 2003 was 25 pounds. It is believed that a large portion of that was eaten around Halloween.

(Source: U.S. Census Bureau)

Mini Jack-o'-Lantern Basket

(Pictured below left)

I painted bright pumpkins on some small baskets I happened to have on hand. When they were dry, I filled them with candy and gave them to trick-or-treaters and co-workers. —Brooke Bock, Tyrone, Pennsylvania

FACE PATTERN

Materials Needed:
Face pattern at right; 2-3/4-inch-high x 2-1/2-inch-long x 1-1/2-inch-wide chip basket; paper towels; water basin; palette or foam plate; orange acrylic craft paint; small piece of new kitchen sponge; black fine-line permanent marker; white correction fluid pen (found in art supply stores) or white opaque paint marker; powdered cosmetic blush; cotton swab; natural raffia; scissors; candy corn.

Finished Size:
Pumpkin basket measures about 2-3/4 inches high x 2-1/2 inches long x 1-1/2 inches wide.

Directions:
Pour a small puddle of the orange paint onto the palette or foam plate. Dampen the piece of kitchen sponge and dip into the paint. Dab the paint on a clean area of the palette or foam plate to evenly distribute the paint. Gently dab the paint onto the outside of the chip basket and handle. Let dry.

Referring to the face pattern above right, use a black fine-line permanent marker to draw the jack-o'-lantern face onto one long side of the basket.

When dry, add the white details using a white correction fluid pen or opaque paint marker.

When dry, use a cotton swab to apply cosmetic blush to each cheek.

Tie several strands of raffia around the handle above the face and make a bow. If desired, tear the ends to create a fringed look.

Fill the basket with candy corn.

Chocolate Caramel Apples

Cut into wedges, these scrumptious apples dressed up with melted chocolate, nuts and toffee bits are easy to share. —Linda Smith, Frederick, Maryland

- 1 package (14 ounces) caramels
- 2 tablespoons water
- 4 wooden sticks
- 4 large tart apples
- 2 cups chopped pecans *or* peanuts
- 1 cup (6 ounces) semisweet chocolate chips
- 1 teaspoon shortening
- 1 cup English toffee bits *or* almond brickle chips

In a microwave-safe bowl, combine the caramels and water. Microwave, uncovered, on high for 1 minute; stir. Microwave 30-45 seconds longer or until the caramels are melted. Insert wooden sticks into apples; dip apples into the caramel mixture, turning to coat. Coat with nuts; set on waxed paper to cool.

Melt chocolate chips and shortening; drizzle over apples. Sprinkle with toffee bits. Set on waxed paper to cool. Cut into wedges to serve. **Yield:** 8 servings.

Editor's Note: This recipe was tested in an 850-watt microwave.

Pear 'n' Apple Cobbler

(Pictured below)

Nutmeg adds homemade flavor to this comforting dessert, which tops apple pie filling and canned pears with tender biscuits. The only way to improve a big bowlful of this cobbler is to add a scoop of vanilla ice cream. It's truly an old-fashioned delight.
—Shirley Brown, Pocatello, Idaho

    2 teaspoons cornstarch
  1/4 teaspoon plus 1/8 teaspoon ground nutmeg,
        divided
  2/3 cup orange juice
    1 can (21 ounces) apple pie filling
    1 can (15-1/4 ounces) sliced pears, drained
1-1/2 cups biscuit/baking mix
    2 tablespoons plus 2 teaspoons sugar, *divided*
  1/2 cup milk
    2 tablespoons butter, melted

In a large saucepan, combine the cornstarch, 1/4 teaspoon of nutmeg and orange juice until smooth. Gently stir in pie filling and pears. Bring to a boil; cook and stir for 1-2 minutes or until thickened. Keep warm.

In a bowl, combine the biscuit mix, 2 tablespoons sugar, milk and butter just until blended. Pour hot filling into an ungreased 11-in. x 7-in. x 2-in. baking dish. Drop batter in six mounds onto fruit mixture. Combine the remaining sugar and nutmeg; sprinkle over the top.

Bake at 350° for 35-40 minutes or until bubbly and a toothpick inserted in the biscuit topping comes out clean. Serve warm. **Yield:** 6 servings.

Candy Apple Pie

(Pictured above)

Like a combination of apple and pecan pie, this sweet treat usually tops off our special autumn meals.
—Cindy Kleweno, Burlington, Colorado

    6 cups thinly sliced peeled tart apples
    2 tablespoons lime juice
  3/4 cup sugar
  1/4 cup all-purpose flour
  1/2 teaspoon ground cinnamon *or* nutmeg
  1/4 teaspoon salt
Pastry for double-crust pie (9 inches)
    2 tablespoons butter
TOPPING:
  1/4 cup butter
  1/2 cup packed brown sugar
    2 tablespoons heavy whipping cream
  1/2 cup chopped pecans

In a large bowl, toss apples with lime juice. Combine dry ingredients; add to the apples and toss lightly. Place bottom pastry in a 9-in. pie plate; fill with apple mixture. Dot with butter. Cover with top crust. Flute edges high; cut steam vents. Bake at 400° for 40-45 minutes or until golden brown and apples are tender.

Meanwhile, for topping, melt butter in a small saucepan. Stir in brown sugar and cream; bring to a boil, stirring constantly. Remove from the heat and stir in pecans. Pour over top crust. Return to the oven for 3-4 minutes or until bubbly. Serve warm. **Yield:** 8 servings.

and cinnamon; mix well. Gradually beat in milk and eggs just until blended. Pour into crust. Place pan on a baking sheet. Bake at 350° for 55-60 minutes or until center is almost set.

Combine the sour cream, sugar and vanilla; spread over filling. Bake 5 minutes longer. Cool on a wire rack for 10 minutes. Carefully run a knife around edge of pan to loosen; cool 1 hour longer. Chill overnight.

Remove sides of pan; let stand at room temperature 30 minutes before slicing. Sprinkle with cinnamon. Refrigerate leftovers. **Yield:** 12-14 servings.

Pumpkin Cheesecake with Sour Cream Topping

(Pictured above)

This luscious cheesecake is a special way to enjoy fall flavors. —Dorothy Smith, El Dorado, Arkansas

    1-1/2 cups graham cracker crumbs
      1/4 cup sugar
      1/3 cup butter, melted
FILLING:
        3 packages (8 ounces *each*) cream cheese,
          softened
        1 cup packed brown sugar
        1 can (15 ounces) solid-pack pumpkin
        2 tablespoons cornstarch
      1/2 teaspoon ground nutmeg
    1-1/4 teaspoons ground cinnamon
        1 can (5 ounces) evaporated milk
        2 eggs
TOPPING:
        2 cups (16 ounces) sour cream
      1/3 cup sugar
        1 teaspoon vanilla extract
Additional ground cinnamon

In a bowl, combine crumbs and sugar; stir in butter. Press onto the bottom and 1-1/2 in. up the sides of a greased 9-in. springform pan. Bake at 350° for 5-7 minutes or until set. Cool for 10 minutes.

In a mixing bowl, beat cream cheese and brown sugar until smooth. Add the pumpkin, cornstarch, nutmeg

Ghostly Custards

(Pictured below)

Here's a treat that will get everyone into the "spirit" of the season! These cute custards are fun and yummy.
        —Suzanne Strocsher, Bothell, Washington

        1 can (16 ounces) pumpkin
        1 can (12 ounces) evaporated milk
      1/3 cup sugar
        2 tablespoons honey
        1 teaspoon ground cinnamon
      3/4 teaspoon ground allspice
        2 eggs
        2 cups frozen whipped topping, thawed
Mini chocolate chips

In a mixing bowl, combine the first seven ingredients; beat on low until smooth. Place eight ungreased 4-oz. custard cups in two 8-in. square baking pans. Fill each cup with 1/2 cup of pumpkin mixture. Pour hot water around cups into the pans to a depth of 1 in.

Bake at 325° for 40-50 minutes or until a knife inserted near the center comes out clean. Remove from pans to cool on wire racks. Before serving, top each with dollops of whipped topping in the shape of a ghost; add chocolate chips for eyes. **Yield:** 8 servings.

Microwave Chocolate Cake

This cake cooks into a light, moist dessert. Topped with chocolate sauce, it's too tempting to resist.
—Mary Brenneman, Tavistock, Ontario

1-1/2 cups all-purpose flour
    1 cup sugar
    3 tablespoons baking cocoa
    1 teaspoon baking soda
    1/4 teaspoon salt
    1 cup cold water
    1/3 cup vegetable oil
    1 tablespoon white vinegar
    1 teaspoon vanilla extract
CHOCOLATE SAUCE:
    1 cup sugar
    3 tablespoons cornstarch
    2 tablespoons baking cocoa
    1 cup boiling water
Dash salt
    1 tablespoon butter
    1 teaspoon vanilla extract

In a bowl, combine the first five ingredients. Stir in water, oil, vinegar and vanilla until well blended. Pour into an ungreased 8-in. square microwave-safe dish. Microwave on high for 6-8 minutes, turning the dish every 2 minutes, or until a toothpick inserted near the center comes out clean.

In a 1-qt. microwave-safe bowl, combine sugar, cornstarch and cocoa. Stir in water and salt. Microwave on high for 2-3 minutes, stirring occasionally, or until mixture boils. Microwave 1 minute more. Stir in butter and vanilla. Spoon over pieces of cake. **Yield:** 9 servings.

Editor's Note: This recipe was tested in a 700-watt microwave.

Caramel Apples

(Pictured above)

Nothing tastes better at this time of year than a sweet-to-eat caramel apple! This recipe, which is my favorite, has rich homemade flavor that can't be beat.
—Karen Ann Bland, Gove, Kansas

    1 cup butter
    2 cups packed brown sugar
    1 cup light corn syrup
    1 can (14 ounces) sweetened condensed milk
    1 teaspoon vanilla extract
    8 to 10 wooden sticks
    8 to 10 medium tart apples

In a heavy 3-qt. saucepan, combine the butter, brown sugar, corn syrup and milk; bring to a boil over medium-high heat. Cook and stir until the mixture reaches 248° (firm-ball stage) on a candy thermometer, about 30-40 minutes.

Remove from heat; stir in vanilla. Insert sticks into apples. Dip each into hot caramel mixture; turn to coat. Set on waxed paper to cool. **Yield:** 8-10 apples.

Pumpkin Ice Cream Pie

(Pictured above)

Although it looks like you fussed, this layered pie is easy to make. —Suzanne McKinley, Lyons, Georgia

3 English toffee candy bars (1.4 ounces *each*), crushed, *divided*
3 cups vanilla ice cream, softened, *divided*
1 chocolate crumb crust (9 inches)
1/2 cup canned pumpkin
2 tablespoons sugar
1/2 teaspoon ground cinnamon
1/4 teaspoon ground nutmeg

Combine two-thirds of the crushed candy bars and 2 cups ice cream. Spoon into crust; freeze for 1 hour or until firm. In a bowl, combine the pumpkin, sugar, cinnamon, nutmeg and remaining ice cream. Spoon over ice cream layer in crust. Sprinkle with remaining crushed candy bars. Cover and freeze for 8 hours or up to 2 months. Remove from the freezer 10-15 minutes before serving. **Yield:** 8 servings.

Clove Apple Cake

(Pictured at right)

This spicy cake is so good with the sweet custard sauce. —Kim Marie Van Rheenen, Mendota, Illinois

6 tablespoons butter, softened
3/4 cup sugar
1 teaspoon ground cloves
2 eggs
1-1/3 cups all-purpose flour
1 teaspoon baking powder
1/2 cup milk
1-1/2 cups chopped peeled tart apples
CUSTARD SAUCE:
1/4 cup sugar
2 tablespoons all-purpose flour
2 cups milk
1 egg, beaten
3 tablespoons butter, softened
1/2 teaspoon vanilla extract
Additional ground cloves, optional

In a mixing bowl, cream butter, sugar and cloves. Add eggs, one at a time, beating well after each addition. Combine flour and baking powder; add to creamed mixture alternately with milk. Fold in apples.

Transfer batter to a greased and floured 9-in. round baking pan. Bake at 375° for 35-40 minutes or until a toothpick inserted near the center comes out clean. Cool on a wire rack.

Meanwhile, in a saucepan, combine sugar, flour and milk until smooth. Bring to a boil over medium-high heat; cook and stir for 2 minutes or until thickened and bubbly. Remove from the heat.

Stir a small amount into egg; return all to pan. Bring to a gentle boil. Reduce heat; cook and stir for 2 minutes. Remove from the heat; whisk in butter and vanilla. Serve over warm cake. Sprinkle with ground cloves if desired. **Yield:** 6-8 servings.

Gingersnap Pumpkin Pudding

Crushed cookies give yummy crunch to this creamy dessert. If you like, try molasses cookies instead of gingersnaps. —Mary Smith, Litchfield, Michigan

1-3/4 cups cold milk
   1 package (3.4 ounces) instant cheesecake *or* vanilla pudding mix
   1/2 cup canned pumpkin
   1/4 to 1/2 teaspoon pumpkin pie spice
   10 gingersnaps
   1 cup whipped topping

In a bowl, whisk the milk and pudding mix for 2 minutes. Stir in the pumpkin and pumpkin pie spice. Let stand for 2 minutes or until soft-set. Set aside three gingersnaps; crush the rest.

Fold the whipped topping into the pumpkin pudding; spoon pudding into dessert bowls. Sprinkle with the gingersnap cookie crumbs. Serve with whole gingersnaps. **Yield:** 3 servings.

Clay Pumpkin Pin

(Pictured below right)

When I found that I didn't have any festive accessories for Halloween, I created a whimsical jack-o'-lantern pin using clay, beads and a wood button. It was easy! —Paula Del Favero, Deerfield Beach, Florida

Materials Needed:
Oven-bake polymer clay—one 2-ounce package each of orange and green; waxed paper; ruler; craft knife or other sharp knife; small square of corrugated cardboard; shallow glass baking dish; photocopy paper or baker's parchment to line baking dish; 3/8-inch wooden furniture button; black acrylic craft paint; small flat paintbrush; five 5mm black beads; 1-inch pin back; E-6000 or Crafter's Goop adhesive.

Finished Size:
Pin is about 1-3/4 inches high x 2 inches wide.

Directions:
To prevent colors of clay from mixing, work each color on a separate sheet of waxed paper. Clean your hands before beginning to work with clay and before switching colors.

Knead each color of clay until smooth and pliable.

Roll a 1-inch ball of orange clay. Flatten ball into a 1/4-inch-thick x 1-3/4-inch-high x 2-inch-wide pumpkin shape.

Place corrugated cardboard on a flat surface. Gen-

tly but firmly press front of clay pumpkin onto ridges of cardboard, creating a vertical ridge pattern on pumpkin.

Paint the wooden furniture button black for the nose. Let dry. Press nose onto center of the pumpkin.

Use tip of knife to make small cuts for the mouth and eyebrows. Use flat side of knife to make indentations around the outside of the pumpkin to create a scalloped edge.

Press three beads onto mouth. Press two beads above nose for eyes.

Roll a short 1/4-inch-wide rope of green clay and cut a 1/4-inch length for the stem. Gently press stem into top of pumpkin.

Line the inside of baking dish with paper or parchment and place the pumpkin inside. Bake according to the clay manufacturer's instructions. Let cool.

Glue pin back across back of pumpkin. Let dry.

Spooktacular
Treats

Recipes

Projects

Sugar Cookie Scarecrow And Pumpkins

(Pictured below right)

To add bushels of fall flavor to your next bash, try baking up this cookie scarecrow shaped and decorated by the Taste of Home kitchen staff. They used a yummy cookie recipe from Vickie Wade of Bourbonnais, Illinois to make the colorful character.

    1 cup butter, softened
1-1/2 cups confectioners' sugar
    1 egg
    1 teaspoon almond extract
    1 teaspoon vanilla extract
2-1/2 cups all-purpose flour
    1 teaspoon baking soda
    1 teaspoon cream of tartar
    4 tablespoons water
Blue, green, red and yellow liquid *or* paste food coloring
    3/4 cup vanilla frosting, *divided*
Pastry tips—#18 open star and #5 round
    1 large green gumdrop, sliced into thirds
    1 large red gumdrop, sliced into thirds
    1 large black gumdrop, sliced into fourths
    1 yard thin ribbon, cut into 6 pieces

In a mixing bowl, cream butter and sugar. Add egg and extracts. Combine dry ingredients; gradually add to creamed mixture; mix well. Cover and refrigerate 3 hours or overnight.

On a lightly floured surface, roll the dough to 1/4-in. thickness. Cut into two 4-in. squares, four 4-in. x 2-in. rectangles, a 5-in. x 1-1/2-in. rectangle and a 3-in. x 3/4-in. rectangle.

Place the 5-in. and 3-in. rectangles together on an ungreased baking sheet to form scarecrow's hat. Place remaining pieces 2 in. apart on ungreased baking sheets. Round edges of one 4-in. square to form head. With a straw or toothpick, make holes so cookie pieces

can be attached later with ribbon (there should be one hole in hat, two holes in head, five holes in 4-in. body and one hole in each arm and leg). Cut out remaining dough with a 2-1/2-in. round cookie cutter for pumpkins. Place on ungreased baking sheets.

Bake at 350° for 12-15 minutes or until lightly browned. Immediately remove small round cookies to wire racks to cool. With straw or toothpick, reopen holes in scarecrow pieces. Carefully remove scarecrow pieces to wire racks.

Place a tablespoon of water in each of four small bowls; tint each with a different color of food coloring. Using a small pastry brush, paint hat, arms, body and legs as shown in photo below. Combine red and yellow water to make orange. Use orange- and green-tinted water to paint round cookies like pumpkins.

Tint 1/2 cup of vanilla frosting yellow. Cut a small hole

n the corner of a pastry or plastic bag; insert star tip. Fill bag with yellow frosting. Pipe straw on head, body, arms and legs. Attach gumdrop pieces with frosting to form eyes, nose, cheeks, buttons and patches.

Tint remaining frosting black. Prepare a second plastic or pastry bag; insert round tip. Fill bag with black frosting. Pipe a stitch pattern around eyes, mouth and patches. Let frosting dry for 30 minutes. Place scarecrow pieces on a covered board; carefully tie together with ribbon. Arrange pumpkins around the scarecrow. **Yield:** 1 scarecrow and about 1 dozen pumpkins.

Pumpkin Spice Cake

(Pictured at right)

When Carole Lajeunesse of Aurora, Colorado shared her favorite spice cake recipe with our home economists, they turned it into a pretty pumpkin. It's a "vine" way to sweeten a fabulous fall affair.

   2 packages (18-1/4 ounces *each*) spice
     cake mix
   6 eggs
   1 can (16 ounces) solid-pack pumpkin
2/3 cup evaporated milk
2/3 cup vegetable oil
   2 cups (12 ounces) vanilla baking chips
   2 cans (16 ounces *each*) vanilla frosting
Red, yellow and green paste *or* liquid food coloring
Textured paper towel
   2 pastry bags *or* small heavy-duty resealable
     plastic bags
Pastry tips—#5 round and #352 leaf
   1 cup flaked coconut

In a mixing bowl, combine cake mixes, eggs, pumpkin, milk and oil. Beat on low speed for 30 seconds; beat on medium for 2 minutes. Stir in chips. Fill two greased muffin cups two-thirds full. Pour remaining batter into two greased and floured 12-cup fluted tube pans.

Bake at 350° for 20 minutes for cupcakes and 40-45 minutes for cakes or until a toothpick inserted near the center comes out clean. Cool in pans for 25 minutes; remove to wire racks to cool completely.

Level the bottom of each cake. Spread one cake bottom with frosting; put cake bottoms together to form a pumpkin. Set aside. Combine red and yellow food coloring to make orange; tint about three-fourths of the frosting. Tint remaining frosting green.

Place one cupcake right side up in the center of the cake to support the stem. Put a dollop of green frosting on the cupcake and top with an upside-down cupcake; frost with green frosting. Frost the cake with orange frosting. Let stand, uncovered, until frosting is slightly firm, about 30 minutes. To create texture, place paper towel over frosting and press lightly, then remove.

Cut a small hole in the corner of a pastry or plastic bag; insert round tip. Fill bag with green frosting. Pipe curly vines from pumpkin stem and base. Prepare another bag with green frosting; insert leaf tip. Holding bag at a 45° angle, pipe leaves randomly along the vines. Combine coconut with green food coloring; sprinkle around base of cake. **Yield:** 12-16 servings.

Editor's Note: Cakes must be baked in identical cake pans or baked in two batches.

Halloween Fun Fact

These U.S. towns are always in a
Halloween mood:

Transylvania, Louisiana
Skull Valley, Arizona
Witcherville, Arkansas
Gravestown, Mississippi
Eek, Alaska

Haunted House Cake

(Pictured at right)

When this eerie abode appears at Halloween parties, guests will surely move right in...to get a piece of the treat! Our kitchen staff prepared the ghostly home with handy packaged cake mixes, plus common baking pans you likely already have in your kitchen. To complete the frightfully delightful scene, they decorated it with edible details including cookie tombstones, cereal shingles and a chocolate door.

Materials Needed:
1 package (18-1/4 ounces) chocolate cake mix; 1 package (18-1/4 ounces) white cake mix; 2 Nutter Butter cookies; 3/4 cup shortening; 3/4 cup butter, softened; 6 cups confectioners' sugar; 3 tablespoons plus 1-1/2 teaspoons milk; 1-1/2 teaspoons vanilla extract; milk chocolate candy bar (1.55 ounces); 1 orange M&M miniature baking bit; orange liquid or paste food coloring; 1 cup Golden Grahams cereal; stick of orange-striped fruit gum; chocolate jimmies; 1/4 cup gold rock candy; 14- x 10-inch serving board or platter; purple gift wrap; clear cellophane; tape; standard baking supplies.

Finished Size:
Cake measures about 13 inches long x 9 inches wide x 7 inches high.

Directions:
Cover the serving board with gift wrap, taping wrap on the back side of board. Cover wrapped board with clear cellophane in the same way. Set board aside.
Cake: Prepare chocolate cake batter according to package directions. Spoon 3 cups into a greased and floured 8- x 4- x 2-inch loaf pan. Set remaining batter aside. Bake at 350° for 55-60 minutes or until a toothpick inserted near the center comes out clean. Cool for 10 minutes before removing from pan to a wire rack to cool completely.

Prepare white cake batter and pour into a greased and floured 13- x 9- x 2-inch baking pan. Drop reserved chocolate batter by 1/4 cupfuls onto white batter. Cut through batter with a knife to swirl. Bake at 350° for 35-40 minutes or until a toothpick inserted near the center comes out clean. Cool for 10 minutes before removing from pan to a wire rack to cool completely.
Assembly: Place the 13- x 9-inch cake on the covered board. Using a serrated knife, level top of loaf cake and cut it in half widthwise. Referring to photo at far right for position, place one half on the corner of the 13- x 9-inch cake for the house.

For the roof, slice the remaining half of loaf cake in half diagonally. Position the two halves together so they form a triangular shape on top of house.

Cut each cookie in half widthwise and set aside.

In a mixing bowl, cream shortening and butter. Gradually add the confectioners' sugar, milk and vanilla, mixing until smooth. Frost house, roof, sides of 13- x 9-inch cake and cookie halves.

Break candy bar into rectangles. Place one on front of house for door (save remaining pieces for another use). Place a dot of frosting on left side of door and attach M&M baking bit for doorknob. Tint remaining frosting orange and frost the top of 13- x 9-inch cake.

Place cereal on roof of house for shingles. Cut gum in half widthwise and then lengthwise. Place two pieces above the door for shutters. Use jimmies to outline the window.

For tombstones, attach jimmies to the cookies to read "RIP" and "BOO." Place cookies on the cake, lightly pushing them into frosting.

Place rock candy in front of door for walkway.
Yield: 12-15 servings.

Haunted House Tips

FEEL FREE to be creative when you're decorating the Haunted House Cake. If you like, try using different candies to give this creepy cottage your own look. For example, you could substitute candy corn for the cereal on the roof and replace the rock candy with M&M's for the walkway.

You could even create an eerie pumpkin patch along with (or in place of) the tombstones. Just arrange some candy pumpkins next to the house. Add gummy worms for an extra spooky effect.

Ghostly "Boo-Day" Cake

(Pictured at far right)

Taste of Home's cooks prepared speedy frosting and created a ghoulish design to decorate a homemade chocolate cake. To form your own ghost shape, simply enlarge and use the pattern below right.

      1 cup water
  1/2 cup butter
  1/2 cup shortening
      3 tablespoons baking cocoa
      2 cups all-purpose flour
      2 cups sugar
      1 teaspoon baking soda
  1/2 teaspoon salt
      2 eggs
  1/2 cup buttermilk
      1 teaspoon vanilla extract
CHOCOLATE FROSTING:
      1 cup heavy whipping cream
      1 cup (6 ounces) semisweet chocolate chips
 1-3/4 to 2 cups confectioners' sugar
WHITE FROSTING:
  1/4 cup butter, softened
  1/4 cup shortening
      2 cups confectioners' sugar
 4-1/2 teaspoons milk
  1/2 teaspoon vanilla extract
Orange and purple paste *or* gel food coloring

In a saucepan, combine the water, butter, shortening and cocoa; cook and stir until butter and shortening are melted. In a large mixing bowl, combine the flour, sugar, baking soda and salt. Add the butter mixture; mix well. Add the eggs, buttermilk and vanilla; mix well.

Pour into a greased and waxed paper-lined 15-in. x 10-in. x 1-in. baking pan. Bake at 350° for 20-25 minutes or until a toothpick inserted near the center comes out clean. Cool for 10 minutes before removing from pan to a wire rack to cool completely. Gently peel off waxed paper. Transfer to a 17-in. x 12-in. covered board.

In a saucepan, heat the cream until bubbles begin to form around sides of pan. Remove from the heat; stir in chocolate chips until melted. Place pan in a bowl of ice water; stir constantly until cooled. Gradually whisk in enough confectioners' sugar to achieve spreading consistency. Frost the top and sides of cake.

In a small mixing bowl, cream the butter and shortening. Beat in confectioners' sugar, milk and vanilla until smooth. Place 1/3 cup in a small bowl; tint orange.

Place 3 tablespoons in another bowl; tint purple.

Enlarge and trace the pattern below onto waxed per. Cut out. With a sharp knife, trace the ghost or chocolate frosting. Gently spread the white frostin ghost shape. Place orange frosting in a pastry or pl bag; cut a hole in one corner. Pipe banner on gl Cut a hole in corner of another pastry or plastic insert #2 round pastry tip and purple frosting. Pipe "I py Boo-Day" on banner. **Yield:** 12-15 servings.

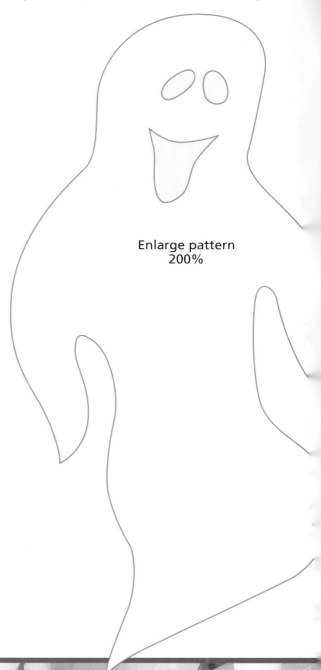

Enlarge pattern
200%

2 tablespoons dried cranberries
2 tablespoons golden raisins
2 tablespoons chopped dried apricots
2 tablespoons chopped dried apples

In a mixing bowl, beat the eggs and sugar. Add sour cream and maple flavoring. Combine the flour, baking soda and salt; add to sour cream mixture and mix well. Fold in pecans. Pour into two greased and floured 9-in. round baking pans.

Bake at 350° for 30 minutes or until a toothpick inserted near the center comes out clean. Cool for 10 minutes before removing from the pans to wire racks to cool completely.

For the frosting, in a mixing bowl, cream the butter and confectioners' sugar. Add the maple syrup; mix well. Spread the frosting between the layers and over the top and sides of the cake.

In a microwave-safe bowl, melt chocolate and peanut butter chips; stir until smooth. Transfer to a pastry or plastic bag; cut a small hole in the corner of the bag. Pipe a tree and branches on top of the frosted cake. Combine the dried fruit; sprinkle around the base of the tree and at the ends of the branches to resemble leaves. **Yield:** 12 servings.

Maple Tree Cake
(Pictured at right)

o top off this scrumptious maple-flavored cake from orraine Tishmack of Casselton, North Dakota, our itchen staff added a festive fall scene. They piped on simple tree shape using melted chocolate and eanut butter chips. Then they sprinkled on dried ranberries and other fruit for the leaves.

        4 eggs
        2 cups sugar
        2 cups (16 ounces) sour cream
        2 teaspoons maple flavoring
2-1/2 cups all-purpose flour
        2 teaspoons baking soda
Dash salt
    1/2 cup chopped pecans
FROSTING:
    1/4 cup butter, softened
        3 cups confectioners' sugar
    1/2 cup plus 1 tablespoon maple syrup
    1/4 cup semisweet chocolate chips
    1/4 cup peanut butter chips

Popcorn Witch

(Pictured below)

This spellbinding snack started with a popcorn ball recipe from Roberta Holiday of Fort Worth, Texas. Know[ing?] that the balls are a cinch to shape, our kitchen staff conjured up a bewitching Halloween table topper. The [ma-]terials needed to make it are simple—just   popcorn, candies, pretzels and other easy-to-find supplies.

Materials Needed:

...ge roasting pan; heavy saucepan; candy thermome-
...; 15-inch-square covered board; 5 quarts popped
...pcorn; 2 cups sugar; 1 cup packed brown sugar; 1
... water; 2/3 cup corn syrup; green liquid food color-
...; 11 pieces of candy corn; 2 pretzel sticks; 2 pieces
...urple cellophane or plastic wrap—one 15 x 12 inch-
...and one 6-inch square; 2 pieces of red shoestring
...orice—one 24 inches and one 12 inches; one 10-
...h wooden skewer; 7 pieces of black rope licorice—
...nches each; 1 ice cream sugar cone; 2 tablespoons
...nilla frosting; 2 brown M&M's; 1 pretzel rod; 1/4 cup
...tato sticks; 1/2 cup chocolate sandwich cookie
...umbs; standard kitchen utensils.

Finished Size:

...e witch with broom measures approximately 11 inch-
...tall x 6 inches wide.

Directions:

...ace popcorn in a large roasting pan and keep warm
... a 200° oven.

...In a heavy saucepan, combine sugars, water and
...rn syrup. Cook and stir over medium heat until a can-
...y thermometer reads 235° (soft-ball stage). Remove
...om the heat and add the green liquid food coloring.
...our the mixture over the popcorn and stir to coat
...enly. Cool for 10 minutes.

Forming Feet: With
...ands dipped in cold wa-
...er, shape 2 cups of pop-
...orn into a 6-inch heart
...bout 1/2 inch thick on a
...overed board. For toes,
...nsert 10 pieces of candy
...corn around rounded
...edges of heart (see photo
...1 at right).

1.

Forming Body: Firmly
shape 5 cups of popcorn
into a 6- x 3-inch cylinder
for the body. Center over
the feet.

For the arms, firmly
cover half of each pretzel
stick with 1/2 cup of popcorn. Insert uncovered
ends of the pretzel sticks
into the popcorn body
(see photo 2 at right).

For dress, center the
15- x 12-inch cellophane

2.

piece over body. Gather at
waist and tie with the 24-
inch piece of red licorice
(see photo 3 at right).

Forming Head: Firmly
shape 2 cups of popcorn
into a 3-1/2-inch ball. Add
a few more pieces to form
a pointed chin. Attach
head by carefully insert-
ing skewer through top of
head into body and base
(see photo 4 at right). If
there is any popcorn re-
maining, shape into 1-1/2-
inch balls; cover with plastic wrap and set aside.

For the hair, cut the
black licorice into 1/8-inch
strips to within 1/2 inch of
one end. Attach uncut
ends to the sides and back
of head with toothpicks.

With a sharp serrated
knife, carefully cut sugar
cone 3 inches from point-
ed end. Cover the 3-inch
pointed end of cone with
the cellophane square. Tie
the 12-inch piece of red
licorice around cone bot-
tom to secure; place hat
on head.

With some of vanilla
frosting, attach the brown
M&M's for eyes and the
remaining piece of candy
corn for the nose.

3.

4.

5.

For the broom, spread the remaining frosting on
1-1/2 inches of one end of the pretzel rod. Attach the
potato sticks for the straw of the broom (see photo 5
above right).

Lean the broom against the witch as shown in the
photo at far left. Sprinkle the chocolate sandwich
cookie crumbs on the covered board for the dirt.
Arrange reserved popcorn balls around the witch or
place them in a serving bowl next to the covered board.
Yield: 14-16 servings (1 witch and 4-6 popcorn balls).

Editor's Note: We recommend you test your candy thermometer before each use by bringing water to
a boil; the thermometer should read 212°. Adjust your
recipe temperature up or down based on your test.

Frightful Feline Pin

(Pictured below)

People are glad when this black cat crosses their paths. The spooky jewelry can be counted on fearlessly for a good number of grins. Plus, it's a "purrfect" project to share with children. You craft the pin by twisting together er chenille "bumps" to make the cat, then gluing it to a circle of felt. It's easy enough for almost anyone.

—*Crystal Ogle, Falmouth, Virginia*

Materials Needed:
One black bump chenille stem (available at craft stores); two 5mm wiggle eyes; 6 inches of 1/8-inch-wide orange satin ribbon; 3-inch craft broom; 5-inch square of lightweight cardboard; 5-inch square of yellow felt; 1-1/2-inch pin back; compass with pencil; craft glue; craft scissors.

Finished Size:
Black cat pin measures 4 inches wide x 4 inches high.

Directions:
Glue yellow felt square onto cardboard square with edges matching. Let dry.

Cut black bump chenille stem into four pieces as shown below.

Shape legs into an inverted U. Bend back piece to match curve of legs. Place back over curve of legs and twist ends of back around legs to secure.

Insert narrow end of tail between back and leg pieces on right edge and twist to attach. Bend tail up as shown in photo at right.

Insert head piece between back and leg pieces on left and bend ends of head piece up for ears. Grasp ears at head and body and twist one full turn to create neck.

Glue the eyes to the head as shown in the photo.

Tie ribbon in a bow and glue to neck.

Use compass to draw a 4-in. circle on back of cardboard and felt square. Cut out circle.

Glue craft broom to felt side of circle as shown in photo. Glue cat to felt so its feet are on the handle of the craft broom.

Glue pin back onto the back. Let dry.

Cutting bump chenille stem

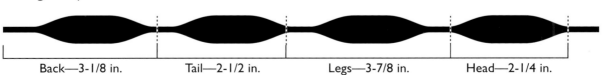

Back—3-1/8 in.   Tail—2-1/2 in.   Legs—3-7/8 in.   Head—2-1/4 in.

Spirited Shindigs

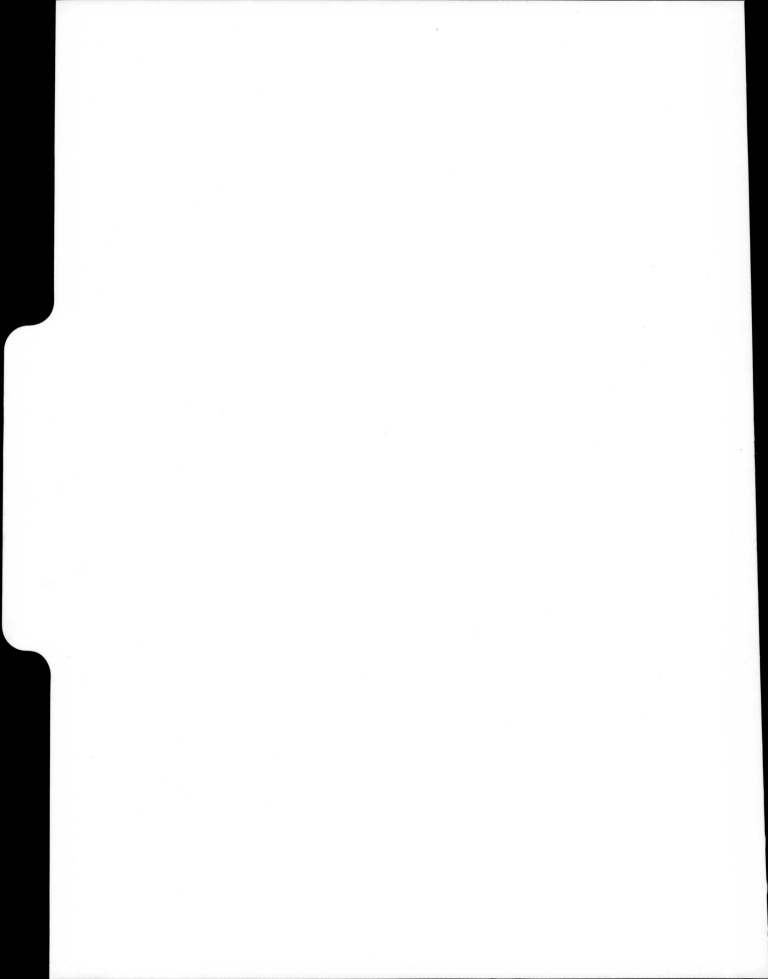

CONTENTS | Spirited Shindigs

spooktacular party tips

YOUR Halloween party will be a hair-raising hit with these hints and tips. From trick-or-treating safety tips to games that will get your guests howling with laughter, these easy ideas guarantee chills and thrills for every ghost, witch or goblin who haunts your house on October 31.

HALLOWEEN PARTY PLANNER

Advanced planning is the key to any successful party. You won't be terrorized to throw a Halloween bash with this spooktacular timeline!

SIX WEEKS BEFORE:

■ Plan the kind of party you want to host. Will it be a ghoulish gala for grown-ups, a spine-tingling time for little tykes or a frightfully fun family affair? Will you have a theme (such as haunted house, mad scientist lab, etc.)?

■ Plan your menu. Are you serving a full dinner or just some snacks and desserts? Select foods that tie into your theme.

■ Create your guest list and send out invitations. Make sure the invitations indicate if it's a costume party.

FOUR WEEKS BEFORE:

■ Choose costumes for your family.

■ Start compiling a shopping list for food.

■ Plan the party games and shop for supplies.

■ Begin browsing party supply stores for decorations. Don't forget to create a spooky scene outside as well as in. The Internet is also a super source for finding unusual Halloween party decorations and supplies.

THREE WEEKS BEFORE:

■ Call any guests who haven't responded.

■ Set up your outdoor decorations. But don't carve the pumpkins just yet!

■ Shop for non-perishable food items.

THE WEEK OF YOUR PARTY:

■ Clean the house.

■ Start preparing your foods.

■ Set up the tables and indoor decorations.

■ Carve your pumpkins.

■ Prepare treat bags for your guests.

THE DAY OF YOUR PARTY:

■ Spot-clean the house.

■ Finish decorating.

■ Prepare any last-minute foods.

■ Check over party details.

■ Put on your costume and help the rest of the family with theirs.

■ Relax and have fun!

TRICK-OR-TREATING SAFETY TIPS

Here are some things to keep in mind when heading out to trick-or-treating:

- Masks can make it hard for young children to see and breathe. Consider face paint or make-up instead.

- Costumes that are too long pose a tripping hazard. Hem or pin them up if they're too long. Also, footwear should fit properly.

- Walk, don't run, from house to house. Stick to one side of the street instead of zigzagging back and forth. When you do cross, hold your child's hand and look both ways for cars.

- If trick-or-treating at night, add reflective tape to costumes. Or place glow sticks inside trick-or-treat bags. Older kids can carry flashlights.

- Only go to well-lit houses and go to the front door, not the garage or back door.

- Be careful of pumpkins with lit candles inside. Costumes can catch fire if they get too close.

- Grown-ups should inspect all candy before being eaten. If in doubt, throw it out.

- Travel in groups and never go into someone's house alone.

- Adults, be especially careful when driving around during trick-or-treating hours. Watch for kids darting out into the road. At home, be sure to make a clear pathway to your door. And make sure your outside is well lit.

GOODIE BAG TREAT IDEAS

No kid's Halloween party is complete without treat bags for each guest to take home. Make goodie bags (like those shown on page 171) or buy them at a party supply or discount department store.

Instead of filling treat bags with candy, consider these alternatives:

- **Balloons**
- **Crayons and markers**
- **Fast-food coupons**
- **Individual bags of pretzels, crackers or popcorn**
- **Juice boxes**
- **Key chains**
- **Pencils or pens and erasers**
- **Pennies**
- **Plastic spiders, worms or bugs**
- **Small coloring books**
- **Small toys, such as bubbles and yo-yos**
- **Stickers or tattoos**

spooktacular party tips

SCARY INVITATIONS

Creative Halloween invitations hint at the ghostly good times guests will have when they attend your party. Consider these options:

- Write your invitations using a blood-red marker on a mask, rubber hand or other scary item.
- Write in invisible ink and include instructions for your guests to reveal the message.
- Record the details of your invite on a cassette tape or compact disc using a scary voice with Halloween music or spooky sounds in the background.
- Hand-deliver mini pumpkins with the party details written on the back and a face drawn on the front.
- Create a mini poster for a horror movie with your party details woven into the poster.

IF-YOU-DARE DECORATIONS

In a flash, your home can become happily haunted for Halloween. Here are some easy decorating ideas your guests will find frightfully delightful.

- Line your drive or walkway with paper-bag, carved-pumpkin or other Halloween-type luminaries.
- Hang fake spiders and webs from your front porch, bushes or trees.

- Turn your front yard into a horrifying cemetery by cutting tombstones out of cardboard. Paint them gray and write creepy or silly names on them like "Hal O. Ween," "Ima Nut" and "Scared E. Kat." Attach metal spikes to the back with duct tape and poke the tombstones into the ground around the yard.
- Inside, string more fake spiders and webs. Cover the furniture with white sheets to give your home the appearance of an abandoned house.
- Put scary decorations (fake severed head, skull, rubber hand, etc.) in unexpected places like inside the coat closet, bathroom, etc.
- Hang "ghosts" around. Blow up large white balloons and tie them off with long pieces of black string. Cut a tiny hole in the center of old sheets or purchased pieces of white fabric (about a yard for each ghost) and slip the string through the holes. Draw two black eyes and a scary mouth, then hang the ghosts with the black string from the ceiling and in trees outside.

More Ways to Set a Spooky Scene

- Rent videos or DVDs of some classic horror films and play them in the background during the party. Check out "Creature from the Black Lagoon," "Dracula," "Frankenstein," "The Invisible Man," "The Mummy" and "The Wolf Man."
- At the door where guests will enter your home, greet them with spooky sounds from a purchased cassette or compact disc.
- For an eerie glow, replace some of your regular light bulbs with green, black or orange bulbs, which can be found at hardware and party supply stores.

SPOOKY SMOKE

To create mysterious, mood-setting fog at your party like the creepy cauldron at right, order dry ice from your local grocery store's seafood department or ice supplier two weeks before your party.

- Plan to pick up your dry ice as close as possible to the time you will need it. Bring an insulated container like an ice chest or Styrofoam cooler. Store the dry ice in the same type of container to slow sublimation (changing from a solid to a gas).
- Try to open and close the container as little as possible. Do not store dry ice in an air-tight container, because it could explode.
- DO NOT TOUCH dry ice with your fingers as severe burns can result. Keep dry ice out of the reach of children. Use tongs or thick gloves when handling it and use it in a well-ventilated area.
- To create fog, put chunks of dry ice in a water-tight container; cover with water. Warm water creates more fog, but the ice will disappear quickly. Cooler water will produce less dense fog, but the ice will last longer.
- If the amount of fog decreases during your party, add more dry ice and water.

spirited
snacks &
beverages

THREE-IN-ONE POPCORN CRUNCH

Carma Blosser, Livermore, Colorado

Folks with a sweet tooth will dig into these bite-size snacks. Candy corn is a colorful addition, so this mouth-watering mix is suitable for any autumn event.

4	quarts popped popcorn
2	cups dry roasted peanuts
1⅓	cups sugar
1⅓	cups packed brown sugar
1	cup dark corn syrup
½	cup water
½	cup butter
½	teaspoon salt
1½	cups candy corn

Place popcorn and peanuts in large buttered heatproof containers or bowls; set aside. In a large heavy saucepan, combine the sugars, corn syrup, water, butter and salt. Cook over medium heat until a candy thermometer reads 285° (soft-crack stage), stirring occasionally.

Pour over popcorn mixture; stir gently to coat. Stir in candy corn. Drop into bite-size pieces onto waxed paper. Cool completely. Store in an airtight container.

YIELD: 6 quarts.

EDITOR'S NOTE: We recommend that you test your candy thermometer before each use by bringing water to a boil; the thermometer should read 212°. Adjust your recipe temperature up or down based on your test.

BONE SLICES

A savory seafood filling is featured in these cre bone pieces from our home economists. For e more fun, stack slices on a platter to resemb backbone.

½	cup mayonnaise
1	package (3 ounces) cream cheese, softened
2	tablespoons *each* finely chopped celery green pepper and onion
1	tablespoon lemon juice
1	teaspoon ground mustard
1	teaspoon Worcestershire sauce
⅛	teaspoon lemon-pepper seasoning
⅛	to ¼ teaspoon hot pepper sauce
1½	cups cooked *or* canned crabmeat, drain flaked and cartilage removed
4	flour tortillas (10 inches)

In a mixing bowl, beat mayonnaise and cre cheese until smooth. Add the celery, green pep onion, lemon juice, mustard, Worcestershire sa lemon-pepper and hot pepper sauce; mix well. in the crab.

Spread about ½ cup filling over each tortilla. up tightly; wrap in plastic wrap. Refrigerate fe hours or until chilled. Cut into ½-in. slices.

YIELD: about 6 dozen.

freaky fac

More than 2,000 years ago, the C celebrated the new year on Novem 1, which marked the end of the sumr harvest (representing life), and the ginning of the dark, cold winter (r resenting death).

They believed ghosts and spir roamed the Earth on October 31 cause trouble and ruin crops. So Celts built sacrificial bonfires a donned masks and costumes made animal skins and heads to avoid be recognized as human.

spirited snacks & beverages

CREAMY ONION SPREAD

Janet Joecks, Menomonee Falls, Wisconsin

My daughter came across this recipe a few years ago, and I have adapted it to our tastes.

1   large sweet onion, finely chopped
1   garlic clove, minced
1   tablespoon olive oil
$1/4$ cup sliced green onions
$3/4$ teaspoon salt
$1/2$ teaspoon pepper
$1/8$ to $1/4$ teaspoon cayenne pepper
$3/4$ cup sour cream
$3/4$ cup mayonnaise
$1/2$ cup whipped cream cheese
Additional sliced green onions
Breadsticks and sweet red and yellow pepper strips

In a skillet, saute onion and garlic in oil for 1 minute. Reduce heat to medium-low. Cover and cook for 8 minutes or until onion begins to turn golden brown. Add the green onions, salt, pepper and cayenne. Cook and stir for 2 minutes. Remove from the heat; cool to room temperature, about 15 minutes.

Meanwhile, in a small mixing bowl, combine the sour cream, mayonnaise and cream cheese until smooth. Stir in onion mixture. Garnish with additional green onions. Cover and refrigerate for at least 1 hour. Serve with breadsticks and peppers.

YIELD: about 2 cups.

GHOULISH FINGERS

Marilee Davieau, Allentown, Pennsylvania

We serve this fun finger food at our an Halloween party alongside sandwich rolls a variety of condiments.

3   packages (8 ounces *each*) assorted lunch meats
1   package (3 ounces) cream cheese, softened
12   grape tomatoes, halved lengthwise

Roll up each slice of lunch meat; spread a s amount of cream cheese at seam to secure Insert a tomato half at one end of each roll t semble a fingernail; secure the tomato in place a small amount of cream cheese. Place seam down on a platter. Cover and refrigerate u serving.

YIELD: 2 dozen.

ORANGE HALLOWEEN PUNCH

Edie DeSpain, Logan, Utah

This eye-catching orange punch is a Halloween dition at my house. It's refreshing, frothy and to stir up—with only five ingredients.

1   can (46 ounces) pineapple juice, chilled
3   cups lemon-lime soda, chilled
3   cups orange drink
2   liters ginger ale, chilled
$1/2$ gallon orange sherbet

In a punch bowl, combine the juice, soda and ora drink. Stir in ginger ale. Top with scoops of sher Serve immediately.

YIELD: about 6 quarts.

with floured 2 1/2-in. Halloween-shaped cookie cutters. Place 1 in. apart on ungreased baking sheets. Bake at 425° for 4-6 minutes or until lightly browned. Remove to wire racks to cool.

Meanwhile, in a large skillet, saute apples, sugar a.. cinnamon in butter until apples are tender. Combine flour and cold water until smooth; stir into skillet. Bring to a boil; cook and stir for 2 minutes or until thickened. Spoon into a serving dish. Serve warm with cinnamon-sugar crisps.

YIELD: 3 cups dip (2 to 3 dozen crisps).

SUGAR SPICED ALMONDS

Sherri Jackson, Chillicothe, Ohio

These zippy almonds are spicy yet sweet. Once you start eating them, you can't stop!

1/4   cup sugar
2   tablespoons vegetable oil
1   teaspoon cayenne pepper
1/2   teaspoon garlic salt
1/2   teaspoon chili powder
1/4   teaspoon crushed red pepper flakes
2   cups unblanched whole almonds

In a bowl, combine the first six ingredients. Add almonds; toss to coat. Spread into a greased 15-in. x 10-in. x 1-in. baking pan. Bake at 250° for 30 minutes or until lightly browned, stirring occasionally. Cool. Store in an airtight container.

YIELD: 2 cups.

PPLE DIP WITH CRISPS

i Karcher, Geneva, Nebraska

sister created this recipe for a family celebration, it's great anytime. With the tempting taste of a e-baked pie, this finger food pairs warm spiced les with cute cutout shapes from a prepared st.

INAMON-SUGAR CRISPS:

try for double-crust pie (9 inches)
    tablespoons sugar
    teaspoon ground cinnamon

PLE DIP:

    medium tart apples, peeled and coarsely chopped
    cup sugar
    teaspoon ground cinnamon
    cup butter
    cup all-purpose flour
    cup cold water

cinnamon-sugar crisps, on a lightly floured face, roll pastry to 1/8-in. thickness. Combine jar and cinnamon; sprinkle over pastry. Cut

Meanwhile, in a bowl, combine the ketchup, le[mon] juice, peel, horseradish, Worcestershire sauce [and] pepper sauce. On a serving platter, arrange shr[imp] in groups of three to resemble dragon claws. S[erve] with sauce; garnish with lemon wedges if desi[red].

YIELD: 6 servings (1¼ cups sauce).

PEPPER POPPER FINGERS

Our creative home economists had a hand in m[ak]ing these Halloween-inspired jalapeno popp[ers.] They're baked instead of fried, so making them [is a] real snap.

1   package (8 ounces) cream cheese, softened
1   cup (4 ounces) shredded sharp cheddar cheese
1   cup (4 ounces) shredded Monterey Jack cheese
6   bacon strips, cooked and crumbled
¼   teaspoon garlic powder
¼   teaspoon chili powder
12   medium jalapeno peppers, stems removed, halved lengthwise and seede[d]
½   cup dry bread crumbs
2   tablespoons ketchup
¼   cup sliced almonds

In a large mixing bowl, combine the cheeses, ba[con] and seasonings. Spoon about 1 tablespoonful i[nto] each pepper half. Dip tops of stuffed peppers i[n] bread crumbs.

Place a small amount of ketchup at the end [of] each popper; top with a sliced almond to resem[ble] a fingernail. Place in a greased 15-in. x 10-in. x [1-] in. baking pan. Bake, uncovered, at 300° for 25-[30] minutes or until golden brown.

YIELD: 2 dozen.

EDITOR'S NOTE: When cutting or seeding [hot] peppers, use rubber or plastic gloves to protect y[our] hands. Avoid touching your face.

DRAGON CLAWS WITH BLOOD SAUCE

Stand back and watch guests gobble up this cold appetizer from our Test Kitchen!

10   cups water
1   teaspoon salt
1   pound uncooked medium shrimp, peeled and deveined
1   cup ketchup
2   tablespoons lemon juice
2   teaspoons grated lemon peel
4   teaspoons prepared horseradish
¼   teaspoon Worcestershire sauce
⅛   to ¼ teaspoon hot pepper sauce
Lemon wedges, optional

In a large saucepan, combine water and salt; bring to a boil. Add shrimp. Reduce heat; simmer, uncovered, for 2-3 minutes or until shrimp turn pink, stirring occasionally. Drain. Cool in ice water; drain. Refrigerate until serving.

HALLOWEEN PARTY MIX

Jeanette Urbom, Overland Park, Kansas

This colorful mix has a light coating that also makes it perfect for gatherings.

1   package (11 ounces) pretzels
1   package (10$^{1}/_{2}$ ounces) miniature peanut butter filled butter-flavored crackers
1   cup dry roasted peanuts
1   cup sugar
$^{1}/_{2}$ cup butter
$^{1}/_{2}$ cup light corn syrup
2   tablespoons vanilla extract
1   teaspoon baking soda
1   package (10 ounces) M&M's
1   package (18$^{1}/_{2}$ ounces) candy corn

In a large bowl, combine the pretzels, crackers and peanuts. In a large saucepan, combine sugar, butter and corn syrup. Bring to a boil over medium heat; boil for 5 minutes.

Remove from the heat; stir in vanilla and baking soda (mixture will foam). Pour over pretzel mixture and stir until coated. Pour into a greased 15-in. x 10-in. x 1-in. baking pan. Bake at 250° for 45 minutes, stirring every 10-15 minutes. Break apart while warm. Toss with M&M's and candy corn. Cool completely. Store in airtight containers.

YIELD: 16 cups.

LICORICE CARAMELS

Donna Higbee, Riverton, Utah

Fans of black licorice won't be able to stop ea these gooey caramels.

1   teaspoon plus 1 cup butter, *divided*
2   cups sugar
1$^{1}/_{2}$ cups light corn syrup
1   can (14 ounces) sweetened condensed milk
$^{1}/_{2}$ teaspoon salt
2   teaspoons anise extract
$^{1}/_{4}$ teaspoon black food coloring

Line an 8-in. square baking pan with heavy-duty butter foil with the 1 teaspoon butter. Set as In a heavy saucepan, combine the sugar, corn sy sweetened condensed milk, salt and remair butter; bring to a boil over medium heat. C and stir until a candy thermometer reads 2 (firm-ball stage).

Remove from the heat; stir in extract and food oring (keep face away from mixture as odc very strong). Pour into prepared pan (do not sc saucepan). Cool completely before cutting. Lift and candy out of pan; remove foil. Cut into squares; wrap each in waxed paper.

YIELD: about 5 dozen.

EDITOR'S NOTE: We recommend that you your candy thermometer before each use bringing water to a boil; the thermometer she read 212°. Adjust your recipe temperature u down based on your test.

CANDY CORN SNACK MIX

Denise Neal, Yorba Linda, California

It's no trick—this Halloween party treat requires ly three ingredients and 5 minutes to prepare.

1   cup *each* candy corn, milk chocolate M&M's and salted peanuts

In a serving bowl, combine all ingredients. Stor an airtight container.

YIELD: 3 cups.

spirited snacks & beverages

CREAMY CHIPPED BEEF FONDUE

Beth Fox, Lawrence, Kansas

My mother often served fondue at parties, and I've since followed in that tradition. It's nice to offer a hearty appetizer that requires very little work.

1⅓ to 1½ cups milk
2   packages (8 ounces *each*) cream cheese, softened
1   package (2½ ounces) thinly sliced dried beef, chopped
¼   cup chopped green onions
2   teaspoons ground mustard
1   loaf (1 pound) French bread, cubed

In a saucepan, heat milk and cream cheese over medium heat; stir until smooth. Stir in beef, onions and mustard; heat through. Transfer to a fondue pot or slow cooker; keep warm. Serve with bread cubes.

YIELD: about 4 cups.

PECAN CEREAL CLUSTERS

Debbie Zorn, Vidalia, Georgia

Featuring crunchy cereal, colorful candies, pecans and loads of peanut butter flavor, these chocolaty bites offer plenty of make-ahead convenience. They're a cinch to whip up when you're in a hurry.

¾   cup peanut butter
1   cup (6 ounces) semisweet chocolate chips
3   cups Cheerios
1   package (14 ounces) milk chocolate M&M's
¾   cup pecan halves

Line three 15-in. x 10-in. x 1-in. baking pans with waxed paper. In a large heavy saucepan over low heat, cook and stir the peanut butter and chocolate chips until chips are melted. Remove from the heat; stir in Cheerios, M&M's and pecans until evenly coated. Drop by rounded tablespoonfuls onto prepared pans. Refrigerate for 4 hours or until firm.

YIELD: about 5 dozen.

EDITOR'S NOTE: Reduced-fat or generic brands of peanut butter are not recommended for this recipe.

INGERSNAP DIP

ssie Hughes, Marion, Virginia

s easy-to-fix dip is a fun way to dress up a pack-
e of gingersnaps. It's great for fall gatherings
d makes a sweet snack for the holidays.

    package (8 ounces) cream cheese, softened
    cup confectioners' sugar
    teaspoons pumpkin pie spice
    carton (8 ounces) frozen whipped topping, thawed
    package (16 ounces) gingersnaps

a small mixing bowl, combine the cream cheese,
nfectioners' sugar and pumpkin pie spice. Beat in
hipped topping until blended. Refrigerate until
ving. Serve with gingersnaps.

ELD: 3 cups.

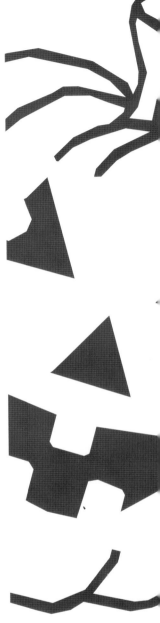

spirited shindigs

CAULDRON DIP

This witch's cauldron holds a Halloween snack that's frightfully fun. Our Test Kitchen formed a pot by toasting a slice of rye bread, then filled it with a creamy dip that's perfect with the pretzel "logs" and sweet pepper "flames" placed underneath.

1	cup (8 ounces) sour cream
1	tablespoon dried parsley flakes
1	teaspoon sugar
1/2	teaspoon onion powder
1/4	teaspoon garlic salt
1/4	teaspoon pepper
1	slice soft dark rye bread
1	*each* medium sweet red, yellow and orange pepper, julienned
10	pretzel rods, broken in half

In a small bowl, combine sour cream, parsley, sugar, onion powder, garlic salt and pepper. Cover and refrigerate.

Flatten bread with a rolling pin. Press over an inverted greased 10-oz. custard cup. Top with another 10-oz. custard cup. Place on an ungreased baking sheet. Bake at 350° for 7 minutes. Carefully remove top dish. Bake 3-5 minutes longer or until bread is lightly toasted. Immediately remove the bread from dish. Cool.

Fill bread bowl with dip. Arrange peppers and pretzels under and around bowl.

YIELD: 1 cup.

HOT APPLE CIDER

Sue Gronholz, Beaver Dam, Wisconsin

A hot beverage like this is savored here when ch weather returns after summer. The clove-studc orange slices are so attractive.

1	medium navel orange, cut into 1/2-inch slices
50	to 60 whole cloves
6	cups apple cider *or* juice
1	cinnamon stick (4 inches)
2 1/4	cups unsweetened pineapple juice
1/4	cup honey
3	tablespoons lemon juice
1	teaspoon grated lemon peel
1/4	teaspoon ground nutmeg

Additional cinnamon sticks, optional

Cut orange slices in half. Using a wooden toothpi poke holes in the peel of each orange slice at 1 in. intervals. Insert a clove into each hole; s aside.

In a large saucepan, bring apple juice and cinnam stick to a boil. Reduce heat; cover and simmer f 5 minutes. Stir in the pineapple juice, honey, lem juice and peel and nutmeg; return to a boil. Redu heat; cover and simmer for 5 minutes. Disca cinnamon stick. Garnish with orange slices. Ser warm with additional cinnamon sticks for stirre if desired.

YIELD: 8-10 servings.

spirited snacks & beverages

ARSHMALLOW WITCHES

ready for an assembly line because these no-
e marshmallow witches from our Test Kitchen
easy to prepare, and kids will love helping.
y're perfect for gatherings because a dozen can
ut together in just 30 minutes.

cup vanilla frosting, *divided*

miniature semisweet chocolate chips

large marshmallows

drop *each* green, red and yellow
food coloring

cup flaked coconut

chocolate wafers

miniature peanut butter cups

milk chocolate kisses

the face of each witch, place a dab of frosting
the bottom of three chocolate chips; press two
eyes and one for nose onto each marshmallow.

hair, combine green food coloring and a drop of
er in a small resealable plastic bag; add coconut
shake well. Spread a small amount of frosting
sides of marshmallows; press coconut hair into
ting. Place 3 tablespoons of frosting in a small

heavy-duty resealable plastic bag; tint orange
with red and yellow food coloring. Set aside.

For hats, spread some of the remaining frosting in
the center of chocolate wafers; press peanut butter cups upside down into frosting. Lightly spread
bottoms of chocolate kisses with frosting; place
on peanut butter cups.

Cut a small hole in the corner of plastic bag; insert
a small star tip. Fill the bag with reserved orange
frosting and pipe stars around the base of each
peanut butter cup. Secure a hat to each witch
with a dab of frosting.

YIELD: 1 dozen.

spooky tip

Whip up an extra batch of Marshmallow Witches, put them in plastic
wrap and tie with curly orange or black
ribbon for festive party favors.

spirited shindigs

GHOSTLY HOT COCOA

Ruby Gibson, Newton, North Carolina

Chocolate pudding mix is the convenient start to this clever cocoa mix. Kids of all ages get a kick out of the marshmallow ghost floating on top.

$6\,2/3$	cups nonfat dry milk powder
1	cup instant chocolate drink mix
1	package (5 ounces) cook-and-serve chocolate pudding mix
$1/2$	cup confectioners' sugar
$1/2$	cup powdered nondairy creamer
$1/2$	cup baking cocoa

ADDITIONAL INGREDIENTS:

30	cups boiling water
30	Peeps ghost candy

In a very large bowl, combine the first six ingredients. Store in an airtight container in a cool dry place for up to 3 months.

TO PREPARE HOT COCOA: Dissolve $1/3$ cup co
mix in 1 cup boiling water. Float a Peeps ghos
each cup of hot cocoa.

YIELD: 1 serving per batch.

PUMPKIN SEED CHEESE BALL

Save some of your home-roasted pumpkin seeds
coat this creamy green onion spread from our ho
economists.

1	package (8 ounces) cream cheese, softened
1	cup (4 ounces) shredded part-skim mozzarella cheese
$1/2$	cup chopped green onions
1	teaspoon Italian seasoning
$1/2$	teaspoon dried parsley flakes
$1/8$	teaspoon cayenne pepper
$1/4$	cup roasted pumpkin seeds
$1/4$	cup unsalted sunflower kernels

Assorted crackers *or* fresh vegetables

In a small mixing bowl, combine the first six ing
dients. Cover and refrigerate for 30 minutes
until easy to handle. Meanwhile, on a plate, combi
pumpkin seeds and sunflower kernels; set aside.

Shape cream cheese mixture into a ball; gently r
in pumpkin seed mixture (lightly press seeds in
cream cheese mixture if necessary). Wrap in pla
tic wrap. Refrigerate for at least 2 hours or un
firm. Serve with crackers or vegetables.

YIELD: 1 cheese ball ($1\,3/4$ cups).

freaky fact

Halloween is the second-most comme
cially successful holiday, with Christma
being the first.

YIELD: 30 batches (7 cups total).

spice, vanilla and ginger; beat until smooth. Serve warm or chilled with goblins. Refrigerate leftover dip.

YIELD: About 40 goblins and 3 1/2 cups dip.

SPOOKY SNACKS

Andrea Chapman, Helena, Oklahoma

These clever crawlers come together in a snap!

1/2	cup plus 1 tablespoon peanut butter
48	butter-flavored crackers
1/2	cup chow mein noodles
1/4	cup raisins

Spread 1 teaspoon of peanut butter on the tops of 24 crackers. Place three noodles on each side of each cracker for legs; top with the remaining crackers. Spread a small amount of peanut butter on each raisin; place two on each cracker for eyes.

YIELD: 2 dozen.

MUSHROOM PARTY PUFFS

Patricia Kile, Greentown, Pennsylvania

Full of cheese and seasonings, these puffs are satisfying by themselves.

36	medium fresh mushrooms
3	tablespoons butter
1	cup mayonnaise
1	cup (4 ounces) finely shredded Swiss cheese
1/4	cup Dijon mustard
1/4	cup minced fresh parsley
1/2	teaspoon onion powder
2	egg whites

Remove and discard mushroom stems. In a skillet, saute mushroom caps in butter. In a bowl, combine mayonnaise, cheese, mustard, parsley and onion powder. Beat egg whites until stiff; fold into mayonnaise mixture. Spoon into mushroom caps. Place in an ungreased 15-in. x 10-in. x 1-in. baking pan. Bake at 450° for 8-10 minutes or until golden.

YIELD: 12-15 servings.

EDITOR'S NOTE: Reduced-fat or fat-free mayonnaise may not be substituted for regular mayonnaise in this recipe.

ﾟBLINS WITH ﾟMPKIN DIP

￾isty Johnson, Columbus, Ohio

￾re up some fun at your Halloween bash with ￾e ghostly good chips and pleasing pumpkin dip.

￾BLINS:

	cup sugar
	to 2 teaspoons ground cinnamon
	flour tortillas (10 inches)

￾MPKIN DIP:

	package (8 ounces) cream cheese, softened
	cups confectioners' sugar
	can (15 ounces) solid-pack pumpkin
	teaspoons pumpkin pie spice
	teaspoon vanilla extract
	teaspoon ground ginger

￾ bowl, combine sugar and cinnamon; set aside. ￾ tortillas with a ghost-shaped 3 1/2-in. cookie cut-￾ place on baking sheets coated with nonstick ￾king spray. Spritz goblins with nonstick cooking ￾y; sprinkle with reserved cinnamon-sugar. Bake ￾50° for 6-8 minutes or until edges are lightly ￾ned. Remove to wire racks.

￾ small mixing bowl, beat cream cheese and con-￾ioners' sugar. Gradually add the pumpkin, pie

SERPENT TONGUE POTATOES

Sue Murphy, Greenwood, Michigan

Seasoned with chili powder and cayenne pepper, these paper-thin chips are surefire crowd-pleasers.

4	medium unpeeled baking potatoes
4	teaspoons salt, *divided*
4	cups ice water
1	tablespoon chili powder
1	teaspoon garlic salt
1	teaspoon dried parsley flakes
1/4	to 1/2 teaspoon cayenne pepper

Oil for deep-fat frying

Using a vegetable peeler or metal cheese slicer, cut potatoes into very thin lengthwise strips. Place in a large bowl; add 3 teaspoons salt and ice water. Soak for 30 minutes; drain. Place potatoes on paper towels and pat dry. In a small bowl, combine the chili powder, garlic salt, parsley, cayenne and remaining salt; set aside.

In an electric skillet or deep-fat fryer, heat oil to 375°. Cook potatoes in oil in batches for 2-3 minutes or until deep golden brown, stirring frequently. Remove with a slotted spoon; drain on paper towels. Immediately sprinkle with reserved seasoning mixture. Store in an airtight container.

YIELD: 10 cups.

SPOOKY CITRUS PUNCH

Irene Kusler, Eureka, South Dakota

There's no doubt this refreshing beverage will quench your thirst. Food coloring makes it fun for Halloween.

1	can (12 ounces) frozen limeade concentrate, thawed
3/4	cup lemonade concentrate
2	cups water
1/4	cup sugar, optional
2	liters ginger ale, chilled

Food coloring of your choice, optional

Ice cubes

In a large punch bowl, combine the limeade lemonade concentrates. Stir in water and suga desired. Stir in the ginger ale and food colorir desired. Serve immediately over ice.

YIELD: about 3 quarts.

SPIDERWEB DIP WITH BAT TORTILLA CHIPS

Sonia Candler, Edmonton, Alberta

Every year, our daughter and her friends anticip our annual Halloween party. Among the menu it is this taco dip with bat-shaped tortilla chips.

20	chipotle chili and pepper tortillas *or* flo tortillas (8 inches)
3/4	teaspoon garlic salt
3/4	teaspoon ground coriander
3/4	teaspoon paprika
1/4	teaspoon plus 1/8 teaspoon pepper

DIP:

1	package (8 ounces) cream cheese, softened
3/4	cup salsa
1/2	cup prepared guacamole
1	to 2 tablespoons sour cream

Cut tortillas into bat shapes with a 3 3/4-in. co cutter. Place tortillas on baking sheets coa with nonstick cooking spray. Spritz tortillas v nonstick cooking spray. Combine the garlic s coriander, paprika and pepper; sprinkle over tillas. Bake at 350° for 5-8 minutes or until ed just begin to brown.

In a small mixing bowl, combine cream che and salsa. Spread into a 9-in. pie plate. Caref spread guacamole to within 1 in. of edges. P sour cream in a small resealable plastic bag; c small hole in a corner of bag. Pipe thin concer circles an inch apart over guacamole. Begin with the center circle, gently pull a knife thro circles toward center edge. Wipe knife cle Repeat to complete spiderweb pattern. Se with tortilla bats.

YIELD: about 7 dozen chips and 1 1/2 cups dip.

BENT TONGUE POTATOES

CINNAMON CARAMEL APPLES

Our Test Kitchen staff used cinnamon and chocolate to give a fun and tasty twist to traditional caramel apples. Rolled in nuts, coconut or colorful candies, they'll delight kids of all ages.

2   packages (14 ounces *each*) caramels
3   tablespoons milk chocolate chips
3   tablespoons water
1   teaspoon ground cinnamon
3/4 teaspoon vanilla extract
8   Popsicle sticks
8   large tart apples

Chocolate-covered toffee bits, finely chopped salted peanuts and cashews, flaked coconut, M&M miniature baking bits *and/or* chocolate sprinkles

In a microwave-safe bowl, combine the caramels, chocolate chips, water, cinnamon and vanilla. Microwave, uncovered, on high for 1 1/2 minutes; stir. Microwave 30-60 seconds longer or until caramels are melted. Insert Popsicle sticks into the apples; dip into caramel mixture, turning to coat. Roll in or press on desired toppings. Place on waxed paper; let stand until set.

YIELD: 8 servings.

EDITOR'S NOTE: This recipe was tested in a 1,100-watt microwave.

PUMPKIN SEED TRAIL M

Our home economists combine a bounty of fall g
ies to create this hearty, colorful snack mix.

1   cup seeds from freshly cut pumpkin, washed and dried
2   tablespoons vegetable oil
1/4 teaspoon salt
1   cup roasted salted almonds
1   cup salted cashew halves
1   cup Reese's pieces
2/3 cup *each* raisins, golden raisins and drie
    cranberries

In a large skillet, saute seeds in oil for 5 minu
or until lightly browned. Using a slotted spc
transfer seeds to an ungreased 15-in. x 10-in. x 1
baking pan; spread into a single layer. Sprinkle v
salt. Bake at 325° for 15-20 minutes or until cr
Remove to paper towels to cool completely.

In a large bowl, combine the almonds, cashe
Reese's pieces, raisins, golden raisins and dried cr
berries. Add pumpkin seeds; toss to combine. St
in an airtight container.

YIELD: 6 cups.

SLOW COOKER CHEESE DI

Marion Bartone, Conneaut, Ohio

I brought this slightly spicy cheese dip to a gath
ing with friends, where it was a huge hit.

1   pound ground beef
1/2 pound bulk hot pork sausage
2   pounds process American cheese, cubec
2   cans (10 ounces *each*) diced tomatoes a
    green chilies

Tortilla chips

In a skillet, cook beef and sausage over mediu
heat until no longer pink; drain. Transfer to a 5-
slow cooker. Add cheese and tomatoes; mix w
Cover and cook on low for 4 hours or until t
cheese is melted, stirring occasionally. Serve w
tortilla chips.

YIELD: 3 quarts.

spirited snacks & beverages

OBLIN EYEBALLS

nome economists had great vision when creat-
:hese devilish deviled eggs. Guests at your
ween party will be "goblin" them up!

- eggs
- food coloring
- cup mayonnaise
- tablespoon prepared mustard
- and pepper to taste
- large stuffed olives, halved widthwise

e eggs in a single layer in a large saucepan; add
.gh cold water to cover eggs by 1 in. Bring to
il over high heat. Reduce heat; cover and sim-
for 15 minutes. Drain; let stand until cool
.gh to handle. Gently crack eggs (do not peel).

a large bowl with hot water; add food coloring
nt water a dark red. Add eggs, making sure they
completely covered by water; let stand for 30
utes. Remove eggs from water; peel (eggs
ld have a veined appearance).

eggs in half widthwise; place yolks in a bowl.
whites aside. Mash yolks with a fork; stir in
mayonnaise, mustard, salt and pepper. To make
s stand better on serving plate, slice a small
e from the bottom of egg white halves. Stuff
i yolk mixture. Place an olive half in the center
ach to resemble an eyeball. Refrigerate until
'ing.

:LD: 2 dozen.

freaky fact

It's thought that the tradition of bob-
bing for apples originated from the
Roman harvest festival that honors
Pamona, the goddess of fruit trees.

HERBED CHEESE SPREAD

Laurel Leslie, Sonora, California

Flavored with several herbs, this appetizer certainly
lives up to its name. It's one of the best cream cheese
spreads I've tried.

1   package (8 ounces) cream cheese,
    softened
¼   cup butter, softened
1   tablespoon minced fresh parsley
2   teaspoons minced chives
2   teaspoons minced fresh chervil *or* ½
    teaspoon dried chervil
1   to 2 garlic cloves, minced
¾   teaspoon minced fresh tarragon *or* ¼
    teaspoon dried tarragon
¼   teaspoon lemon-pepper seasoning

Assorted crackers

In a mixing bowl, beat cream cheese and butter
until smooth. Add the parsley, chives, chervil, garlic,
tarragon and lemon-pepper; mix well. Transfer
to a serving dish. Cover and refrigerate for 4
hours or overnight. Remove from the refrigerator
15 minutes before serving. Serve with crackers.

YIELD: 1½ cups.

haunting
halloween
buffets

JACK-O'-LANTERN SANDWICHES

Be prepared for happy faces when you make these eye-catching jack-o'-lanterns from our Test Kitchen cooks. They loaded the sandwiches with flavorful fillings, then easily formed fun pumpkin shapes using cookie cutters.

1/2   cup mayonnaise
2   teaspoons Italian salad dressing mix
16   slices whole wheat *or* white bread
8   slices American cheese
1   pound shaved deli chicken *or* turkey
8   lettuce leaves

In a bowl, combine the mayonnaise and salad dressing mix; spread on each slice of bread. Top half of the slices with cheese, chicken and lettuce. Top with remaining bread. Cut sandwiches with a 4-in. pumpkin-shaped cutter. Remove top slice; cut out eyes and nose with a small triangle cutter. Use cutout pieces for mouth.

YIELD: 8 servings.

CRANBERRY APPETIZER MEATBALLS

Jim Ulberg, Elk Rapids, Michigan

A tangy non-traditional sauce nicely coats t[ ] meatballs for a memorable fall party snack.

2   eggs, beaten
1   cup dry bread crumbs
1/3   cup minced fresh parsley
1/3   cup ketchup
2   tablespoons finely chopped onion
2   tablespoons soy sauce
2   garlic cloves, minced
1/2   teaspoon salt
1/4   teaspoon pepper
2   pounds ground beef

CRANBERRY SAUCE:

1   can (16 ounces) whole-berry cranberr[ ] sauce
1   bottle (12 ounces) chili sauce
1   tablespoon brown sugar
1   tablespoon prepared mustard
1   tablespoon lemon juice
2   garlic cloves, minced

In a large bowl, combine the eggs, bread cru[ ] parsley, ketchup, onion, soy sauce, garlic, salt[ ] pepper. Crumble beef over mixture and mix [ ] Shape into 1-in. balls.

Place meatballs on a rack in a shallow baking [ ] Bake, uncovered, at 400° for 15 minutes or un[ ] longer pink. Transfer with a slotted spoon to a [ ] cooker or chafing dish.

Combine sauce ingredients in a saucepan; sin[ ] for 10 minutes, stirring occasionally. Pour [ ] meatballs. Serve warm.

YIELD: about 7 dozen.

UMBO JOES

ey Wranosky, Eagle River, Wisconsin

guys in our family like to spoon the zesty beef
over both halves of the roll and eat it with a
Now that I no longer work outside of the home,
I myself in the kitchen reading recipes, cooking
baking.

- pounds ground beef
- large onion, chopped
- cup chopped green pepper
- can (10 3/4 ounces) condensed chicken gumbo soup, undiluted
- cup ketchup
- cup packed brown sugar
- tablespoons cider vinegar
- tablespoon prepared horseradish
- bay leaf
- teaspoon salt
- teaspoon pepper
- sandwich rolls, split

In a large skillet, cook beef, onion and green pepper over medium heat until meat is no longer pink; drain. Stir in soup, ketchup, brown sugar, vinegar, horseradish, bay leaf, salt and pepper. Cover and simmer for 30 minutes. Discard bay leaf. Spoon onto rolls.

YIELD: 12 servings.

spooky tip

Gumbo Joes are great to serve at parties. Prepare the filling the day before and chill. Reheat and place in a slow cooker to keep warm.

Complete the meal with baked beans, potato chips, pickles and a festive Halloween dessert.

CRANBERRY CHEESE SPREAD

Nancy Johnson, Laverne, Oklahoma

Here's a creamy sweet-tart spread that's ideal for a holiday buffet.

1   package (8 ounces) cream cheese, softened
1/2   cup sour cream
2   tablespoons honey
1/4   teaspoon ground cinnamon
1   can (16 ounces) whole-berry cranberry sauce
1/3   cup slivered almonds, toasted
Assorted crackers

In a small mixing bowl, beat the cream cheese, sour cream, honey and cinnamon until smooth. Spread onto a serving dish or plate. In a bowl, stir cranberry sauce until it reaches spreading consistency; spread over cream cheese mixture. Sprinkle with almonds. Cover and refrigerate for 2-3 hours. Serve with crackers.

YIELD: 12-14 servings.

LIKE 'EM HOT WINGS

Myra Innes, Auburn, Kansas

These spicy chicken wings are wonderfully seasoned. They're an easy crowd-pleasing snack.

12   whole chicken wings (about 2 1/2 pounds)
1   bottle (2 ounces) hot pepper sauce (about 1/4 cup)
1   to 2 garlic cloves, minced
1 1/2   teaspoons dried rosemary, crushed
1   teaspoon dried thyme
1/4   teaspoon salt
1/4   teaspoon pepper
Celery and carrot sticks and blue cheese salad dressing, optional

Cut chicken wings into three sections; discard wing tips. In a large resealable plastic bag, combine the hot pepper sauce, garlic and seasonings. Add wings;

toss to evenly coat. Transfer to a well-grea[sed] 13-in. x 9-in. x 2-in. baking dish. Bake, uncovere[d] 425° for 30-40 minutes or until chicken juices [run] clear, turning every 10 minutes. Serve with ce[lery,] carrots and blue cheese dressing if desired.

YIELD: 4-6 servings.

EDITOR'S NOTE: 2 pounds of uncooked chic[ken] wing sections may be substituted for the wh[ole] chicken wings. Omit the first step of the recip[e.]

MINI MEXICAN QUICHES

Linda Hendrix, Moundville, Missouri

This fun finger food is great for a party or when[ev]er you want to munch a yummy treat.

1/2   cup butter, softened
1   package (3 ounces) cream cheese, softened
1   cup all-purpose flour
1   cup (4 ounces) shredded Monterey Jac[k] cheese
1   can (4 ounces) chopped green chilies, drained
2   eggs
1/2   cup heavy whipping cream
1/4   teaspoon salt
1/8   teaspoon pepper

In a small mixing bowl, cream butter and cre[am] cheese. Add flour; beat until well blended. Shap[e in]to 24 balls; cover and refrigerate for 1 hour. P[ress] balls onto the bottom and up the sides of grea[sed] miniature muffin cups. Sprinkle a rounded [tea]spoonful of cheese and 1/2 teaspoon of chilies [into] each shell.

In a bowl, beat eggs, cream, salt and pepper. Sp[oon] into shells. Bake at 350° for 30-35 minutes or [un]til golden brown. Let stand for 5 minutes be[fore] serving. Refrigerate leftovers.

YIELD: 2 dozen.

ALIAN SAUSAGE NDWICHES

e Yaeger, Brookings, South Dakota

en my wife and I have friends over, we love erve these sandwiches. This is a convenient e, since it can be prepared the day before and ated.

Italian sausages
large green peppers, thinly sliced
cup chopped onion
can (12 ounces) tomato paste
can (15 ounces) tomato sauce
cup water
tablespoon sugar
garlic cloves, minced
teaspoons dried basil
teaspoon dried oregano
teaspoon salt
sandwich buns
dded part-skim mozzarella cheese, optional

large Dutch oven, brown sausages a few at a
; discard all but 2 tablespoons drippings. Saute
ers and onion in drippings until crisp-tender;
. Return sausages to pan along with tomato
e, tomato sauce, water, sugar, garlic, basil,
ano and salt; bring to a boil. Reduce heat; cov-
d simmer for 30 minutes. Serve on buns. Top
cheese if desired.

LD: 20 servings.

GINGER SQUASH SOUP

Laurel Leslie, Sonora, California

Everyone likes the lovely golden color and creamy consistency of this soup. A touch of ginger sparks the mild squash flavor.

3   cups chicken broth
2   packages (10 ounces *each*) frozen cooked winter squash, thawed
1   cup unsweetened applesauce
3   tablespoons sugar
1   teaspoon ground ginger
1/2   teaspoon salt
1/2   cup heavy whipping cream, whipped

In a large saucepan, simmer broth and squash. Add the applesauce, sugar, ginger and salt. Bring to a boil. Reduce heat to low; stir in cream. Cook for 30 minutes or until soup reaches desired consistency, stirring occasionally.

YIELD: 6 servings.

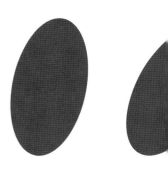

spirited shindigs

DINNER IN A PUMPKIN

SuAnn Bird, Lindon, Utah

Scoop out hearty helpings of meat, rice and cooked pumpkin in this fun fall entree.

4 medium pie pumpkins (2$^1/_2$ pounds *each*)
1$^1/_4$ pounds ground beef
$^1/_2$ cup chopped onion
$^1/_2$ cup chopped celery
$^1/_4$ cup chopped green pepper
1 can (10$^3/_4$ ounces) condensed cream of chicken soup, undiluted
1 can (4 ounces) mushroom stems and pieces, drained
$^1/_4$ cup soy sauce
2 tablespoons brown sugar
2 cups hot cooked rice
2 tablespoons vegetable oil

Wash each pumpkin; cut a 4-in. circle around stem. Remove top and set aside; discard seeds and loose fibers from inside. Place pumpkins in a shallow sturdy baking pan; set aside.

In a large skillet, cook the beef, onion, celery and green pepper over medium heat until meat is no longer pink and vegetables are tender; drain. Stir in the soup, mushrooms, soy sauce and brown sugar. Cook for 3-4 minutes or until heated through. Fold in rice; spoon into pumpkins and replace tops. Brush outside of pumpkins with oil.

Bake at 350° for 50-60 minutes or just until pumpkin is tender (do not overbake). Place on individual serving plates.

YIELD: 4 servings.

SPOOKY MONSTER SANDWICHES

Why serve chicken salad on ordinary rolls v you can make these spooky sandwiches from Test Kitchen?

2 cups cubed cooked chicken breast
$^1/_2$ cup dried cranberries, optional
$^1/_2$ cup mayonnaise
$^1/_4$ cup finely chopped onion
$^1/_4$ cup chopped celery
$^1/_4$ teaspoon salt
$^1/_4$ teaspoon pepper
12 dinner rolls, split and toasted
1 jar (15 ounces) process cheese sauce
24 pimiento-stuffed olives
12 pimiento strips
6 whole baby dill pickles, cut in half lengthwise

In a bowl, combine the chicken, cranberries if sired, mayonnaise, onion, celery, salt and pepper rolls with chicken mixture. Heat cheese sauc soften; drizzle or pipe over top of each sandw to resemble hair. For each monster sandwich, tach olives for eyes, pimiento strips for noses pickles for fangs.

YIELD: 1 dozen.

spooky tip

You can make Spooky Mons Sandwiches with a variety of f ings, including tuna salad and slor joes, and a variety of cheeses a lunch meats. Get creative to suit yc family's taste...and enlist the kids help with assembling!

haunting halloween buffets

Thaw bread dough according to package directi[ons];
let rise until doubled.

Meanwhile, in a large skillet over medium heat, c[ook]
the sausage until no longer pink; drain and tra[ns]fer to a large bowl. Add the spinach, chees[e,]
oregano and garlic powder; set side. Roll each [loaf]
of bread into a 14-in. x 12-in. rectangle. Spre[ad]
sausage mixture lengthwise down the cente[r of]
each rectangle. Gently press the filling down; [brush]
with butter.

Bring edges of dough to the center over filling; pi[nch]
to seal. Place each loaf seam side down o[n a]
greased baking sheet. Tuck ends under and form[in]to a snake shape. Place an egg yolk in each of t[wo]
small bowls. Tint one orange with red and yell[ow]
food coloring and the other with green food col[or]ing if desired. Brush stripes on snake. Bake [at]
350° for 25-30 minutes or until golden brown.

Cut out small holes in olives; gently press into bre[ad]
for eyes. Cut a slit in each loaf; insert a red pepp[er]
strip for tongues.

YIELD: 2 loaves.

SAUSAGE-STUFFED SLITHERY SNAKES

This cheese-, spinach- and sausage-filled bread from
our Test Kitchen is a *ssss*erious party pleaser! It
ties in well with any Halloween theme.

2	loaves (1 pound *each*) frozen bread dough, thawed
1	pound bulk Italian sausage
1	package (10 ounces) frozen chopped spinach, thawed and squeezed dry
4	cups (1 pound) shredded part-skim mozzarella cheese
1/4	cup grated Parmesan cheese
1	teaspoon dried oregano
1/2	teaspoon garlic powder
2	tablespoons butter
2	egg yolks
4	drops *each* red, yellow and green food coloring, optional
4	pitted ripe olives
2	roasted sweet red pepper strips

BARBECUED FRANKS

Dorothy Anderson, Ottawa, Kansas

Guests won't be able to resist "goblin" up the[se]
special sausages at your Halloween party!

2	teaspoons cornstarch
2	tablespoons cold water
1	jar (18 ounces) peach preserves
1	cup barbecue sauce
2	packages (1 pound *each*) miniature hot dogs *or* smoked sausages

In a large saucepan, combine the cornstarch a[nd]
water until smooth. Stir in the preserves a[nd]
barbecue sauce. Bring to a boil; cook and stir f[or]
2 minutes or until thickened. Stir in hot dogs un[til]
coated. Cover and cook for 5 minutes or until hea[t]ed through.

YIELD: 20 servings.

AJUN PORK
ANDWICHES

e Kruse, Monee, Illinois

s recipe's specially seasoned rub gives tender juicy
k a slightly spicy flavor. You'll watch in delight
hese delicious, open-faced sandwiches disappear
m your buffet table!

    pork tenderloins (1 pound *each*), trimmed
    teaspoons vegetable oil
    tablespoons paprika
    teaspoons dried oregano
    teaspoons dried thyme
'2 teaspoons garlic powder
    teaspoon pepper
    teaspoon salt, optional
    teaspoon ground cumin
    teaspoon ground nutmeg
    teaspoon cayenne pepper
    French bread slices *or* mini buns
tter *or* mayonnaise
ttuce leaves
in slivers of green and sweet red pepper

ice tenderloins in a greased 13-in. x 9-in. x 2-in.
king pan. Rub each with 1 teaspoon oil. In a bowl,
mbine paprika, oregano, thyme, garlic powder,

pepper, salt if desired, cumin, nutmeg and cayenne;
pat over tenderloins. Cover and refrigerate overnight.

Bake at 425° for 25-30 minutes or until a meat
thermometer reads 160°-170°. Let stand for 10
minutes; thinly slice. Spread bread or buns with
butter or mayonnaise; top with lettuce, pork and
green and red pepper.

YIELD: 3 dozen.

SLIMY STEWED WORMS

Shelley Way, Cheyenne, Wyoming

I top spaghetti "worms" with a hearty meat sauce
for a mouth-watering main dish that's guaranteed
to please all of your party guests.

1	pound ground beef
1	can (28 ounces) crushed tomatoes
2	cups water
1	can (14 1/2 ounces) beef broth
1	can (6 ounces) tomato paste
1 1/2	cups chopped onion
1/4	cup minced fresh parsley
2	garlic cloves, minced
3/4	teaspoon dried basil
1/2	teaspoon onion salt
1/2	teaspoon dried oregano
1/2	teaspoon sugar
1/4	teaspoon pepper
1/4	teaspoon dried thyme
8	ounces uncooked spaghetti
1/4	cup grated Parmesan cheese

In a Dutch oven or soup kettle, cook beef over medium heat until no longer pink; drain. Add the next 13
ingredients; bring to a boil. Reduce heat; cover
and simmer for 15 minutes. Add spaghetti; cover
and simmer for 15-20 minutes or until spaghetti
is tender, stirring occasionally. Stir in Parmesan
cheese.

YIELD: 8-10 servings.

WITCH'S HAT SOUP

Get into the Halloween spirit with this cute soup created by our Test Kitchen. With a mix of vegetables, beans and seasonings, it's a thick broth with a kick of spice that heats up October 31 menus.

4	flour tortillas (8 inches)
1	envelope taco seasoning, *divided*
1	pound ground beef
1/3	cup chopped onion
2	cups water
2	cups frozen mixed vegetables
1	can (15 1/2 ounces) chili beans, undrained
1	can (15 ounces) black beans, rinsed and drained
1	can (14 1/2 ounces) diced tomatoes with mild green chilies, undrained
1/2	teaspoon sugar

Canned pasteurized cheddar cheese snack

Spritz the tortillas with nonstick cooking spray; sprinkle with 1/2 teaspoon taco seasoning. With a 2 1/2 -in. round cookie cutter, cut out four circles from each tortilla (discard scraps). Cut a slit into the center of eight circles; shape each into a cone and secure with toothpicks. Place circles and cones on an ungreased baking sheet. Bake at 400° 8-10 minutes or until crisp.

Meanwhile, in a large saucepan, cook beef and on over medium heat until meat is no longer pink; dr Stir in the water, vegetables, beans, tomatoes, s ar and remaining taco seasoning. Cover and simr for 10 minutes or until heated through, stirring casionally.

Discard toothpicks from cones. To assemble h. place cones on circles; pipe a band of cheese arou base of cones. Ladle soup into bowls and top v hats.

YIELD: 8 servings (2 quarts).

BAKED MACARONI 'N' CHEESE

Karen Ochs, Erie, Pennsylvania

Folks love the cheesy goodness so much, I'm asl to bring this dish to many gatherings. It's comf food at its finest.

1	package (16 ounces) elbow macaroni
2	pounds process American cheese, cubec
8	ounces Swiss cheese, cubed
1	medium green pepper, chopped
1	medium onion, chopped
1	jar (2 ounces) diced pimientos, drained
4	eggs
4	cups milk
1	teaspoon salt
1/2	teaspoon pepper
1/4	teaspoon paprika

Cook macaroni according to package direction Drain and rinse in cold water. Add cheese, gre pepper, onion and pimientos. Combine eggs, mi salt and pepper; pour over macaroni mixture a mix well.

Pour into two greased 13-in. x 9-in. x 2-in. baki dishes. Sprinkle with paprika. Bake, uncovered, 350° for 30-35 minutes or until bubbly ar browned.

YIELD: 18 servings (3/4 cup each).

OUTHWESTERN PIZZA

oline Grooms, Dickinson, North Dakota

soned ground beef, corn and black beans
ciously top off a cornmeal crust in this hearty
etizer pizza.

- cups all-purpose flour
- cup cornmeal
- cup sugar
- teaspoons baking powder
- teaspoon cayenne pepper
- teaspoon chili powder
- teaspoon salt
- cup milk
- cup vegetable oil
- egg
- cup *each* shredded cheddar and
  Monterey Jack cheese

PING:

- pounds ground beef
- cup water
- envelopes taco seasoning, *divided*
- cups (16 ounces) sour cream
- cups (10 ounces) *each* shredded cheddar
  and Monterey Jack cheese, *divided*
- can (15 1/4 ounces) whole kernel corn,
  drained

1   can (15 ounces) black beans, rinsed
      and drained

1   cup salsa

In a large bowl, combine the flour, cornmeal, sugar, baking powder, cayenne, chili powder and salt. Combine the milk, oil and egg; stir into dry ingredients just until moistened. Stir in the cheeses. Spread into a greased 15-in. x 10-in. x 1-in. baking pan. Bake at 400° for 10-12 minutes or until a toothpick comes out clean.

In a large skillet, cook beef over medium heat until no longer pink; drain. Stir in water and one envelope of taco seasoning. Bring to a boil. Reduce heat; simmer, uncovered, for 5 minutes. Set aside.

In a small bowl, combine the sour cream and remaining taco seasoning; mix well. Spread over crust. Sprinkle with the beef mixture and half of the cheeses. Combine the corn, beans and salsa; spoon over cheese. Sprinkle with remaining cheese. Broil 5-10 minutes or until cheese is melted.

YIELD: 12-15 servings.

TRULY TEXAN CHILI

Betty Brown, San Antonio, Texas

I am a native Texan, and this is the best chili re‹
I've ever tasted. It's meaty and spicy. I'd make ‹
whenever I was homesick during the years we s‹
away from Texas due to my husband's military ca‹

3	pounds ground beef
2	to 3 garlic cloves, minced
3	tablespoons chili powder (or to taste)
1	tablespoon ground cumin
1/4	cup all-purpose flour
1	tablespoon dried oregano
2	cans (14 1/2 ounces *each*) beef broth
1	teaspoon salt
1/4	teaspoon pepper
1	can (15 ounces) pinto beans, rinsed and‹ drained, optional

Optional garnishes: shredded cheddar cheese,‹
tortilla chips, sour cream *and/or* lime wedges

In a large kettle or heavy saucepan, cook b‹
over medium heat until no longer pink; dra‹
Reduce heat; stir in garlic. Combine chili pow‹
cumin, flour and oregano; sprinkle over meat, s‹
ring until evenly coated. Add broth, salt and pep‹
bring to a boil, stirring occasionally.

Reduce heat; cover and simmer for 1 1/2 to 2 hou‹
stirring occasionally. (Chili can be transferred t‹
slow cooker for simmering if desired.) Cool. Co‹
and refrigerate overnight.

Reheat in a heavy saucepan, double boiler or sl‹
cooker over low heat. If desired, add beans and h‹
through. Garnish individual bowls, if desired, w‹
cheese, tortilla chips, sour cream and/or li‹
wedges.

YIELD: 4-6 servings (5 cups).

ITALIAN BEEF HOAGIES

Lori Piatt, Danville, Illinois

You'll need just five ingredients to feed a crowd these
tender tangy sandwiches. On weekends, I start the
roast the night before, so I can shred it in the
morning.

1	boneless sirloin tip roast (about 4 pounds), halved
2	envelopes Italian salad dressing mix
2	cups water
1	jar (16 ounces) mild pepper rings, undrained
18	hoagie buns, split

Place roast in a 5-qt. slow cooker. Combine the
salad dressing mix and water; pour over roast.
Cover and cook on low for 8 hours or until meat is
tender. Remove meat; shred with a fork and return to slow cooker. Add pepper rings; heat through.
Spoon 1/2 cup meat mixture onto each bun.

YIELD: 18 servings.

haunting halloween buffets

In a large skillet, cook beef over medium heat until no longer pink; drain. Stir in the tomatoes, tomato paste, parsley and garlic; remove from the heat. In a large bowl, combine the eggs, cheeses, salt and pepper. Layer three noodles in a greased 13-in. x 9-in. x 2-in. baking dish. Top with half of the cottage cheese mixture, 1 cup mozzarella cheese and half of the meat sauce. Repeat layers.

Cover and bake at 375° for 30 minutes. Uncover; bake 25-30 minutes longer or until edges are bubbly. Let stand for 10 minutes before cutting.

YIELD: 12-15 servings.

PUMPKIN CHILI

Betty Butler, Greencastle, Indiana

This unique chili freezes well...but it still doesn't last around our farmhouse very long, especially when my five children and 13 grandchildren are around! They often are—we are a very close-knit family.

3	pounds ground beef
1	medium onion, chopped
1	cup canned pumpkin
1	teaspoon salt
1	teaspoon pepper
2	teaspoons pumpkin pie spice
2	cans (10 3/4 ounces *each*) condensed tomato soup, undiluted
2	cans (16 ounces *each*) chili sauce
1	teaspoon sugar
1	teaspoon chili powder

In a large Dutch oven or soup kettle, cook beef and onion over medium heat until meat is no longer pink; drain. Add remaining ingredients; stir to mix well. Add water if desired to reduce thickness. Bring to a boil; reduce heat and simmer 1 hour.

YIELD: 10-12 servings (11 cups).

OTLUCK LASAGNA

lleen Wolfisberg, Everson, Washington

s is a variation on a lasagna dish a co-worker de for a company potluck. When I was expect- our third son, I often prepared meals and froze m. It was so nice to have a substantial entree like s one on hand to bake.

	pound ground beef
	can (14 1/2 ounces) Italian stewed tomatoes, cut up
	can (6 ounces) tomato paste
	tablespoon minced fresh parsley
	teaspoon minced garlic
	eggs
/2	cups small-curd cottage cheese
/2	cups ricotta cheese
	cup grated Parmesan cheese
	teaspoon salt
	teaspoon pepper
	lasagna noodles, cooked and drained
	cups (8 ounces) shredded part-skim mozzarella cheese

SPOOKY JOES

Darla Webster, Meriden, Iowa

Where we live, trick-or-treating is difficult. So I plan at-home Halloween parties for my son and his friends. These sloppy joes are a highlight!

2   pounds ground beef
2   cans (10¾ ounces *each*) condensed tomato soup, undiluted
1   teaspoon onion salt
2   cups (8 ounces) shredded cheddar cheese
8   hamburger buns, split
8   slices cheddar cheese

In a large skillet, cook beef over medium heat until no longer pink; drain. Stir in the soup and onion salt; heat through. Stir in shredded cheddar cheese until melted. Spoon about ½ cup onto the bottom of each bun. Cut cheese slices with 2½-in. Halloween cookie cutters; place over beef mixture. Serve with bun tops on the side.

YIELD: 8 servings.

FINGERS OF FRIGHT

Kids' eyes usually widen at the sight of these chewy digits made with circus peanut candies.

5   red, black *and/or* green jelly beans
10   circus peanut candies

Cut jelly beans in half lengthwise. Press each half into the end of a circus peanut.

YIELD: 10 servings.

SPIDER CUPCAKES

These sweet treats are creepy—and easy! Make a chocolate cupcake into a spider by adding a half-marshmallow "body" under the frosting, licorice legs and mini M&M eyes. Add chocolate sprinkles for a "hairy" effect.

1   package (18¼ ounces) chocolate cake mix
2   cups sugar
½   cup baking cocoa
½   cup butter, cubed
½   cup milk

2   teaspoons vanilla extract
12   large marshmallows
Chocolate sprinkles
48   M&M's miniature baking bits
192   pieces black licorice (3 inches)

Prepare cake batter according to package directions. Fill 24 greased or paper-lined muffin cups. Bake at 350° for 21-26 minutes or until a toothpick comes out clean. Cool for 5 minutes before removing from pans to wire racks to cool completely.

For frosting, combine the sugar, cocoa, butter and milk in a small saucepan. Bring to a boil over medium heat, stirring constantly. Remove from the heat; stir in vanilla. Cool to 110°. Beat with a wooden spoon until thickened and mixture begins to lose its gloss, about 8 minutes.

Cut marshmallows in half widthwise; place a half on each cupcake. Frost the marshmallows and tops of cupcakes. Dip cupcakes in chocolate sprinkles. Place a dab of frosting on each baking bit and press on cupcakes for eyes.

For spider legs, use a metal or wooden skewer to poke four holes on opposite sides of cupcakes; insert a piece of licorice into each hole.

YIELD: 2 dozen.

GREAT PUMPKIN BROWNIE

To make this eye-catching treat, simply bake brownie batter in a pizza pan and decorate as desired; follow my easy instructions.

1   package fudge brownie mix (13-inch x 9-inch pan size)
1   can (16 ounces) vanilla frosting
Orange paste food coloring
16   green milk chocolate M&M's
22   yellow milk chocolate M&M's
13   orange milk chocolate M&M's
8   dark brown milk chocolate M&M's
20   pieces candy corn

Prepare brownie batter according to package directions for fudge-like brownies. Spread on a greased 12-in. pizza pan to within 1 in. of edges. Bake

for 20-25 minutes or until a toothpick in-
...ed near the center comes out clean. Cool on a
 rack.

...frosting orange; frost entire top of brownie. For
..., arrange green M&M's in a square pattern at
...of pumpkin. For each eye, arrange 11 yellow
...M's in a triangle. For nose, arrange orange
...M's in a triangle. For mouth, place brown
...M's in a horizontal line; surround with candy
... tips pointing out. Cut into squares to serve.

...D: 16-20 servings.

...LLOWEEN
...RAMEL APPLES

...n making this treat, be sure to start with the
...es at room temperature so the caramel won't slip
...e it tends to on chilled apples.

package (11½ ounces) milk
chocolate chips

tablespoons shortening

packages (14 ounces *each*) caramels

cup water

large tart apples, room temperature

| 8 | Popsicle sticks |
| 3 | to 4 Butterfinger candy bars (2.1 ounces *each*), coarsely crushed |

In a microwave-safe bowl, melt chocolate chips and
shortening; set aside. In another microwave-safe
bowl, microwave the caramels and water, uncovered, on high for 1 minute; stir. Heat 30-45 seconds
longer or until caramels are melted.

Line a baking sheet with waxed paper and grease
the paper; set aside. Wash and thoroughly dry
apples. Insert a Popsicle stick into each; dip into
caramel mixture, turning to coat.

Place on prepared pan. Drizzle with melted chocolate. Sprinkle with crushed candy bars. Refrigerate
until set. Remove from refrigerator 5 minutes before
serving; cut into wedges.

YIELD: 8 servings.

EDITOR'S NOTE: This recipe was tested in a 1,100-
watt microwave.

HALLOWEEN CARAMEL APPLES
SPIDER CUPCAKES
SPOOKY JOES
GREAT PUMPKIN BROWNIE

spirited shindigs **129**

bewitching
breads &
salads

CRUNCHY APPLE SALAD

Julie Pearsall, Union Springs, New York

This old-fashioned salad is part of my favorite meal that Mom used to make. Crunchy apples, celery and walnuts blend well with the creamy mayonnaise.

4   large red apples, diced
1   cup chopped celery
1   cup raisins
1   cup chopped walnuts
1/2   cup mayonnaise

In a large bowl, combine the apples, celery, raisins and walnuts. Blend in mayonnaise. Cover and refrigerate until serving.

YIELD: 16 servings.

AUTUMN SALAD WITH ORANGE VINAIGRETTE

A light orange dressing nicely accents sweet dried cranberries and crunchy almonds in this salad from our Test Kitchen. If you prefer, you can use your favorite salad greens in place of the ready-to-serve package.

3   tablespoons olive oil
1   tablespoon sugar
1   tablespoon red wine vinegar
2   teaspoons orange juice concentrate

1/8   teaspoon salt
Pinch coarsely ground pepper
4   cups ready-to-serve salad greens
1/2   cup sliced almonds, toasted
1/4   cup dried cranberries
1/4   cup thinly sliced red onion

In a jar with a tight-fitting lid, combine the first six ingredients; shake well. In a large bowl, com[bine] the salad greens, almonds, cranberries and on[ion.] Add vinaigrette; toss to coat.

YIELD: 4 servings.

SPICED SWEET POTATO BISCUITS

Flo Burtnett, Gage, Oklahoma

A pumpkin cookie cutter can be used for sw[eet] treats and for savory biscuits as well. These [bis]cuits are a fun addition to any meal in fall.

1 1/2   cups all-purpose flour
2   teaspoons baking powder
1/2   teaspoon salt
1/4   teaspoon ground cinnamon
1/8   teaspoon ground nutmeg
1/3   cup cold butter
1   cup cold mashed sweet potatoes (prepared without milk *or* butter)
1/3   cup milk
1   egg, lightly beaten
1/2   teaspoon sugar

In a bowl, combine the first five ingredients. C[ut in] butter until crumbly. Combine sweet potato [and] milk; stir into crumb mixture just until moiste[ned.] Turn onto a floured surface; knead 10-15 times. [Roll] out to 1/2-in. thickness; cut with a floured 2 1/[2-in.] pumpkin-shaped cookie cutter or biscuit cutte[r.]

Place 2 in. apart on a greased baking sheet. B[rush] with egg; sprinkle with sugar. Bake at 425°[for] 10-12 minutes or until golden brown. Serve wa[rm.]

YIELD: 1 dozen.

ICED SWEET POTATO BISCUITS

PUMPKIN SPICE BREAD

Delora Lucas, Belle, West Virginia

This recipe is at least 40 years old. It makes a very moist bread that tastes like pumpkin pie without the crust.

3   cups sugar
1   cup vegetable oil
4   eggs, lightly beaten
1   can (16 ounces) solid-pack pumpkin
3½   cups all-purpose flour
1   teaspoon baking soda
1   teaspoon salt
1   teaspoon ground cinnamon
1   teaspoon ground nutmeg
½   teaspoon baking powder
½   teaspoon ground cloves
½   teaspoon ground allspice
½   cup water

In a large bowl, combine sugar, oil and eggs. Add pumpkin and mix well. Combine dry ingredients; add to the pumpkin mixture alternately with water. Pour into two greased 9-in. x 5-in. x 3-in. loaf pans.

Bake at 350° for 60-65 minutes or until a toothpick inserted near the center comes out clean. Cool in pans 10 minutes before removing to a wire rack; cool completely.

YIELD: 2 loaves.

PARSLEY TORTELLINI TOSS

Jacqueline Graves, Lawrenceville, Georgia

Tortellini, cheese, ham, turkey and a harvest of veggies make this pasta toss satisfying enough for a main meal.

1   package (16 ounces) frozen cheese tortellini
1½   cups cubed provolone cheese
1½   cups cubed part-skim mozzarella cheese
1   cup cubed fully cooked ham
1   cup cubed cooked turkey
1   cup frozen peas, thawed
2   medium carrots, shredded
½   medium sweet red pepper, diced
½   medium green pepper, diced
1   cup minced fresh parsley
½   cup olive oil
3   tablespoons red wine vinegar
2   tablespoons grated Parmesan cheese
2   garlic cloves, minced

Cook tortellini according to package directions; rinse in cold water and drain. Place in a large bowl; add the next eight ingredients. In a jar with a tight-fitting lid, combine the remaining ingredients and shake well. Pour over salad and toss to coat. Cover and refrigerate until serving.

YIELD: 12-15 servings.

bewitching breads & salads

CHEESY ONION BREAD
Kay Daly, Raleigh, North Carolina

It's impossible to stop nibbling on warm pieces of this cheesy onion bread. The sliced loaf fans out for a fun presentation.

1   unsliced large round loaf bread (about 1½ pounds)
1   pound sliced Monterey Jack cheese
½   cup chopped green onions
⅓   cup butter, melted
2   to 3 teaspoons poppy seeds

Cut the bread lengthwise and widthwise in a curvy pattern without cutting through the bottom crust. Insert cheese between cuts. Combine onions, butter and poppy seeds; drizzle over the bread. Wrap in foil; place on a baking sheet. Bake at 350° for 15 minutes. Unwrap; bake 10 minutes longer or until the cheese is melted.

YIELD: 8 servings.

WALNUT PEAR SALAD
Marian Platt, Sequim, Washington

This nutty salad is absolutely beautiful with mixed greens. Pears and apricot nectar add fruity sweetness.

⅓   cup apricot nectar
2   tablespoons olive oil
2   tablespoons red wine vinegar
1   teaspoon minced fresh mint or ¼ teaspoon dried mint
⅛   teaspoon salt
⅛   teaspoon ground mustard
3   medium pears, peeled, halved and sliced
12 cups mixed salad greens
¾   cup chopped walnuts, toasted

In a jar with a tight-fitting lid, combine the first six ingredients; shake well. Combine the pears and dressing in a large serving bowl. Cover and refrigerate until chilled. Just before serving, add greens to pear mixture; toss to coat. Sprinkle with walnuts.

YIELD: 6 servings.

CRANBERRY SWEET POTATO MUFFINS
Jane Musil, Lyons, Illinois

The autumn flavors of sweet potatoes, cranberries and cinnamon give seasonal appeal to these golden muffins.

2   cups all-purpose flour
    cup sugar
    teaspoons baking powder
    teaspoon salt
    teaspoon ground cinnamon
    teaspoon ground nutmeg
    egg
    cup milk
    cup cold mashed sweet potatoes (without added butter or milk)
    cup butter, melted
    cup chopped fresh or frozen cranberries
    Cinnamon-sugar

In a bowl, combine flour, sugar, baking powder, salt, cinnamon and nutmeg. In a small bowl, combine egg, milk, sweet potatoes and butter; stir into dry ingredients just until moistened. Stir in cranberries.

Fill greased or paper-lined muffin cups half full. Sprinkle with cinnamon-sugar. Bake at 375° for 18-22 minutes or until a toothpick comes out clean. Cool in pan 10 minutes before removing to a wire rack.

YIELD: 1 dozen.

spirited shindigs

135

CRANBERRY ORANGE BREAD

Marsha Ransom, South Haven, Michigan

I found this recipe in a children's storybook. Now it's a family favorite.

1/4   cup butter, softened
1   cup sugar
1   egg
1   teaspoon grated orange peel
2   cups all-purpose flour
1   teaspoon baking powder
1   teaspoon salt
1/2   teaspoon baking soda
3/4   cup orange juice
1   cup chopped fresh *or* frozen cranberries
1   cup golden raisins

In a large mixing bowl, cream butter and sugar. Beat in egg and orange peel. Combine the dry ingredients; add to creamed mixture alternately with juice. Fold in cranberries and raisins. Pour into a greased 9-in. x 5-in. x 3-in. loaf pan.

Bake at 350° for 60-65 minutes or until a toothpick inserted near the center comes out clean. Cool for 10 minutes; remove from pan to a wire rack to cool completely.

YIELD: 1 loaf (16 slices).

SUNFLOWER CORN MUFFINS

Nadine Brimeyer, Denver, Iowa

These golden mini muffins with a rich corn taste ture the flavor of fall.

1   cup (8 ounces) sour cream
1   can (8 ounces) whole kernel corn, drain
1   can (8 ounces) cream-style corn
1/2   cup shredded cheddar cheese
1/4   cup sliced green onions
1/4   cup butter, melted
1   egg, beaten
1   package (8 1/2 ounces) corn bread/muf
        mix
3   tablespoons sunflower kernels

In a bowl, combine the first seven ingredients; in corn bread mix just until moistened. Spoon greased miniature muffin cups. Sprinkle v sunflower kernels. Bake at 375° for 30-35 min or until a toothpick comes out clean. Cool f minutes before removing from pans to a v rack. Serve warm.

YIELD: 3 1/2 dozen mini muffins.

SLIMY RED GOOP SALAD

Judy Nix, Toccoa, Georgia

This frightfully fun salad features cola, which a to the bright, sparkling taste.

1   can (15 ounces) mandarin oranges
1/2   cup water
2   packages (3 ounces *each*) cherry gelat
1   can (21 ounces) cherry pie filling
3/4   cup cola

Drain mandarin oranges, reserving juice; set aside. In a large saucepan, bring mandarin ora juice and water to a boil; remove from the heat. in gelatin until dissolved. Stir in pie filling and

Pour into a 1 1/2-qt. serving bowl. Refrigerate 50 minutes or until slightly thickened. Fo reserved oranges. Refrigerate 3 hours longe until firm.

YIELD: 8 servings.

bewitching breads & salads

PARMESAN ROLLS

Marietta Slater, Augusta, Kansas

My family just can't seem to get enough of these fun, cheesy rolls. They have a delightful texture from the cornmeal and are a great switch from traditional dinner rolls. I like to serve them with spaghetti, lasagna and stew.

2	packages (¹/₄ ounce *each*) active dry yeast
¹/₂	cup warm water (110° to 115°)
1	cup warm milk (110° to 115°)
¹/₂	cup grated Parmesan cheese
¹/₃	cup butter, melted
3	tablespoons sugar
1	teaspoon salt
1	cup cornmeal
2	eggs
4¹/₂	to 5 cups all-purpose flour

TOPPING:

¹/₄	cup butter, melted
¹/₄	cup grated Parmesan cheese

In a large mixing bowl, dissolve yeast in water. Add milk, Parmesan cheese, butter, sugar, salt, cornmeal and eggs; mix well. Add 3 cups of flour and beat until smooth. Add enough remaining flour to form a soft dough. Turn onto a floured surface; knead until smooth and elastic, about 6-8 minutes. Place in a greased bowl, turning once to grease top. Cover let rise in a warm place until doubled, about 1 h

Punch dough down. Shape into 24 ovals; dip into melted butter and Parmesan cheese. Plac greased baking sheets. Cover and let rise u doubled, about 30 minutes. Bake at 375° for 2(minutes or until golden brown. Remove from | to cool on wire racks.

YIELD: 2 dozen.

COCONUT PUMPKIN LOAVES

Anne Smithson, Cary, North Carolina

A friend made this moist bread for us years Because it makes three loaves, I can give one lo a neighbor, enjoy one with my family and fr one for later.

5	eggs
2	cups canned pumpkin
2	cups sugar
1¹/₄	cups vegetable oil
3	cups all-purpose flour
2	packages (3.4 ounces *each*) instant coconut pudding mix
3	teaspoons ground cinnamon
2	teaspoons baking soda
1	teaspoon ground nutmeg
³/₄	cup chopped pecans

In a large mixing bowl, beat the eggs and pu kin until smooth. Add sugar and oil; mix v Combine the flour, pudding mixes, cinnamon, I ing soda and nutmeg; add to the pumpkin mixt Stir in nuts.

Transfer to three greased and floured 8-in. x 4 x 2-in. loaf pans. Bake at 350° for 60-65 min or until a toothpick inserted near the center co out clean. Cool for 10 minutes before removing f pans to wire racks to cool completely.

YIELD: 3 loaves.

bewitching breads & salads

ROSTY CRANBERRY ALAD CUPS

rnadine Bolte, St. Louis, Missouri

stead of traditional cranberry sauce, consider se individual fruit salads. They're a make-ahead at terrific for autumn potlucks.

- can (16 ounces) jellied cranberry sauce
- can (8 ounces) crushed pineapple, drained
- cup (8 ounces) sour cream
- cup confectioners' sugar
- cup miniature marshmallows

d food coloring, optional

a bowl, combine the first five ingredients; add d food coloring if desired. Fill foil- or paper-lined uffin cups two-thirds full. Cover and freeze until m, about 3 hours.

ELD: 16 servings.

EASY BANANA BREAD

Sharon Ward, King Ferry, New York

I taught my four children to bake using guaranteed-to-be-good recipes like this.

1/3	cup shortening
1/2	cup sugar
2	eggs
1 3/4	cups all-purpose flour
1	teaspoon baking powder
1/2	teaspoon baking soda
1/2	teaspoon salt
1	cup mashed ripe bananas (2 medium)

In a mixing bowl, cream shortening and sugar. Add eggs; mix well. Combine flour, baking powder, baking soda and salt; add to creamed mixture alternately with bananas, beating well after each addition. Pour into a greased 8-in. x 4-in. x 2-in. loaf pan.

Bake at 350° for 50-55 minutes or until a toothpick inserted near the center comes out clean. Let stand for 10 minutes before removing from pan; cool on a wire rack.

YIELD: 1 loaf.

cookie & bar boo-nanza

In a microwave-safe bowl, heat the shortening [and] remaining chocolate chips on high for 1 minut[e] until chips are melted; stir until smooth. Drizzle [over] cookies. Let stand for 30 minutes or until choco[late] is set. Store in an airtight container.

YIELD: 6 dozen.

MELTED WITCH PUDDLES

In honor of the doomed wicked witch in "The Wi[zard] of Oz," our home economists had fun fashio[ning] these simply delicious snacks.

1	teaspoon water
4	drops yellow food coloring
1 1/2	cups flaked coconut
2	cups (12 ounces) semisweet chocolate chips
6	tablespoons shortening, *divided*
36	cream-filled chocolate sandwich cookie[s]
36	Bugles
4	cups vanilla *or* white chips
36	pretzel sticks

In a large resealable plastic bag, combine water [and] food coloring; add coconut. Seal bag and shake to [tint] coconut; set aside. In a microwave, melt choco[late] chips and 2 tablespoons shortening; stir until smo[oth].

For witch's hats, place about 1/3 cup chocol[ate] mixture in a resealable plastic bag; cut a sm[all] hole in a corner of bag. Pipe a small amount [of] chocolate on a cookie. Dip a Bugle in some of [the] remaining chocolate; allow excess to drip [off]. Position over chocolate on cookie, forming a wit[ch's] hat. Set on waxed paper to dry. Repeat with [re-] maining chocolate, Bugles and cookies.

For brooms, melt vanilla chips and the remain[ing] shortening; stir until smooth. Place mixture i[n a] large heavy-duty resealable plastic bag; cu[t a] small hole in a corner of bag. Pipe mixture into [the] shape of a puddle onto waxed paper-lined baki[ng] sheets. Immediately place a witch's hat on the pu[d-] dle. Place a pretzel stick alongside the hat; spr[in-] kle reserved tinted coconut at the end of the pr[et-] zel stick. Repeat with remaining puddles, hats a[nd] brooms. Chill for 15 minutes or until set. Store in [an] airtight container.

YIELD: 3 dozen.

TRIPLE-CHOCOLATE BROWNIE COOKIES

Linda Robinson, New Braunfels, Texas

Our family of chocolate lovers gets triply excited when these cookies come out of the oven. They have the texture and taste of fudge brownies.

3/4	cup butter, cubed
4	squares (1 ounce *each*) unsweetened chocolate
2	cups sugar
4	eggs
1 1/2	cups all-purpose flour
1/2	cup baking cocoa
2	teaspoons baking powder
1/2	teaspoon salt
2	cups (12 ounces) semisweet chocolate chips, *divided*
2	teaspoons shortening

In a small saucepan over low heat, melt butter and unsweetened chocolate; cool. Transfer to a large mixing bowl; add sugar and eggs. Beat until smooth. Combine the flour, cocoa, baking powder and salt; gradually add to chocolate mixture. Stir in 1 1/2 cups chocolate chips. Cover and refrigerate for 2 hours or until easy to handle.

Drop by tablespoonfuls 2 in. apart onto greased baking sheets. Bake at 350° for 7-9 minutes or until edges are set and tops are slightly cracked. Cool for 2 minutes before removing from pans to wire racks to cool completely.

cookie & bar boo-nanza

CHOCOLATE-GLAZED BROWNIES

Deb Anderson, Joplin, Missouri

These moist and fudgy brownies are ideal for taking to bake sales and family gatherings. For holidays, I like to dress them up with colorful candy sprinkles.

- 1/3 cup butter, softened
- 1 cup sugar
- 3 egg whites
- 1 teaspoon vanilla extract
- 2/3 cup all-purpose flour
- 1/2 cup baking cocoa
- 1/2 teaspoon baking powder
- 1/4 teaspoon salt

CHOCOLATE GLAZE:
- 2/3 cup confectioners' sugar
- 2 tablespoons baking cocoa
- 1/4 teaspoon vanilla extract
- 3 to 4 teaspoons hot water

Halloween candy sprinkles, optional

In a mixing bowl, cream butter and sugar. Add egg whites; beat well. Beat in vanilla. Combine the flour, cocoa, baking powder and salt; gradually add to creamed mixture. Spread into an 8-in. square baking pan coated with nonstick cooking spray.

Bake at 350° for 20-25 minutes or until a tooth[pick] inserted near the center comes out clean. Coo[l] a wire rack.

For glaze, in a small bowl, combine confection[ers'] sugar, cocoa, vanilla and enough water to ach[ieve] desired consistency. Spread over brownies. Deco[rate] with candy sprinkles if desired. Cut into bars.

YIELD: 1 dozen.

HAZELNUT CRUNCHERS

Ruth Sayles, Pendleton, Oregon

I often make ice cream sandwiches using th[ese] yummy cookies. They're also scrumptious a[ll by] themselves!

- 1/2 cup butter, softened
- 1/2 cup packed dark brown sugar
- 1/3 cup sugar
- 1 egg
- 1/2 teaspoon vanilla extract
- 1 cup plus 2 tablespoons all-purpose flou[r]
- 1/2 teaspoon baking soda

Pinch salt
- 1 cup vanilla *or* white chips
- 1 cup chopped hazelnuts *or* filberts, toast[ed]

In a large mixing bowl, cream butter and sug[ar.] Add egg and vanilla; mix well. Combine dry ing[re]dients; add to creamed mixture and mix well. S[tir] in chips and nuts.

Shape into 1 1/2-in. balls; place on greased bak[ing] sheets. Flatten to 1/2-in. thickness with a gl[ass] dipped in sugar. Bake at 350° for 10-12 minu[tes] or until lightly browned. Remove to a wire rack[to] cool.

YIELD: about 2 dozen.

freaky fac[t]

Orange and black are Halloween col[ors] because orange represents the color[of] fall harvest and black represents [the] darkness of winter.

NNAMON
ACKLE COOKIES

Lair, Apple Valley, Minnesota

recipe is the compilation of many years of bak-
make these cookies year-round for our family.
freeze well.

 cup butter, softened
 cup shortening
 cup sugar
 cup packed brown sugar
 egg
 teaspoon vanilla extract
 teaspoon almond extract
 cups all-purpose flour
 tablespoon ground cinnamon
 teaspoons baking soda
 teaspoons cream of tartar
 teaspoons ground nutmeg
 teaspoons grated orange peel
 teaspoon grated lemon peel
 teaspoon salt
tional sugar

mixing bowl, cream butter, shortening and sug-
Add egg and extracts; mix well. Combine the
 eight ingredients; gradually add to the
ned mixture.

e into 1-in. balls; roll in sugar. Place 2 in. apart
greased baking sheets. Bake at 350° for 10-
inutes or until lightly browned.

D: about 6 dozen.

EASY OWL COOKIES

"Who" wouldn't love these adorable cookies? Our
Test Kitchen cooks use a roll-out refrigerated cookie dough, chocolate-chip eyes and a candy-corn nose,
making these a cinch to assemble. If you don't have
chocolate chips on hand, use M&M's instead for a
kid-friendly fall treat.

1   tube (18 ounces) refrigerated peanut
      butter cookie dough
$1/2$ cup all-purpose flour
18   yellow candy coating disks
18   semisweet chocolate chips
9   pieces candy corn

In a large mixing bowl, beat cookie dough and flour
until combined. Set aside $4^1/2$ teaspoons of dough
for the ears. Drop dough by $1/4$ cupfuls into nine
mounds 2 in. apart on ungreased baking sheets.
Coat the bottom of a glass with nonstick cooking
spray; flatten dough with glass to $1/8$-in. thickness.

Position two candy coating disks on each cookie for
eyes. Place a chocolate chip on each disk. Use $1/4$
teaspoon of reserved dough to shape each ear; position on top of head.

Bake at 350° for 8-10 minutes or until golden
brown. Immediately position a piece of candy
corn on each cookie for beak. Cool for 2 minutes before removing from pans to wire racks.

YIELD: 9 cookies.

CANDY-TOPPED BARS

Renee Anderson, Franklin, Tennessee

These yummy, colorful bars have a nutty shortbread crust and a sweet cream cheese filling.

1	cup all-purpose flour
1/3	cup packed brown sugar
1/2	cup cold butter
1/2	cup chopped pecans
1	package (8 ounces) cream cheese, softened
1/4	cup sugar
1	egg
2	tablespoons milk
1	tablespoon lemon juice
1/2	teaspoon vanilla extract
1/2	to 1 cup M&M miniature baking bits

In a large bowl, combine flour and brown sugar. Cut in butter until mixture resembles coarse crumbs. Stir in pecans. Set aside 1/2 cup for topping. Press remaining crumb mixture into a greased 9-in. square pan. Bake at 350° for 12-15 minutes or until edges are lightly browned.

In a mixing bowl, beat cream cheese and sugar. Add egg, milk, lemon juice and vanilla; mix well. Pour over warm crust. Sprinkle with reserved crumb mixture. Bake for 25-30 minutes or until set. Immediately sprinkle with baking bits. Cool on a wire rack. Cut into bars. Refrigerate leftovers.

YIELD: 16 servings.

PB&J BARS

Mitzi Sentiff, Alexandria, Virginia

Big and little kids alike will love these four-ingredient bars that offer a cookie crust, a layer of jam and a crunchy peanut butter and granola topping.

1	package (18 ounces) refrigerated sugar cookie dough, *divided*
2/3	cup strawberry jam
3/4	cup granola cereal without raisins
3/4	cup peanut butter chips

Line a 9-in. square baking pan with foil and grease the foil. Press two-thirds of the cookie dough into

prepared pan. Spread jam over dough to w
1/4 in. of edges. In a mixing bowl, beat the gra
peanut butter chips and remaining dough
blended. Crumble over jam.

Bake at 375° for 25-30 minutes or until go
brown. Cool on a wire rack. Using foil, lift out of
Cut into bars and remove from foil.

YIELD: 9-12 servings.

SWEET SANDWICH COOKIES

Pat Schar, Zelienople, Pennsylvania

This caramel cookie is a past winner of our far
holiday bake-off. The tender brown sugar co
melts together with the rich browned butter f
for a yummy flavor combination.

1	cup butter, softened
3/4	cup packed brown sugar
1	egg yolk
2	cups all-purpose flour
1/4	teaspoon salt

BROWNED BUTTER FILLING:

2	tablespoons butter
1 1/4	cups confectioners' sugar
1/2	teaspoon vanilla extract
4	to 5 teaspoons milk

In a small mixing bowl, cream butter and b
sugar. Beat in egg yolk. Combine flour and
gradually add to creamed mixture. Cover and r
erate for 20 minutes.

Shape into 1-in. balls. Place 1 1/2 in. apart o
greased baking sheets; flatten with a fork, for
a crisscross pattern. Bake at 325° for 8-10 mi
or until golden brown. Remove to wire racks to

For filling, heat butter in a saucepan over me
heat until golden brown. Remove from the hea
in confectioners' sugar, vanilla and enough m
achieve spreading consistency. Spread on the bc
of half of the cookies; top with remaining cook

YIELD: about 1 1/2 dozen.

ACK-O'-LANTERN
ROWNIES

Burtnett, Gage, Oklahoma

sting a Halloween party? Use a cookie cutter to
ily cut these homemade chocolate brownies in-
oumpkin shapes, then give them personality
h orange, black and green frosting. Our grandchil-
n think these are great.

2 cups sugar

   cup butter, melted

2 teaspoons vanilla extract

   eggs

   cup all-purpose flour

   cup baking cocoa

   teaspoon baking powder

   teaspoon salt

   can (16 ounces) vanilla frosting

ange paste food coloring

en and black decorating gel

ndy corn and M&M's, optional

In a large mixing bowl, combine the sugar, butter and
vanilla. Beat in the eggs until well blended. Combine
the flour, cocoa, baking powder and salt; gradually
add to sugar mixture. Line a greased 13-in. x 9-in. x
2-in. baking pan with waxed paper; grease the paper.
Spread batter evenly in pan. Bake at 350° for 18-
22 minutes or until brownies begin to pull away from
sides of pan. Cool on a wire rack.

Run a knife around edge of pan. Invert brownies onto a work surface and remove waxed paper. Cut
brownies with a 3-in. pumpkin cookie cutter, leaving
at least $1/8$ in. between each shape. (Discard scraps
or save for another use.) Tint frosting with orange
food coloring; frost brownies. Use green gel to create the pumpkin stems and black gel and candy corn
and M&M's if desired to decorate the faces.

YIELD: about 1 dozen.

spirited shindigs

GRANOLA BLONDIES

Janet Farley, Snellville, Georgia

A mix of good-for-you ingredients makes these chewy blond brownies impossible to pass up. The granola adds crunch while dried fruit lends pleasing sweetness. I serve them to just about anybody who walks in our front door.

1   egg
1   egg white
1 1/4   cups packed brown sugar
1/4   cup vegetable oil
1   cup all-purpose flour
1   teaspoon baking powder
1/2   teaspoon salt
2   cups granola with raisins
1   cup dried cranberries *or* cherries

In a mixing bowl, combine the egg, egg white, brown sugar and oil; mix well. Combine the flour, baking powder and salt; stir into sugar mixture just until blended. Stir in granola and cranberries (batter will be thick).

Spread into a 9-in. square baking pan coated with nonstick cooking spray. Bake at 350° for 25-30 minutes or until golden and set. Cool on a wire rack. Cut into bars.

YIELD: 1 dozen.

PRETZEL PUMPKIN GRAHAMS

This sweet-and-salty snack from our Test Kit is easy enough for kids to make. Miniature pre make great pumpkin shapes.

12   whole chocolate graham crackers
1/2   pound white candy coating, chopped
24   miniature pretzels
Orange colored sugar *or* sprinkles
6   green gumdrops, cut into four lengthw
        slices

Cut graham crackers in half, making squares. microwave, melt white candy coating; stir smooth. Dip one pretzel in candy coating; let ex drip off.

Place on a graham cracker square. If desire pretzel holes with candy coating. Decorate orange sugar or sprinkles. For stem, dip the of one gumdrop piece into candy coating; p above the pumpkin. Repeat. Let stand until about 30 minutes.

YIELD: 2 dozen.

reaky fac

The Irish placed candles in hollov out turnips to keep away spirits. (time, people began using pump instead.

cookie & bar boo-nanza

GERMAN CHOCOLATE BARS

Jennifer Sharp, Murfreesboro, Tennessee

My mom gave me this recipe at Christmas wh
wanted to make something different and yumm
gifts. The chewy bars can be cut into larger pie
but they're very rich.

1   package (18 1/4 ounces) German choco
    cake mix
2/3 cup cold butter
1   cup (6 ounces) semisweet chocolate ch
1   can (15 ounces) coconut-pecan frosting
1/4 cup milk

Place cake mix in a bowl; cut in butter until crum
Press 2 1/2 cups into a greased 13-in. x 9-in. x 2
baking pan. Bake at 350° for 10 minutes; immedi
ly sprinkle with chocolate chips. Drop frosting by
blespoonfuls over the chips. Stir milk into the rem
ing crumb mixture; drop by teaspoonfuls over to

Bake 25-30 minutes longer or until bubbly aro
the edges and top is cracked. Cool on a wire r
Refrigerate for 4 hours before cutting.

YIELD: 4 dozen.

BUTTERSCOTCH PEANUT BARS

Margery Richmond, Fort Collins, Colorado

With lots of peanuts and butterscotch flavor
plus a rich, buttery crust, these easy-to-make bars
are so good.

1/2   cup butter, softened
3/4   cup packed brown sugar
1 1/2 cups all-purpose flour
1/2   teaspoon salt
3   cups salted peanuts

TOPPING:
1   package (10 to 11 ounces) butterscotch
      chips
1/2   cup light corn syrup
2   tablespoons butter
1   tablespoon water

Line a 15-in. x 10-in. x 1-in. baking pan with alu-
minum foil. Coat the foil with nonstick cooking
spray; set aside. In a small mixing bowl, cream
butter and brown sugar. Add flour and salt; mix
well. Press into prepared pan. Bake at 350° for 6
minutes. Sprinkle with peanuts.

In a large saucepan, combine topping ingredients.
Cook and stir over medium heat until chips and butter are melted. Spread over hot crust. Bake for 12-
15 minutes or until topping is bubbly. Cool on a wire
rack. Cut into bars.

YIELD: 4 dozen.

freaky fac

According to Hallmark, about 90%
American families (roughly 50 mill
people) participate in Halloween eve
each year.

cookie & bar boo-nanza

CHOCOLATE CHUNK COOKIES

Elaine Anderson, New Galilee, Pennsylvania

It's such a pleasure to serve delicious cookies like these to neighbors and family. I love to bake cookies more than anything else. My four young daughters are eager to help with mixing, measuring and stirring!

6	squares (1 ounce *each*) white baking chocolate, *divided*
1	cup butter, softened
1/2	cup sugar
1/2	cup packed brown sugar
2	eggs
2	teaspoons vanilla extract
2 1/2	cups all-purpose flour
1	teaspoon baking soda
1/4	teaspoon salt
1	package (11 1/2 ounces) semisweet chocolate chunks *or* 2 cups semisweet chocolate chips

Melt three squares of white chocolate; cool. In a large mixing bowl, cream butter and sugars. Add eggs, one at a time, beating well after each addition. Beat in melted chocolate and vanilla. Combine the flour, baking soda and salt; gradually add to the creamed mixture. Stir in semisweet chocolate chunks.

Drop by tablespoonfuls onto ungreased baking sheets. Bake at 375° for 10-12 minutes or until golden brown. Cool for 1 minute before removing to wire racks. Melt remaining white chocolate; drizzle over cookies.

YIELD: 3 dozen.

HORTBREAD CUTOUTS

an Henderson, Montgomery, Texas

ound this recipe in a magazine over 30 years ago d have made the cutouts year-round ever since. ur ingredients make them an oh-so-simple recipe whip up.

	cup butter, softened
	cup sugar
/2	cups all-purpose flour
lored sugar, optional	

a mixing bowl, cream butter and sugar; gradu- y add flour. Divide dough in half.

a lightly floured surface, roll out each portion dough to 1/4-in. thickness. Cut with 2-in. to 3-in. okie cutters dipped in flour. Place 1 in. apart on greased baking sheets. Sprinkle with colored sug- if desired.

ke at 300° for 20-25 minutes or until lightly owned. Remove to wire racks to cool.

ELD: about 2 dozen.

spirited shindigs

CUTOUT PUMPKIN SANDWICH COOKIES

Schelby Thompson, Winter Haven, Florida

Apricot preserves peek out of these buttery, tender sugar cookies. Make them throughout the year with a variety of cookie cutter shapes.

1	cup butter, softened
1 1/4	cups sugar, *divided*
2	eggs, *separated*
2 1/2	cups all-purpose flour
1/4	teaspoon salt
	Confectioners' sugar
1/2	cup ground almonds
3/4	cup apricot preserves

In a large mixing bowl, cream butter and 3/4 cup sugar. Add egg yolks, one at a time, beating well after each addition. Combine flour and salt; gradually add to creamed mixture. Shape dough into a ball; chill for 1 hour or until firm.

On a surface dusted with confectioners' sugar, roll dough to 1/8-in. thickness; cut with a 3-in. pumpkin-shaped cookie cutter. Cut a 1 1/2-in. pumpkin from the center of half the cookies and remove (set aside small pumpkin cut-outs to bake separately).

Place on greased baking sheets. Beat egg whites until frothy. Combine almonds and remaining sugar. Brush each cookie with egg whites; sprinkle with almond mixture. Bake at 350° for 6-8 minutes or until lightly browned. Remove immediately to wire racks to cool completely.

Spread 1 1/2 teaspoons of apricot preserves over the plain side of solid cookies. Place cookies with centers cut out, almond side up, on top of the preserves, making a sandwich.

YIELD: 2 dozen.

HOLIDAY PEANUT BARS

Peg Woitel, Fairbanks, Alaska

Oats, peanut butter and M&M's give these mass appeal. When I have free time, I often ba pan and pop it in the freezer to take to a fu potluck or bake sale.

2	cups quick-cooking oats
1 1/2	cups all-purpose flour
3/4	cup packed brown sugar
1 1/2	teaspoons baking soda
1/2	teaspoon salt
3/4	cup butter, melted
1	package (14 ounces) peanut M&M's
1	can (14 ounces) sweetened condensed milk
1/2	cup chunky peanut butter
1	tablespoon vanilla extract

In a mixing bowl, combine the oats, flour, bro sugar, baking soda and salt. Add butter; mix u crumbly. Set aside 1 cup. Press the remaining cru mixture into a greased 13-in. x 9-in. x 2-in. bak pan. Bake at 350° for 9-11 minutes or until ed are lightly browned (bars will puff up slightly).

Meanwhile, set aside 1 cup M&M's; chop remain M&M's. In a mixing bowl, combine the milk, pea butter and vanilla; mix well. Stir in chopped M& Pour over crust; carefully spread evenly. Sprin with reserved M&M's; gently press into peanut b ter mixture. Sprinkle with reserved crumb m ture. Bake 18-22 minutes longer or until edges lightly browned. Cool on a wire rack before cutti

YIELD: 3 dozen.

spooky tip

Plastic spiders are an easy way to a a bit of creepiness to your Hallowe party. Buy them in bulk and place the on the tabletop as well as servi platters. You can also hang the s ders from the ceiling with fish line.

ghostly
good
desserts

COCONUT CHOCOLATE CAKE

Rene Schwebach, Dumont, Minnesota

I tuck a coconut filling into this moist chocolate c
It's easy to assemble with convenience products
cluding a boxed cake mix, instant pudding mix
prepared frosting.

4	eggs
³/₄	cup vegetable oil
³/₄	cup water
1	teaspoon vanilla extract
1	package (18¹/₄ ounces) chocolate cake mix
1	package (3.9 ounces) instant chocolate pudding mix

FILLING:

2	cups flaked coconut
¹/₃	cup sweetened condensed milk
¹/₄	teaspoon almond extract
1	can (16 ounces) chocolate frosting

In a mixing bowl, beat the eggs, oil, water and va
la. Add the cake and pudding mixes; beat for 5 m
utes. Pour 3 cups into a greased and floured 10
fluted tube pan. Combine the coconut, milk a
extract; mix well. Drop by spoonfuls onto batt
Cover with remaining batter.

Bake at 350° for 50-60 minutes or until a too
pick inserted near the center comes out cle
Cool for 10 minutes before removing from pan
a wire rack to cool completely. Frost with chocol
frosting.

YIELD: 12-15 servings.

PEANUT BUTTER TARTS

These tiny tarts will surely become a big part of your
recipe collection because they chill while you're en-
joying the rest of the meal. Children especially like
having their own "little pie" to help decorate.

1	cup peanut butter chips
1	tablespoon vegetable oil
1	package (3.9 ounces) instant chocolate pudding mix
1³/₄	cups cold milk
1	package (6 count) individual graham cracker tart shells

Whipped topping
Halloween candy, sprinkles *and/or* cake
decorations

In the top of a double boiler over simmering
water, melt chips with oil, stirring until smooth.
Remove top pan from water and cool for 5 minutes.

Meanwhile, in a bowl, whisk pudding and milk
until thick. Fold in peanut butter mixture. Spoon
into tart shells. Chill for 15 minutes. Top with a
dollop of whipped topping and decorate as desired.

YIELD: 6 servings.

spooky tip

To keep the punch cold during yo
Halloween party, try this "handy" tric

Fill several rubber gloves with wat
and freeze until ready to use. Run war
water over the gloves and peel awa
from the ice. Float the frozen hands
the punch.

ghostly good desserts

marshmallow creme and butter; beat until smooth. Add the milk, eggs and extracts; mix well.

Combine the sugars, flour, cinnamon and nutmeg; gradually beat into potato mixture until well blended. Pour into pastry shell.

Bake at 350° for 45-50 minutes or until a knife inserted near the center comes out clean. Cool on a wire rack. Serve with whipped topping. Refrigerate leftovers.

YIELD: 8 servings.

CARAMEL BREAD PUDDING

Tammie Peebles, Naples, Florida

My mom gave me the recipe for this easy-to-make pudding. It's a great way to use up day-old bread.

6	slices day-old bread, cut into $1/2$-inch cubes
1	cup hot water
1	cup packed brown sugar
4	eggs, lightly beaten
2	cups warm milk
$1/2$	cup sugar
$1/2$	teaspoon vanilla extract
$1/2$	teaspoon ground cinnamon
$1/8$	teaspoon salt

Place bread in a greased 2-qt. baking dish. Combine the water and brown sugar; pour over bread. Combine the remaining ingredients; pour over bread. Bake at 350° for 50-60 minutes or until a knife inserted near the center comes out clean. Serve warm or cold.

YIELD: 6-8 servings.

WEET POTATO JSTARD PIE

hy Roberts, New Hebron, Mississippi

ve to bake and experiment with ingredients. I he up with a hit when I developed this delicious-ifferent pie.

	small sweet potatoes, peeled and chopped
	cup marshmallow creme
	cup butter, cubed
	can (5 ounces) evaporated milk
	eggs
	teaspoon vanilla extract
	teaspoon almond extract
	cup sugar
	cup packed brown sugar
	tablespoon all-purpose flour
	teaspoon ground cinnamon
	teaspoon ground nutmeg
	unbaked pastry shell (9 inches)
	cup whipped topping

ce sweet potatoes in a large saucepan and cov-with water. Bring to a boil. Reduce heat; cover d simmer for 10 minutes or until tender. Drain po-oes and place in large mixing bowl; mash. Add

BANANA POUND CAKE

Nancy Zimmerman
Cape May Court House, New Jersey

I adapted a basic pound cake recipe from my great-aunt for this treat. It makes a moist cake that pops out of the pan perfectly.

3	teaspoons plus 3 cups sugar, *divided*
1	cup butter, softened
6	eggs
1	cup mashed ripe banana (about 2 medium)
1½	teaspoons vanilla extract
½	teaspoon lemon extract
3	cups all-purpose flour
¼	teaspoon baking soda
1	cup (8 ounces) sour cream

GLAZE:

1½	cups confectioners' sugar
½	teaspoon vanilla extract
3	to 4 teaspoons milk

Grease a 10-in. fluted tube pan. Sprinkle with 3 teaspoons sugar; set aside. In a large mixing bowl, cream butter and remaining sugar until light and fluffy, about 5 minutes. Add eggs, one at a time, beating well after each addition.

Stir in bananas and extracts. Combine flour and baking soda; add to the creamed mixture alternately with sour cream, beating just until combined.

Pour into prepared pan (pan will be full). Bake at 325° for 75-85 minutes or until a toothpick inserted near the center comes out clean. Cool for 10 minutes before removing from pan to a wire rack to cool completely.

In a small bowl, whisk glaze ingredients until smooth; drizzle over cake. Store in refrigerator.

YIELD: 12-15 servings.

APPLE CRANBERRY COBBLER

Regina Stock, Topeka, Kansas

My family enjoys the sweetness of the apples as ' as the tartness of the cranberries in this old-fa ioned treat. It's a great dessert to make during peak of apple season.

5	cups sliced peeled tart apples
1¼	cups sugar
1	cup fresh *or* frozen cranberries
3	tablespoons quick-cooking tapioca
½	teaspoon ground cinnamon
1	cup water
2	tablespoons butter

TOPPING:

¾	cup all-purpose flour
2	tablespoons sugar
1	teaspoon baking powder
⅛	teaspoon salt
¼	cup cold butter
¼	cup milk

In a large saucepan, combine the apples, sug cranberries, tapioca, cinnamon and water. Let st for 5 minutes, stirring occasionally. Cook and : over medium heat until mixture comes to a full b Cook and stir 3 minutes longer. Pour into a grea 2-qt. baking dish. Dot with butter.

For topping, combine the flour, sugar, baking pc der and salt in a bowl. Cut in butter until cruml Stir in milk to form a soft dough. Drop dough tablespoonfuls over hot apple mixture. Bake, unc ered, at 375° for 30-35 minutes or until topping golden brown and a toothpick inserted into topp comes out clean.

YIELD: 8 servings.

ghostly good desserts

ALLOWEEN POKE CAKE

s cute cake, created by our Test Kitchen, will make
r favorite trick-or-treaters smile with delight
en you serve it on Halloween. The moist marble
e features a buttery frosting and fun candy
mpkins on top.

    package (18¹/₄ ounces) fudge marble
    cake mix

    packages (3 ounces *each*) orange gelatin

    cup boiling water

    cup cold water

    cup butter, softened

2   cups confectioners' sugar

    cup baking cocoa

    cup milk

    teaspoon vanilla extract

    to 15 candy pumpkins *or* candy corn

Prepare and bake cake according to package directions, using a greased 13-in. x 9-in. x 2-in. baking
pan. Cool on a wire rack for 1 hour.

In a small bowl, dissolve gelatin in boiling water; stir
in cold water. With a meat fork or wooden skewer, poke holes in cake about 2 in. apart. Slowly pour
gelatin over cake. Refrigerate for 2-3 hours.

For frosting, in a small mixing bowl, cream butter
until fluffy. Beat in the confectioners' sugar, cocoa,
milk and vanilla until smooth. Spread over cake; top
with candy pumpkins or candy corn. Cover and refrigerate until serving.

YIELD: 12-15 servings.

Combine wafer crumbs and butter; press onto bottom and 1 in. up the sides of a greased 1[0]-in. springform pan. Set aside. In a mixing bowl, b[eat] cream cheese and sugars until smooth. Add e[ggs;] beat on low speed just until combined. Whis[k in] pumpkin, cornstarch, vanilla and pumpkin [pie] spice just until blended. Pour into crust. Place [on a] baking sheet. Bake at 350° for 60-65 minute[s or] until center is almost set. Cool on a wire rack fo[r 15] minutes.

Combine topping ingredients; spread over fill[ing.] Bake at 350° for 6 minutes. Cool on a wire r[ack] for 10 minutes. Carefully run a knife around [the] edge of pan to loosen; cool 1 hour lon[ger.] Refrigerate overnight. Remove sides of pan; [set] aside.

For spiderwebs, draw six 3-in. x 2-in. half cir[cles] on two sheets of parchment paper on top; tape b[oth] securely to work surface. In a saucepan, bring [the] sugar, cream of tartar and water to a boil o[ver] medium heat. Boil, without stirring, until mixt[ure] turns a light amber color and candy thermome[ter] reads 350°. Immediately remove from the heat [and] stir. Cool, stirring occasionally, for 10-15 minute[s or] until hot sugar mixture falls off a metal spoon [in a] fine thread.

Using a spoon or meat fork, carefully drizzle sy[rup] over half-circle outlines and inside the outline[s to] form spiderwebs; reheat syrup if needed. Cool co[m-] pletely. Place melted chocolate in a reseala[ble] plastic bag; cut a small hole in a corner of b[ag.] Pipe 1-in. spiders onto parchment or foil; c[ool] completely. With remaining melted chocola[te,] pipe two or three dots on each web; attach spide[rs.]

Remove sides of springform pan. Cut cheeseca[ke;] place a web on top of each slice and remain[ing] spiders on the side. Refrigerate leftovers.

YIELD: 12 servings.

EDITOR'S NOTE: We recommend that you t[est] your candy thermometer before each use [by] bringing water to a boil; the thermometer sho[uld] read 212°. Adjust your recipe temperature up [or] down based on your test.

SPIDERWEB PUMPKIN CHEESECAKE

Bev Kotowich, Winnepeg, Manitoba

This spiced cheesecake makes an appearance on my Halloween table every year. Folks get a kick out of the candy web and chocolate spiders.

- 1¾ cups chocolate wafer crumbs (about 28 wafers)
- ¼ cup butter, melted

FILLING:
- 3 packages (8 ounces *each*) cream cheese, softened
- ¾ cup sugar
- ½ cup packed brown sugar
- 3 eggs
- 1 can (15 ounces) solid-pack pumpkin
- 2 tablespoons cornstarch
- 3 teaspoons vanilla extract
- 1½ teaspoons pumpkin pie spice

TOPPING:
- 2 cups (16 ounces) sour cream
- 3 tablespoons sugar
- 2 teaspoons vanilla extract

SPIDERWEB GARNISH:
- 1 cup sugar
- ⅛ teaspoon cream of tartar
- ⅓ cup water
- 4 squares (1 ounce *each*) semisweet chocolate, melted

ghostly good desserts

RANGE SPICE CAKE

nie Simon, Reed City, Michigan

e to serve slices of this gingerbread-like cake with
oped topping, but it's just as delicious plain.

- cups all-purpose flour
- cup sugar
- teaspoons baking soda
- teaspoon ground ginger
- teaspoon ground cinnamon
- teaspoon ground cloves
- cup orange juice
- cup molasses
- cup vegetable oil
- egg
- cup orange marmalade

ipped topping, optional

a bowl, combine the flour, sugar, baking soda,
ger, cinnamon and cloves. Combine the orange
e, molasses, oil and egg; add to dry ingredients
stir just until combined. Pour into a greased 9-
square baking pan.

e at 350° for 16-20 minutes or until a toothpick
erted near the center comes out clean. Spoon
rmalade over warm cake. Cool on a wire rack.
ve with whipped topping if desired.

ELD: 9 servings.

MOUSSE-FILLED WITCHES' HATS

Our Test Kitchen staff had a "spooktacular" time
coming up with these rich snacks, featuring sugar
cones filled with a creamy homemade mousse.

- $1^3/_4$ cups heavy whipping cream, *divided*
- 1   cup milk chocolate chips
- 4   squares (1 ounce *each*) semisweet chocolate, chopped
- $1/_2$ teaspoon shortening
- 1   package (4$^3/_4$ ounces) chocolate ice cream sugar cones

Halloween sprinkles

- 12   thin chocolate wafers (2$^1/_4$-inch diameter)

In a small saucepan, bring $1/_2$ cup cream to a boil;
remove from heat. Stir in chocolate chips until
smooth. Transfer to a bowl; cool to room temperature, stirring occasionally. In a small mixing bowl,
beat remaining cream until stiff peaks form; fold
into chocolate mixture. Cover; chill.

In a microwave-safe bowl, melt semisweet chocolate and shortening; stir until smooth. Dip pointed
tips of ice cream cones a third of the way into melted chocolate; roll in sprinkles. Refrigerate until set.
Just before serving, spoon mousse into cones. Top
each with a chocolate wafer. Invert onto a serving
platter.

YIELD: 1 dozen.

CARAMEL FLAN

Anelle Mack, Midland, Texas

Sometimes I like to top this Mexican dessert with whipped cream and toasted slivered almonds.

1/2	cup sugar
1²/₃	cups sweetened condensed milk
1	cup milk
3	eggs
3	egg yolks
1	teaspoon vanilla extract

In a large skillet over medium heat, cook sugar until melted, about 12 minutes. Do not stir. When sugar is melted, reduce heat to low and continue to cook, stirring occasionally, until syrup is golden brown, about 2 minutes. Quickly pour into an ungreased 2-qt. round souffle dish, tilting to coat the bottom; let stand for 10 minutes.

In a blender, combine the condensed milk, milk, eggs, yolks and vanilla. Cover and process for 15 seconds or until well blended. Slowly pour over syrup.

Place the souffle dish in a larger baking pan. Add 1 in. of boiling water to baking pan. Bake at 350° for 55-60 minutes or until center is just set (mixture will jiggle). Remove souffle dish from larger pan. Place on a wire rack; cool for 1 hour. Cover and refrigerate overnight.

To unmold, run a knife around edge and invert flan onto a large rimmed serving platter. Cut into wedges or spoon onto dessert plates; spoon sauce over each serving.

YIELD: 8-10 servings.

SPIDERWEB CHEESECAKE

Jan White, Plainview, Nebraska

The trick to this tempting treat is pulling a tooth through rings of melted chocolate to create the effect. This no-bake cream cheese pie goes tog er quickly and tastes delicious.

1	envelope unflavored gelatin
1/4	cup cold water
2	packages (8 ounces *each*) cream chees softened
1/2	cup sugar
1/2	cup heavy whipping cream
1	teaspoon vanilla extract
1	chocolate crumb crust (8 *or* 9 inches)
2	tablespoons semisweet chocolate chips
1	tablespoon butter

In a small saucepan, sprinkle gelatin over water stand for 1 minute. Heat gelatin; stir until dissol Remove from the heat; cool slightly. In a mix bowl, beat the cream cheese and sugar u smooth. Gradually beat in cream, vanilla and g tin mixture until smooth. Pour into crust.

In a microwave, melt chocolate chips and but stir until smooth. Transfer to a heavy-duty res able bag; cut a small hole in a corner of bag. Pip circle of chocolate in center of cheesecake. F evenly spaced thin concentric circles about 1/ apart over filling. Beginning with the center ci gently pull a toothpick through circles toward er edge. Wipe toothpick clean. Repeat to comp web pattern. Cover and refrigerate for at lea hours before cutting.

YIELD: 6-8 servings.

freaky fac

When people fled Ireland's pot famine during the 1840s and came the United States, they brought w them their Halloween customs.

ghostly good desserts

SPIDERWEB CHEESECAKE

PUMPKIN TRIFLE

Lyla Lehenbauer, New London, Missouri

This impressive trifle looks so elegant with alternating layers of gingerbread cake and a blend of pumpkin and butterscotch pudding. Try making it ahead of time for a fuss-free dessert when you're planning to entertain guests.

1   package (14¹/₂ ounces) gingerbread cake mix
1¹/₄ cups water
1   egg
4   cups cold milk
4   packages (1 ounce *each*) instant butterscotch pudding mix
1   can (15 ounces) solid-pack pumpkin
1   teaspoon ground cinnamon
¹/₄ teaspoon *each* ground ginger, nutmeg and allspice
1   carton (12 ounces) frozen whipped topping, thawed

In a mixing bowl, combine the cake mix, water and egg; mix well. Pour into an ungreased 8-in. square baking pan. Bake at 350° for 35-40 minutes or until a toothpick inserted near the center comes out clean. Cool for 10 minutes before removing from pan to a wire rack. When completely cooled, crumble the cake. Set aside ¹/₄ cup crumbs for garnish.

In a bowl, whisk milk and pudding mixes f[...] minutes or until slightly thickened. Let stand [...] minutes or until soft set. Stir in pumpkin and sp[...] mix well.

In a trifle bowl or 3¹/₂-qt. glass serving b[...] layer a fourth of the cake crumbs, half of the pu[...] kin mixture, a fourth of the cake crumbs and [...] of the whipped topping. Repeat layers. Gar[...] with reserved cake crumbs. Serve immediate[...] refrigerate.

YIELD: 18 servings.

EDITOR'S NOTE: This recipe was tested with B[...] Crocker gingerbread cake mix.

CANDY CORN CUPCAKES

Renee Schwebach, Dumont, Minnesota

These moist, tender white cupcakes are per[...] for Halloween. But for fast yet fabulous results [...] time of year, simply choose candy decorat[...] appropriate to the season.

¹/₂ cup shortening
1¹/₂ cups sugar
1   teaspoon vanilla extract
2   cups all-purpose flour
3¹/₂ teaspoons baking powder
1   teaspoon salt
1   cup milk
4   egg whites
Frosting of your choice
Candy corn *or* other decorations

In a mixing bowl, cream shortening and sugar. B[...] in vanilla. Combine flour, baking powder and s[...] add to the creamed mixture alternately with m[...] Beat in the egg whites. Fill greased or paper-li[...] muffin cups half full.

Bake at 350° for 18-22 minutes or until a tooth[...] comes out clean. Cool for 10 minutes before rem[...] ing from pans to wire racks. Frost cooled c[...] cakes; decorate as desired.

YIELD: 2 dozen.

ghostly good desserts

WEET
ACK-O'-LANTERNS

nah Bjerkseth, Three Hills, Alberta

re's no trick to making these Halloween-flavored cakes. By using a convenient cake mix, you can them out in a jiffy. Simplify them even more canned frosting.

package (18 1/4 ounces) yellow cake mix *or* cake mix of your choice

4 cups confectioners' sugar

tablespoons butter, softened

to 3/4 cup milk

to 1 1/2 teaspoons orange paste food coloring

green gumdrops

black jujubes

pare and bake cake according to package direcs for cupcakes. Fill 24 greased muffin cups twods full. Bake at 350° for 15-18 minutes or until oothpick comes out clean. Cool for 5 minutes be-

fore removing from the pans to wire racks to cool completely.

For frosting, in a small bowl, combine confectioners' sugar, butter and enough milk to achieve spreading consistency. Stir in food coloring. Cut a thin slice off the top of each cupcake. Spread frosting on 12 cupcakes. Invert remaining cupcakes and place on top; frost top and sides.

For stems, cut each gumdrop into three lengthwise wedges; place one piece on top of each cupcake. Cut jujubes into thin slices; use a bottom slice for each mouth. From remaining slices, cut one large triangle and two smaller ones. Position two small triangles and a large triangle on each cupcake for eyes and nose.

YIELD: 1 dozen.

BROWNIE PIE A LA MODE

Beverly Thornton, Cortlandt Manor, New York

This is a quick dessert recipe for when you need something good and chocolaty. Cutting them into wedges and topping them with fudge sauce dresses them up.

1/2	cup sugar
2	tablespoons butter
2	tablespoons water
1 1/2	cups semisweet chocolate chips
2	eggs
1	teaspoon vanilla extract
2/3	cup all-purpose flour
1/4	teaspoon baking soda
1/4	teaspoon salt
3/4	cup chopped walnuts

FUDGE SAUCE:

1	cup (6 ounces) semisweet chocolate chips
1/2	cup evaporated milk
1/4	cup sugar
1	tablespoon butter

Vanilla ice cream

In a small saucepan over medium heat, bring sugar, butter and water to a boil. Remove from the heat; stir in chocolate chips until melted. In a mixing bowl, beat eggs and vanilla. Add chocolate mixture; mix well. Combine flour, baking soda and salt; add to chocolate mixture. Stir in walnuts. into a greased 9-in. pie plate. Bake at 350° for 30 minutes or until a toothpick inserted near center comes out clean. Cool on a wire rack.

For fudge sauce, heat chocolate chips, milk, s and butter in a microwave or double boiler chocolate and butter are melted; stir until sm Drizzle some over pie. Cut into wedges; serve ice cream and additional sauce.

YIELD: 6-8 servings.

PUMPKIN CHIFFON PIE

Linda Gartner, Feasterville, Pennsylvania

This delicious pie is so light and fluffy that folks have room for a slice no matter how full they Guests are always delighted with the delicate fl

1	envelope unflavored gelatin
1/2	cup cold water
3/4	cup milk
1	cup packed brown sugar
1	cup canned pumpkin
1/2	teaspoon ground ginger
1/2	teaspoon ground cinnamon
1/4	teaspoon salt
1 1/2	cups whipped topping
1	graham cracker crust (9 inches)

In a small bowl, sprinkle the gelatin over cold ter; let stand for 1 minute. In a saucepan, hea milk over medium heat until bubbles form ar sides of saucepan. Add gelatin mixture; stir unti solved. Stir in the brown sugar until dissol Remove from the heat. Add the pumpkin, gin cinnamon and salt; mix well. Refrigerate until t ened, about 1 1/2 hours.

Fold whipped topping into pumpkin mixture. into crust. Refrigerate for at least 4 hours or firm. Refrigerate leftovers.

YIELD: 6-8 servings.

ghostly good desserts

...TTERSCOTCH
...CAN DESSERT

...ky Harrison, Albion, Illinois

...t and creamy, this terrific treat never lasts long ...n I serve it. The fluffy cream cheese layer topped ... cool butterscotch pudding is a lip-smacking ...bination.

- cup cold butter
- cup all-purpose flour
- cup chopped pecans, *divided*
- package (8 ounces) cream cheese, softened
- cup confectioners' sugar
- carton (8 ounces) frozen whipped topping, thawed, *divided*
- cups milk
- packages (3.4 or 3.5 ounces *each*) instant butterscotch *or* vanilla pudding mix

... bowl, cut the butter into the flour until crum- ...stir in ¹/₂ cup pecans. Press into an ungreased ...1. x 9-in. x 2-in. baking pan. Bake at 350° for 20 ...utes or until lightly browned. Cool.

... mixing bowl, beat the cream cheese and sug- ...ntil fluffy. Fold in 1 cup whipped topping; spread ... crust. Combine the milk and pudding mix ...l smooth; pour over cream cheese layer. ...igerate for 15-20 minutes or until set. Top with ... remaining whipped topping and pecans. ...igerate for 1-2 hours.

...LD: 16-20 servings.

SWEET POTATO LAYER CAKE

Christy Shepard, Marion, North Carolina

This cake is a hit at parties and church functions.

1¹/₂	cups vegetable oil
2	cups sugar
4	eggs, *separated*
1¹/₂	cups finely shredded uncooked sweet potato (about 1 medium)
¹/₄	cup hot water
1	teaspoon vanilla extract
2¹/₂	cups cake flour
3	teaspoons baking powder
1	teaspoon ground cinnamon
1	teaspoon ground nutmeg
¹/₄	teaspoon salt
1	cup chopped pecans

FROSTING:

¹/₂	cup butter
1¹/₃	cups sugar
2	cans (5 ounces *each*) evaporated milk
4	egg yolks, beaten
2²/₃	cups flaked coconut
1	cup chopped pecans
2	teaspoons vanilla extract

In a mixing bowl, beat oil and sugar. Add egg yolks, one at a time, beating well after each addition. Add sweet potato, water and vanilla; mix well. In a small mixing bowl, beat egg whites until stiff; fold into sweet potato mixture. Combine flour, baking pow- der, cinnamon, nutmeg and salt; add to potato mix- ture. Stir in pecans. Pour into three greased 9-in. round cake pans. Bake at 350° for 22-27 minutes or until a toothpick inserted near the center comes out clean. Cool for 10 minutes; remove to wire racks.

For frosting, melt the butter in a saucepan; whisk in sugar, milk and egg yolks until smooth. Cook and stir over medium heat for 10-12 minutes or until thickened and bubbly. Remove from the heat; stir in the coconut, pecans and vanilla. Cool slightly. Place one cake layer on a serving plate; spread with a third of the frosting. Repeat layers.

YIELD: 10-12 servings.

APPLE-RAISIN BUNDT CAKE

Maryellen Hays, Wolcottville, Indiana

This moist, old-fashioned dessert has a pleasant blend of spices and is loaded with nuts and raisins.

3/4	cup butter, softened
1 1/2	cups sugar
1	cup plus 2 tablespoons strawberry jam
3 1/3	cups all-purpose flour
1 1/2	teaspoons baking soda
1 1/2	teaspoons ground nutmeg
3/4	teaspoon *each* ground allspice, cloves and cinnamon
1 1/2	cups buttermilk
1 3/4	cups raisins
3/4	cup chopped walnuts
3/4	cup chopped peeled apple

GLAZE:

1	cup confectioners' sugar
4	teaspoons milk

In a large mixing bowl, cream the butter and sugar. Stir in the jam. Combine the flour, baking soda and spices; beat into creamed mixture alternately with buttermilk. Add the raisins, walnuts and apple; mix well. Pour into a greased and floured 10-in. fluted tube pan.

Bake at 350° for 1 hour or until a toothpick inserted near the center comes out clean. Cool for 10 minutes before removing from pan to a wire rack to cool completely. Combine glaze ingredients; drizzle over cake.

YIELD: 12-16 servings.

PUMPKIN-FACE ICE CREAM SANDWICHES

Pattie Ann Forssberg, Logan, Kansas

These friendly faces will elicit smiles from frie and family. You can use homemade or purcha sugar cookies.

3	tablespoons butter, softened
1 1/2	cups confectioners' sugar
1/2	teaspoon vanilla extract
1	to 2 tablespoons milk
Red and yellow food coloring	
48	round sugar cookies
72	raisins
Red and green decorating icing	
1	quart vanilla ice cream, softened

In a small mixing bowl, combine the butter, con tioners' sugar, vanilla and enough milk to achi spreading consistency. Tint orange with red and low food coloring. Frost the tops of 24 sugar co ies. Make pumpkin faces, using raisins for eyes nose. Add a smile with red icing and stem w green icing. Let dry completely.

Spoon ice cream onto bottom of plain cookies; with frosted cookies. Place in individual plastic ba seal. Freeze until serving.

YIELD: 2 dozen.

PUMPKIN ICE CREAM

Linda Young, Longmont, Colorado

This delicious ice cream really captures the flav of fall. Enjoy it alone or with gingersnaps.

1	cup canned pumpkin
1/4	teaspoon pumpkin pie spice
1	quart vanilla ice cream, softened
Gingersnaps, optional	

In a large bowl, combine the pumpkin and pie sp until well blended. Stir in ice cream. Freeze ur serving. Garnish with gingersnaps if desired.

YIELD: 4-6 servings.

ghostly good desserts

frightfully
fun crafts

JUST as important as the festive foods at Halloween are the devilishly fun decorations that go along with it! The creepy crafts, creative costumes and scarecrow styling ideas on the following pages will help you set an unforgettable All Hallows' Eve atmosphere.

GIFT BAGS

To hold trick-or-treat candy or party favors, these bags will be a hit on Halloween.

1. Purchase inexpensive gift bags in Halloween colors, such as orange, black, purple and green.

2. Use craft foam cutouts, chenille stems, cheese cloth and wiggle eyes to create decorative trims on the bags.

PINT JAR LUMINARIES

Shine a little light on a mantle or tabletop with these cute candle holders.

1. Paint the outside of a pint-size glass canning jar orange, purple or black.

2. Cut Halloween motifs from fabric.

3. Glue motifs around jar.

4. Place a votive pot and votive candle into jar with jar rim supporting votive holder.

5. Wrap a narrow torn fabric strip or strands of raffia around top of jar. Tie ends in a small bow or an overhand knot.

MARBLE/SPIDERWEB PUMPKIN

For a delightfully different way to carve a pump[kin]
try this special method, which uses clear gl[ass]
marbles to create a decorative web.

1. Cut an opening in the bottom of a pump[kin] and remove the seeds.

2. Draw a spiderweb and spider on a piec[e of] tracing paper.

3. Hold the pattern on the pumpkin with a couple of push pins. Use another push pin to pierce the pattern and transfer the design onto the pumpkin. Gently carve away the outside of the pumpkin following  the pin holes to create the solid lines. Us[e a] small drill to drill holes where desired. Ins[ert] clear marbles into the drilled holes. Ca[rve] away the shell of the pumpkin to create [a] spider's body and press marbles into [the] carved-out area.

4. Place a string of white mini lights in the [bot]tom of the pumpkin.

5. Add leaves around the bottom of the pump[kin].

GLUE-STICK SPIDERWEBS

Making these spiderwebs is child's play by using everyday glue sticks!

1. Use a black marker to draw a spiderweb on a piece of paper for pattern.

2. Place parchment paper over pattern.

3. Using a glue gun and glue sticks, apply glue over spiderweb pattern. If desired, sprinkle spiderweb with iridescent glitter before glue dries.

4. Hang from ceiling with monofilament thread in front of a dark velvet curtain.

frightfully fun crafts

Bat Napkin Ring (for one)

1. Trace pattern below onto tracing paper.

2. Cut shape from black felt.

3. Cut slit where shown on pattern.

4. Glue a 1/2-inch black pom-pom to bat for body, being careful not to glue slit closed.

5. Glue two yellow seed beads to bat's head for eyes.

6. With right side out, slip opposite end of wing through slit.

7. Insert napkin into napkin ring.

HALLOWEEN PHOTO ALBUM

Forever capture Halloween memories in t dressed-up mini-photo album.

1. Use a small piece of household spor and orange and gold acrylic craft pa to sponge-paint the outside of a purcha: mini-photo album.

2. Adhere Halloween motif fabric right side to double-stick adhesive.

3. Cut out desired designs.

4. Remove backing from double-stick adhes and attach fabric right side up on front photo album.

5. Adhere "Trick or Treat" craft foam letter: to spine of photo album.

BAT NAPKIN RING PATTERN
Trace 1—tracing paper
Cut 1—black felt
Cut slit
Enlarge pattern 50%

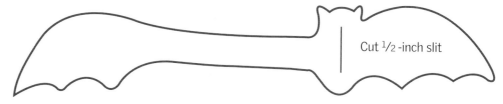

Cut 1/2-inch slit

frightfully fun crafts

LACK VOTIVE CAULDRON

se "terror-ific" candle holders are sure to shed
the right spooky light on your Halloween par-
nack table!

Paint a jelly jar black.

Spray a clear votive holder with crystal spray
or sponge paint with white paint.

Place a small amount of polyester fiberfill
inside black jar and stretch it out to cover outside of jar as shown.

Place votive holder in opening of jar.

Add plastic spiders where desired.

POM-POM CATS

Kids of all ages will have fun making these funny
black cats.

1. Glue two $1^1/_2$ -inch black pom-poms together for the head and body of cat. Glue four
   $^1/_2$-inch black pom-poms to cat's body for legs.

2. Cut two small triangles of black felt and two
   smaller triangles of pink felt. Glue a pink felt
   piece to one side of each black felt piece for
   ears. Glue ear pieces to top of cat's head.

3. Glue two wiggle eyes to cat's head.

4. Cut three $1^1/_2$ -inch-long pieces of nylon
   fishing line for whiskers. Glue center of the
   whiskers together and add a 3mm pink pom-
   pom as shown in photo. Glue whiskers and
   nose to front of cat's head.

5. Glue a $^1/_2$ -inch-long piece of green chenille
   stem to a 1-inch orange pom-pom for the
   stem of the pumpkin. Glue the pumpkin to the
   front of the cat.

GHOSTLY TABLETOP

Nella Parker, Hershey, Michigan

To create a spooky atmosphere and set the mood for a Halloween party, I transformed my table into a ghost.

1. Place a pumpkin in the middle of the table and spread a white sheet evenly over the pumpkin and tabletop.

2. Using white string, gather the fabric at the base of the pumpkin to resemble a ghost.

3. To make the face, cut out eyes and mouth from black felt and glue them on. If you wish, cut out felt bats, spiders, etc. to scatter on the table.

PERKY PUMPKIN CENTERPIECE

Lisa Habig, Beallsville, Ohio

Pumpkin tier decorations are easy to make and ceive many compliments.

1. Find three pumpkins, each slightly sma than the other, to stack.

2. Scoop out the insides of the two bott pumpkins and throw away their lids.

3. Insert dried flowers or leaves between e. tier and place the small whole pumpkin top as the finishing touch.

4. This centerpiece doesn't keep well in a wa house, so make it the day of your party place it on the porch or by a gate.

frightfully fun crafts

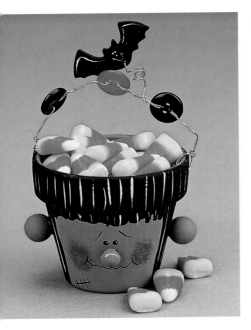

SPIDERS ON SPIDER RIBBON

This table decoration will be a "run-away" hit at your Halloween gathering.

1. Place a length of wire-edge spider-motif ribbon down the length of a table.

2. Twist four black chenille stems together at the center. Shape each end to make eight spider legs.

3. Place the spiders along the ribbon and add a black tea light candle to the center of each spider.

ANKENSTEIN REAT HOLDER

:tta Mateik, Petaluma, California

k to make, these clay pot candy holders are sure ring a smile.

Paint the outside of a 2 1/2 -inch-diameter clay pot black.

Paint a green rectangle on one side of clay pot for face as shown in photo.

Paint two 1/2 -inch wooden balls and a 1/4 -inch furniture plug green for ears and nose.

With a nearly dry brush and red paint, add cheeks to face. Use black fine-line marker to add eyes and remaining details.

Glue ears and nose to face.

Use a liner brush to add white highlights to nose and eyes and to add stripes around the top of the clay pot.

Drill holes in sides of pot. Thread buttons onto craft wire for handle. Insert wire through holes and twist to secure.

Place a plastic portion cup inside pot. Fill pot with candy.

GOURD GHOST FAMILY

This frightful family is a simple centerpiece that's bound to get your guests in the "spirit" of the holiday.

1. Cover a Styrofoam disk with dried moss.

2. Use a black marker to draw two small oval eyes and a larger oval mouth on one side of each white gourd as shown in photo above.

3. Press each gourd into moss-covered disk, making sure each stands upright. Glue as needed to hold.

POPCORN BALL GHOSTS

These ghoulish guys can serve as decorations then go home with guests as favors.

1. Prepare or purchase popcorn balls or [Krispies Treats. Insert a wooden ske into each popcorn ball or mold each [Krispies Treat around a skewer.

2. Wrap ball with plastic wrap.

3. Center a white cloth napkin over wrap ball and fasten with a white chenille ste

4. Cut out small circles for eyes and small o for mouths from black construction pa Glue eyes and mouths to one side of each as shown in photo.

5. Stand each in a glass and drape nap around to hide the glass.

freaky fact

For retailers, Halloween is a $7 billion industry, with $2 billion coming from the sale of candy.

frightfully fun crafts

Bewitching Bashes

CONTENTS

Bewitching Bashes

SPECIAL THANKS
Costumes/Face Painting Photography: Christine Bronico, RR Donnelly; **Additional Photography:** Getty Images, PhotoDisc, JupiterImages, Veer, Punchstock, Doug Croll; **Costume/Face Paint Models:** Alex D., Alex V., Anneli, Davis, Emily, Erin, Hayley, Leo, Luca, Lucy, Mackenzie, Mikaela, Nicholas, Pasquale, Rebecca, Samantha; **Makeup Styling/Face Painting:** Joel Mendenhall and Sadiya Sellers; **Face Painting Kits:** Douglas Drake at Wolfe Brothers Face Art & FX (available at retail outlets and on-line at www.wolfefxproducts.com); **Costume Creation:** Catherine Alston; **Donations:** Julie Ewert and Jeanne Jansch from Michaels, The Arts and Crafts Store (www.michaels.com) for the craft pumpkins and gourds; **Craft Designers:** Alison Palmer Dupree, Richard Erdman II, Suzanne Gaffney, Patricia Graham, Tamara Kirkman, Diane Napolitano; **Additional Thanks To:** Chris Tipton, Deborah Bechtler, Kirk Beason, Roxanne Knoll, Connie Tuccito, Erick Swindell, Elizabeth Tunnicliffe

SNACKS & BEVERAGES

Keep your BOO-rific party guests mingling by providing them with an array of these simple-to-make finger foods. Add a spooky or warming fall beverage to top it all off. You'll win raves and have time to enjoy yourself, too.

BOO-rific black bean dip with chips

Taste of Home Test Kitchen

Your goblin guests will devour this cute chips and dip combo from our home economists. The peppers add a little kick and the beans pack a nutritional punch— much needed on a holiday centered around sweets! Try different Halloween cookie cutters to add a variety of shapes to the chip selection.

9 flour tortillas (7 inches)
4 teaspoons Mexican seasoning
4 bacon strips, diced
¼ cup *each* chopped onion, sweet red and green pepper
2 garlic cloves, minced
2 cans (15 ounces *each*) black beans, rinsed and drained, *divided*
⅓ cup picante sauce
2 tablespoons lime juice
2 teaspoons minced chipotle pepper in adobo sauce
1 teaspoon ground cumin
½ teaspoon salt
2 tablespoons minced fresh cilantro

1 Cut tortillas with a 3-in. ghost-shaped cookie cutter. Place on baking sheets coated with non-stick cooking spray. Spritz tortillas with non-stick cooking spray; sprinkle with Mexican seasoning. Bake at 350° for 8-10 minutes or until edges just begin to brown. Remove to wire racks to cool.

2 In a skillet, cook bacon over medium heat until crisp. Remove to paper towels; drain, reserving 2 teaspoons drippings. In the drippings, saute onion and peppers until tender. Add garlic; saute 1 minute longer.

3 Add one can of beans and mash. Add the picante sauce, lime juice, chipotle peppers, cumin, salt and remaining beans; heat through. Stir in bacon and cilantro. Serve with ghost chips.

Yield: 3 cups dip and 3 dozen chips.

magic potion punch

Michelle Thomas, Bangor, Maine

At a Halloween party, the more creepy the food, the better! I like to tuck gummy worms into an ice ring when I make this great green punch.

2 packages (3 ounces *each*) lime gelatin
2 cup sugar
1 cup boiling water
3 cups cold water
1 quart non-carbonated lemon-lime drink, chilled
2 quarts lemon-lime soda, chilled

Dissolve gelatin and sugar in boiling water; add cold water. Transfer to a punch bowl. Stir in lemon-lime drink and soda.

d: about 4 quarts.

confetti cheese salsa

Deidra Engle, Aledo, Illinois

This creamy cheese dip is so quick and easy that it can be served in any season, but it's always a big hit at Fourth of July picnics. I never have to worry about covering the dish on the picnic table because the mixture disappears in a snap.

2	cups (8 ounces) finely shredded cheddar cheese
2	cups (8 ounces) shredded part-skim mozzarella cheese
2	large tomatoes, seeded and chopped
1	medium green pepper, diced
1	small cucumber, seeded and diced
1	small onion, chopped
1	bottle (8 ounces) ranch salad dressing
2	tablespoons salsa

Corn *or* tortilla chips

1 In a large bowl, combine the first six ingredients. Combine the salad dressing and salsa; pour over cheese mixture and toss gently. Serve with chips. Refrigerate leftovers.

Yield: 7 cups.

festive pumpkin dip

Evelyn Kennell, Roanoke, Illinois

Surprise party guests with this festive fall hors d'oeuvre. Served in a round bread bowl, it'll make an attractive addition to your buffet table. Surround the bread bowl with veggies (as shown) and place a basket of assorted crackers next to it. You'll find that the dip will be gone in no time at all!

12	ounces cream cheese, softened
3/4	cup canned pumpkin
2	tablespoons taco seasoning mix
1/8	teaspoon garlic powder
1/3	cup chopped dried beef
1/3	cup chopped green pepper
1/3	cup chopped sweet red pepper
1	can (2-1/4 ounces) sliced ripe olives, drained
1	round loaf (1 pound) Italian *or* pumpernickel bread

Fresh vegetables, crackers *or* corn chips

1 In a mixing bowl, beat cream cheese, pumpkin, taco seasoning and garlic powder until smooth. Stir in beef, peppers and olives. Cover and refrigerate until ready to serve.

2 Just before serving, cut top off bread; scoop out bread from inside, leaving a 1/2-in. shell (save the bread from inside to make croutons or bread crumbs or save for another use). Fill shell with cream cheese mixture. Serve with vegetables, crackers or corn chips.

Yield: 3 cups.

FUNNY BONE!
What did one ghost say to the other ghost? "Do you believe in people?"

orange-glazed chicken wings

Holly Mann, Amherst, New Hampshire

I normally don't care for wings, but after I tried this recipe that was shared by a co-worker, it changed my mind. A simple overnight marinade coats the wings to create a lovely glaze when baked.

3 pounds chicken wings

2 cups soy sauce

1 cup orange juice

1 teaspoon garlic powder

Cut chicken wings into three sections; discard wing tips. In a large resealable plastic bag, combine the soy sauce, orange juice and garlic powder; add wings. Seal bag and turn to coat. Refrigerate overnight.

Drain and discard marinade. Place chicken wings in a greased foil-lined 15-in. x 10-in. x 1-in. baking pan. Bake at 350° for 1 hour or until juices run clear and glaze is set, turning twice.

Yield: 2-1/2 dozen.

Editor's Note: 3 pounds of uncooked chicken wing sections (wingettes) may be substituted for the whole chicken wings. Omit the first step.

Trick-or-Treat

The tradition of trick-or-treating probably dates back to the early All Souls' Day parades in England. During the festivities, poor citizens begged for food and wealthier families would give them pastries called "soul cakes" in return for a promise to pray for the family's dead relatives.

orange party punch

Brenda Rupert, Clyde, Ohio

This citrus punch was served at every birthday party I had when I was growing up. Now I prepare this fun, frothy drink for my kids.

1 can (12 ounces) frozen orange juice concentrate, thawed

2 liters lemon-lime soda, chilled

1 can (46 ounces) pineapple juice, chilled

1 quart orange *or* pineapple sherbet

1 Prepare orange juice according to package directions; pour into a punch bowl. Stir in soda and pineapple juice. Top with scoops of sherbet. Serve immediately.

Yield: 5-1/2 quarts.

Editor's Note: If you plan on serving this punch in a cauldron, (as shown) make sure it's plastic, not metal. Metal will react with the citrus in the punch resulting in a metallic flavor.

scarecrow veggie pizza

Taste of Home Test Kitchen

At harvest parties, fall festivals or any autumn event, the flavorful fellow here will raise a crop of smiles! Our cooks shaped a scarecrow using red peppers, carrots, broccoli and lots of other fresh veggies. Since you can make the crust with refrigerated dough and quickly prepare a cream cheese spread to put on top, you'll be ready to form your own colorful character in no time.

1	tube (10 ounces) refrigerated pizza dough
1	package (8 ounces) cream cheese, softened
6	tablespoons mayonnaise
3/4	teaspoon dill weed
1/2	teaspoon garlic salt
1/2	teaspoon dried minced onion
1/4	teaspoon onion salt
1	small sweet red pepper
1	small green pepper
1/4	cup shredded Swiss cheese
1	small carrot, chopped
10	fresh green beans
5	pieces Wheat Chex
1	large mushroom, halved
1	small head cauliflower, chopped
1/2	cup chopped broccoli
1	pattypan squash, halved
2	green onion tops, cut into strips
1/4	cup chow mein noodles

1 Press pizza dough onto a greased 14-in. pi pan. Bake at 400° for 10 minutes or until g en brown. Cool on a wire rack.

2 In a small mixing bowl, combine the cre cheese, mayonnaise, dill, garlic salt, onion onion salt. Spread over cooled crust.

3 To make the scarecrow, refer to the photo at for the size of vegetable pieces and the posi of pieces on pizza.

4 From a small piece of red pepper, cut a nar smile for mouth and a triangle for nose. Cho maining red pepper and set aside. Cut one from green pepper for the scarecrow's he Chop remaining green pepper and set asid

5 Position green pepper ring on pizza for scarecrow's head. Fill with shredded Sw cheese. Place two carrot pieces on face for e Add red pepper nose and mouth on face.

6 Use green beans to create the outline of a s and bib overalls below head where show the photo.

7 Combine chopped red pepper and remain chopped carrot. Sprinkle on pizza to fill in shirt. Use chopped green pepper to fill in overalls.

8 Place cereal on the elbows, knees and bi overalls for patches. Add a mushroom hal the bottom of each pants leg for shoes. Arra cauliflower around scarecrow for sky. Arra broccoli at the bottom for grass.

9 Place one squash half above head for hat. the remaining portion of squash in half ag Place green onion strips and one squash q ter on each side of scarecrow for corn husks.

10 For straw, place chow mein noodles be hat, on each side of neck, at the end of each and above shoes.

Yield: 10-12 servings.

Halloween Facts

The U.S. Census estimated that there were 36.1 million potential trick-or-treaters (5- to 13-year-olds) ready to go in 2005. Of course, many other children—older than 13 and younger than age 5—also go trick-or-treating. This mob of candy-loving kids has 108 million (the number of occupied housing units across the nation in 2005) possible stops to make.

cider cheese fondue

Kim Marie Van Rheenen, Mendota, Illinois

ese lovers are sure to enjoy dipping into this creamy, quick-to-fix fondue that has just a hint of apple. You also serve this appetizer with apple or pear wedges.

- 4 cup apple cider **or** apple juice
- 2 cups (8 ounces) shredded cheddar cheese
- 1 cup (4 ounces) shredded Swiss cheese
- 1 tablespoon cornstarch
- 8 teaspoon pepper
- 1 loaf (1 pound) French bread, cut into cubes

In a large saucepan, bring cider to a boil. Reduce heat to medium-low. Toss the cheeses with cornstarch and pepper; stir into cider. Cook and stir for 3-4 minutes or until cheese is melted. Transfer to a small ceramic fondue pot or slow cooker; keep warm. Serve with bread cubes.

Id: 2-2/3 cups.

hot spiced cider

Kim Wallace, Dover, Ohio

Next time you're entertaining, stir up a batch of this nicely spiced cider. The wonderful aroma will make your guests feel welcome on a chilly day.

- 1 gallon apple cider **or** apple juice
- 1 cup orange juice
- 1/4 cup maple syrup
- 1/2 teaspoon orange extract
- 1/2 teaspoon lemon extract
- 4 cinnamon sticks
- 2 teaspoons whole cloves
- 1 teaspoon whole allspice

1 In a Dutch oven, combine the first five ingredients. Place the cinnamon sticks, cloves and allspice on a double thickness of cheesecloth; bring up corners of cloth and tie with string to form a bag. Add to the pan. Cook, uncovered, over medium heat for 10-15 minutes or until flavors are blended (do not boil). Discard spice bag.

Yield: 4-1/2 quarts.

FUNNY BONE!
What is a skeleton's favorite musical instrument? A trombone.

roasted pumpkin seeds

Taste of Home Test Kitchen

Try this zippy twist on a Halloween tradition from o
home economists. It's got just enough heat to take th
chill off autumn afternoons.

2	cups pumpkin seeds
5	teaspoons butter, melted
1	teaspoon Worcestershire sauce
1	teaspoon sugar
1/2	teaspoon salt
1/4	teaspoon garlic powder
1/8	to 1/4 teaspoon cayenne pepper

1 In a bowl, toss pumpkin seeds with butter a
Worcestershire sauce. Combine the sugar, s
garlic powder and cayenne; sprinkle over se
and toss to coat.

2 Line a 15-in. x 10-in. x 1-in. baking pan with f
coat the foil with nonstick cooking spr
Spread seeds in pan. Bake at 250° for 45-60 n
utes or until seeds are dry and lightly brown
stirring every 15 minutes. Cool complete
Store in an airtight container.

Yield: 2 cups.

hot 'n' spicy cranberry dip

Marian Platt, Sequim, Washington

If you want to make this appetizer for a large buffet crowd, double the recipe and use a 16-ounce can of cranb
sauce. Be sure to have extra copies of the recipe—guests will ask for it!

3/4	cup jellied cranberry sauce
1	to 2 tablespoons prepared horseradish
1	tablespoon honey
1-1/2	teaspoons lemon juice
1-1/2	teaspoons Worcestershire sauce
1/8	to 1/4 teaspoon cayenne pepper
1	garlic clove, minced

Miniature hot dogs *or* **smoked sausage links,**
warmed

Sliced apples *or* **pears**

1 In a small saucepan, combine the first seven
gredients; bring to a boil, stirring constan
Reduce heat. Cover and simmer for 5 minu
stirring occasionally. Serve warm with sausa
and/or fruit.

Yield: 3/4 cup.

FUNNY BONE!
What do you use to mend a broken jack-o'-lantern? A pumpkin patch.

lime fruit slushies

Linda Horst, Newville, Pennsylvania

These frosty drinks have a bright green color and refreshing flavor. Divide the mixture between two plastic containers before freezing. They'll thaw to a nice slushy consistency.

4	cup sugar
1	package (3 ounces) lime gelatin
1	cup boiling water
3	cups cold water
3	cups unsweetened pineapple juice
1	can (6 ounces) frozen orange juice concentrate, thawed
1	liter ginger ale, chilled

In a large container, dissolve sugar and gelatin in boiling water. Stir in the cold water, pineapple juice and orange juice concentrate. Freeze.

Remove from the freezer 1-2 hours before serving. Transfer to a punch bowl; stir in the ginger ale.

ld: 12 servings.

hrunken apple heads in citrus cider

nette Engelbert, Bruce Crossing, Michigan

anny Smith apples shaped like shrunken heads will surprise even the scariest lins at your Halloween bash. And the cool cider is so refreshing.

1	cup lemon juice
1	tablespoon salt
4	large Granny Smith apples
16	whole cloves
1	gallon apple cider
1	can (12 ounces) frozen lemonade concentrate, thawed

In a small bowl, combine lemon juice and salt; set aside. Peel apples. Cut each apple from the stem to the blossom end; discard seeds and core. Using a sharp knife, carefully carve a face on the rounded side of each apple half. After carving, dip each apple in lemon juice mixture for 1 minute. Drain on paper towels.

Arrange apple heads on a rack in a shallow baking pan. Bake at 250° for 2 hours or until apples begin to dry and shrink and are lightly browned on the edges. Cool on a wire rack. Insert cloves for eyes. Store in the refrigerator.

Just before serving, combine cider and lemonade in a punch bowl. Float shrunken apple heads in cider.

eld: 4 apple heads and about 1 gallon cider.

SNACKS & BEVERAGES

festive cranberry drink

Dixie Terry, Goreville, Illinois
Served hot or cold, this cranberry drink is so delicious. I found the recipe in my late mother-in-law's collection, handwritten, probably by one of her woman's club friends.

4	cups fresh *or* frozen cranberries
3	quarts water, *divided*
1-3/4	cups sugar
1	cup orange juice
2/3	cup lemon juice
1/2	cup red-hot candies
12	whole cloves

1 In a Dutch oven or large kettle, combine cranberries and 1 qt. water. Cook over medium heat until the berries pop, about 15 minutes. Remove from the heat. Strain through a fine strainer, pressing mixture with a spoon; discard skins. Return cranberry pulp and juice to the pan.

2 Stir in the sugar, juices, red-hots and remaining water. Place cloves on a double thickness of cheesecloth. Bring up corners of cloth and tie with kitchen string to form a bag; add to juice mixture. Bring to a boil; cook and stir until sugar and red-hots are dissolved.

3 Remove from the heat. Strain through a fine mesh sieve or cheesecloth. Discard spice bag. Serve drink warm or cold.

Yield: 3 quarts.

mummy man cheese spread

Rebecca Eremich, Barberton, Ohio
My annual Halloween bash wouldn't be the same without the now famous Mummy Man. When kids first see Mummy Man, they wonder if they can actually eat him. I assure them they can, and we hack off a foot or an arm with some crackers.

2	port wine cheese logs (12 ounces *each*
1	package (8 ounces) cream cheese, softened
1	tablespoon milk
2	whole peppercorns
1	pimiento strip

1 Cut cheese logs into pieces for mumm head, body, arms and legs; arrange on a se ing plate.

2 In small mixing bowl, beat cream cheese milk. Cut a small hole in the corner of a p try or plastic bag; insert basket weave #47. Pipe rows across the mummy, creat bandages. Add peppercorns for eyes pimiento strip for mouth. Chill until servi

Yield: 24 servings.

slow cooker mexican dip

Heather Courtney, Ames, Iowa

My husband, Jamie, and I love to entertain, and this hearty, 7-ingredient dip is always a hit...as well as a request. It couldn't be much easier to put together, and using our slow cooker leaves us free to share some quality time with our guests. After all, isn't that the purpose of a party?

2	pounds ground beef
1	pound bulk hot Italian sausage
1	cup chopped onion
1	package (8.8 ounces) ready-to-serve Spanish rice
1	can (16 ounces) refried beans
1	can (10 ounces) enchilada sauce
1	pound process cheese (Velveeta), cubed
1	package tortilla chip scoops

1 In a Dutch oven, cook the beef, sausage and onion over medium heat until meat is no longer pink; drain. Heat rice according to the package directions.

2 In a 3-qt. slow cooker, combine the meat mixture, rice, beans, enchilada sauce and cheese. Cover and cook on low for 1-1/2 to 2 hours or until cheese is melted. Serve with tortilla scoops.

Yield: 8 cups.

parmesan party mix

Karen Smith, Thornton, Colorado

This is our favorite mix. The combination of seasonings gives it just the right flavor, and it's a snap to toss together.

7	cups Crispix
2	cups cheese-flavored snack crackers
1	cup pretzel sticks
3	tablespoons olive oil
1	teaspoon Italian seasoning
1/4	teaspoon fennel seed, crushed
1/8	teaspoon hot pepper sauce
1/2	cup grated Parmesan *or* Romano cheese

1 In a 2-gal. resealable plastic bag, combine the cereal, crackers and pretzels. In a small bowl, combine the oil, Italian seasoning, fennel seed and hot pepper sauce. Pour over cereal mixture; seal bag and toss to coat. Add Parmesan or Romano cheese; seal bag and toss to coat. Store in an airtight container.

Yield: 8 cups.

FUNNY BONE!
What is a ghost's favorite brand of automobile? A Boo-ick.

BUFFETS

Your party spread will be unforgettable when you use recipes from this special, Halloween-only chapter. From sweet treats to hearty, savory dishes, you'll find what you need to satisfy your Halloween crowd.

the great pumpkin cakes

Sharon Skildum, Maple Grove, Minnesota

This is the ultimate confectionery tribute to Charlie Brown's Great Pumpkin. These little round cakes are surprisingly easy—they're just two cupcakes put together! Just frost and decorate with vines and leaves. Create a pumpkin patch scene (as shown) by sprinkling crushed chocolate wafer cookies on top of a prepared sheet cake. You'll win raves!

1 package (18-1/4 ounces) yellow cake mix *or* cake mix of your choice

2 cans (16 ounces *each*) vanilla frosting, *divided*

1 to 1-1/2 teaspoons orange paste food coloring

2 green gumdrops

2 teaspoon green paste food coloring

Prepare cupcakes according to package directions. Fill 24 greased muffin cups two-thirds full. Bake at 350° for 15-18 minutes or until a toothpick comes out clean. Cool for 5 minutes before removing from pans to wire racks to cool completely.

2 For frosting, in a small bowl, combine 1-1/2 cans frosting; tint orange. Cut a thin slice off the top of each cupcake. Spread frosting on 12 cupcakes. Invert remaining cupcakes and place on top; frost top and sides.

3 For stems, place one gumdrop on top of each pumpkin.

4 Tint remaining frosting green. Cut a small hole in the corner of a pastry or plastic bag; insert #5 round tip and fill with a third of green frosting. Pipe curly vines from pumpkin stems. Using remaining green frosting and a #352 leaf tip, pipe leaves randomly along the vines.

Yield: 1 dozen.

lloween gelatin cutouts

e of Home Test Kitchen

just love these simple-to-make cutouts. The tion of pudding makes them special, too.

4 packages (3 ounces *each*) orange gelatin

5 cups boiling water, *divided*

4 packages (3 ounces *each*) grape gelatin

2 cups cold milk

2 packages (3.4 ounces *each*) instant vanilla pudding mix

In a large bowl, dissolve orange gelatin in 2-1/2 cups boiling water. In another bowl, dissolve grape gelatin in remaining boiling water; set both aside for 30 minutes.

In a bowl, whisk milk and pudding mixes until smooth, about 1 minute. Quickly pour half of the pudding into each bowl of gelatin; whisk until well blended. Pour into two 13-in. x 9-in. x 2-in. dishes coated with nonstick cooking spray. Chill for 3 hours or until set. Cut with 2-in. Halloween cookie cutters.

d: 4 dozen.

sweet and sour spareribs

Ruth Ann Stelfox, Raymond, Alberta

Just the tempting aroma of these ribs will get your party going. Your guests will especially like the thick, tangy sau

5	to 6 pounds pork spareribs
1/2	cup *each* sugar and packed brown sugar
2	tablespoons cornstarch
1	cup ketchup
2/3	cup cider vinegar
1/2	cup cold water

1 Place ribs on a rack in a large shallow roast
pan. Bake, uncovered, at 350° for 1-1/2 hour

2 Meanwhile, in a small saucepan, combine
sugar, brown sugar, cornstarch, ketchup, v
gar and water until smooth. Bring to a b
Cook and stir for 1-2 minutes or until thicke
Remove ribs and rack from pan. Drain and
card fat. Return ribs to roasting pan; dri:
1-1/2 cups sauce over ribs. Bake 30 minu
longer. Cut ribs into serving-size pieces; br
with remaining sauce.

Yield: 5 to 6 servings.

freaky hand sandwiches

Anna Mowan, Spencerville, Indiana

*Serve your guests these fun sandwiches and they'll be
sure to "hand" out compliments!*

2	cups finely chopped cooked chicken
1	small cucumber, finely chopped
2	hard-cooked eggs, finely chopped

1	celery rib, finely chopped
1/3	cup mayonnaise
1/4	teaspoon salt
1/8	teaspoon *each* ground mustard and white pepper
24	slices thin sandwich bread, crusts remov

Sliced almonds

1	tablespoon spreadable cream cheese

Neon green food coloring

1 In a small bowl, combine the first eight ing
dients. Spread 1/4 cup chicken salad ont
bread slices; top with remaining bread.

2 For fingers, cut each of six sandwiches i
four 3/4-in. strips. With a small knife, trim
end of each strip, forming a point. For fing
nails, attach an almond to each strip wit
dab of cream cheese. With a clean paint bru
paint almond nails with green food coloring

3 From each of the remaining sandwiches, cut
one strip for the thumb and one 2-in. oval for
palm. Trim strips; attach almonds and paint
thumbnails. Arrange one palm, four fingers
a thumb on each plate.

Yield: 6 sandwiches.

FUNNY BONE!

How do you tell twin witches apart? You can't tell which witch is which.

italian vegetable salad

Debbie Laubach, La Prairie, Minnesota

Even our two small children eat their vegetables when I serve this colorful, nutritious combination. To make it a main dish, I'll stir pepperoni slices and cooked cooled pasta into the crunchy, creamy blend.

5	cups fresh broccoli florets (1 large bunch)
5	cups fresh cauliflowerets (1 small head)
4	plum tomatoes, chopped
1	medium cucumber, peeled and sliced
1	medium sweet onion, thinly sliced
1	cup sliced fresh carrots
2	cans (2-1/4 ounces *each*) sliced ripe olives, drained
2	cup pimiento-stuffed olives
1	bottle (8 ounces) Italian salad dressing
1	bottle (8 ounces) creamy Italian salad dressing
2	cups (8 ounces) shredded part-skim mozzarella cheese

1 In a large salad bowl, combine the first eight ingredients. Combine salad dressings; pour over vegetable mixture and toss to coat. Cover and refrigerate for at least 4 hours. Stir in cheese just before serving.

Yield: 14 servings.

Halloween Destinations

Traveling for Halloween? North Carolina seems like a great spot, with Transylvania County, Pumpkin Center, and Cape Fear Township in New Hanover County and Cape Fear Township in Chatham County. If you aren't headed there, try Boneyard or Tombstone, Arizona; Skull Creek, Nebraska; Deadwood, California; Frankenstein, Missouri or River Styx, Ohio.

pumpkin cookie dip

Gloria Kirchman, Eden Prairie, Minnesota

A few moments are all you need to whip up this creamy dip that goes perfectly with store-bought gingersnaps.

1	package (8 ounces) cream cheese, softened
2	jars (7 ounces *each*) marshmallow creme
1	can (15 ounces) solid-pack pumpkin
1	teaspoon ground cinnamon
1	teaspoon grated orange peel

Gingersnaps *or* vanilla wafers

1 In a large mixing bowl, beat the cream cheese and marshmallow creme until smooth. Stir in pumpkin, cinnamon and orange peel. Serve as a dip with cookies. Store in the refrigerator.

Yield: 4 cups.

graveyard veggie pizza

Taste of Home Test Kitchen

*Scare your guests with this delicious, yet good-for-you
addition to your next Halloween party!*

2	cups all-purpose flour
2	teaspoons baking powder
1	teaspoon salt
2/3	cup milk
1/4	cup plus 1 tablespoon vegetable oil, *divided*

TOPPING:

3	cups (24 ounces) cottage cheese
1	envelope ranch salad dressing mix
1/2	cup mayonnaise
1/4	cup milk
2	cups (8 ounces) shredded part-skim mozzarella cheese
1	cup chopped fresh broccoli
1	cup chopped fresh cauliflower
2	cans (2-1/4 ounces *each*) chopped ripe olives
1/2	cup chopped celery
1/3	cup shredded carrot
1/4	cup chopped onion
1	jar (2 ounces) sliced pimientos, drained
1	package (3 ounces) cream cheese, soften
4	teaspoons sour cream
10	to 15 crackers

1 For crust, in a bowl, combine the flour, bak powder and salt. Add milk and 1/4 cup oil; well. Shape into a ball; knead 10 times. C lightly floured surface, roll into a 15-in. x 10 rectangle. Transfer to an ungreased 15-in 10-in. x 1-in. baking pan. Press onto the b tom and up the sides of pan. Prick with fo brush with remaining oil. Bake at 425° for 1: minutes or until edges are lightly brown Cool completely on a wire rack.

2 In a small mixing bowl, combine the cott cheese, ranch dressing mix, mayonnaise milk; spread over crust. Sprinkle with cheese, broccoli, cauliflower, olives, celery, rot, onion and pimientos.

3 For tombstones, in another small mixing bo beat cream cheese and sour cream until flu Place mixture in a resealable plastic bag; c small hole in a corner of bag. Pipe "RIP" o crackers. Insert into pizza. Refrigerate u serving.

Yield: 15 servings.

Some think that the tradition of wearing costumes on this spooky holiday can be traced back hundreds of years to the Europeans and Celts. People feared the long, dark autumn nights and believed that ghosts came back from the dead on Halloween. To avoid being recognized by the ghosts, they wore masks and placed bowls of food outside their doors to keep the ghosts from entering their homes.

As Europeans came to America, they brought their customs with them, but the rigid beliefs of many of the settlers prevented the ideas of Halloween from becoming popular. As time went on, the autumnal celebrations of New England began to blend with the beliefs of the new immigrants. By the 1920s Halloween parades were popular, and by the 1950s, kids were trick-or-treating. Today, it's the second largest commercial holiday!

m 'n' cheese spiders

ra Barclay, De Kalb, Illinois

e creepy sandwiches are sure to scare up some fun alloween time! Kids really enjoy eating the spider-ed sandwiches.

- tube (12 ounces) refrigerated flaky buttermilk biscuits, separated into 10 biscuits
- tube (11 ounces) refrigerated breadsticks, separated into 12 breadsticks
- cup chopped fully cooked ham
- tablespoons finely chopped onion
- tablespoons butter, softened
- teaspoons prepared mustard
- slices process American cheese
- egg yolk
- teaspoon water
- tablespoons sliced ripe olives
- tablespoon diced pimientos
- teaspoon poppy seeds

On two greased baking sheets, pat five biscuits nto 3-1/2-in. circles. Cut one breadstick in half engthwise, then in half widthwise, creating our strips. Repeat nine times (save remaining readsticks for another use). Position eight strips of dough around each biscuit to resemble spider legs; twist and press lightly onto baking heet. Tuck a 1/2-in. foil ball under each dough trip so it stands up in the center.

Combine the ham, onion, butter and mustard; spoon 3 tablespoons onto each biscuit circle. Fold cheese slices into quarters and place over ham mixture. Pat remaining biscuits into 4-in. circles; place over filling. Pinch edges to seal.

3 In a small bowl, beat egg yolk and water. Brush over tops of biscuits and breadsticks. On each spider, position two olive slices for eyes; place pimientos in center of olives. Sprinkle with poppy seeds. Bake at 375° for 15-20 minutes or until browned.

Yield: 5 sandwiches.

FUNNY BONE!
What do birds give out on Halloween night? Tweets.

monkey bread

Carol Allen, McLeansboro, Illinois

When my boys hear I'm planning to make Monkey Bread, they're eager to help. Both boys really enjoy helping me, and it seems to taste twice as good when they've helped fix it. It's one of our favorite snacks.

1	package (3-1/2 ounces) cook-and-serve butterscotch pudding mix
3/4	cup sugar
1	tablespoon ground cinnamon
1/2	cup finely chopped pecans, optional
1/2	cup butter, melted
3	tubes (10 ounces *each*) refrigerated bisc

1 In a large resealable plastic bag, combine pudding mix, sugar, cinnamon and pecans i sired. Pour the butter into a shallow bowl. the biscuits into quarters. Dip several piece to the butter, then place in bag and shak coat.

2 Arrange in a greased 10-in. fluted tube Repeat until all the biscuit pieces are coa Bake at 350° for 30-35 minutes or until brow Cool for 30 minutes before inverting onto a s ing plate.

Yield: 10-12 servings.

mummies on a stick

Taste of Home Test Kitchen

These little hot dogs are all "wrapped-up" in Halloween fun. Kids especially enjoy them!

1	package (11 ounces) refrigerated breadsticks
10	Popsicle sticks
10	hot dogs
Prepared mustard	

1 Separate dough; roll 10 pieces into a 24-in. r Insert sticks into hot dogs. Starting at the s end, wrap one dough rope around each hot leaving 2 in. of the hot dog uncovered at the for the mummy head.

2 Place mummies 1 in. apart on a greased ing sheet. Place remaining breadsticks on other baking sheet. Bake at 350° for 18-20 utes. Add dots of mustard for eyes. Save left breadsticks for another use.

Yield: 10 servings.

FUNNY BONE!
What kind of streets do mummies live on? Dead ends.

weet potato biscuits

en McMann, Blairsville, Georgia

…b from the oven, these biscuits are a perfect complement to a hearty casserole or stew—yum!

2 cups self-rising flour

2 teaspoons brown sugar

3 cup shortening

1 egg

2 cup mashed cooked sweet potatoes
(without added butter or milk)

2 tablespoons milk

In a bowl, combine the flour and brown sugar; cut in shortening until mixture resembles coarse crumbs. In another bowl, combine the egg, sweet potatoes and milk. Stir into crumb mixture just until moistened.

Turn onto a floured surface knead 10-12 times or until smooth. Roll dough to 1/2-in. thickness. Cut with a 2-1/2-in. biscuit cutter; place on an ungreased baking sheet.

Bake at 425° for 10-12 minutes or until bottoms are lightly browned. Serve warm.

d: 10 biscuits.

lloween tuna cheese melts

adine Dirmeyer, Harpster, Ohio

…t and little goblins alike are sure to enjoy these easy, cheesy sandwiches at your next Halloween party.

8 slices light rye bread

1 cup butter, softened

1 can (6 ounces) tuna, drained

2 cup sour cream

2 tablespoons mayonnaise

2 teaspoon garlic salt

4 slices process American cheese

1 thin slice green pepper

With a 2-in. pumpkin-shaped cookie cutter, cut a pumpkin from the center of four slices of bread (discard cutouts or save for another use). Butter one side of bread; place buttered side up on a greased baking sheet. Bake at 425° for 5-8 minutes or until lightly browned.

Butter one side of remaining solid slices of bread. In a bowl, combine the tuna, sour cream, mayonnaise and garlic salt. Spread over unbuttered side of solid bread; top with cheese. Place on baking sheet.

Place cutout bread slices over cheese; press down gently. Cut green pepper into small pieces; place on cheese for pumpkin stems. Bake 5-8 minutes longer or until golden brown.

d: 4 servings.

sweet 'n' savory snack treat

Betty Sitzman, Wray, Colorado

Serve this yummy Halloween mix in colorful snack cups, ice cream cones or in cellophane treat bags. You can use different colored M&M's for other festive parties.

3	cups *each* Wheat Chex; Rice Chex and miniature cheese crackers
1	cup fresh pumpkin seeds, washed and dried
1/4	cup butter
1-1/2	teaspoons seasoned salt
1-1/2	teaspoons Worcestershire sauce
1/4	teaspoon garlic powder
1/4	teaspoon hot pepper sauce
2	cups milk chocolate M&M's

1 In a large bowl, combine the cereal, crackers and pumpkin seeds. In a small saucepan, melt butter. Stir in the seasoned salt, Worcestershire sauce, garlic powder and hot pepper sauce. Drizzle over cereal mixture and toss to coat.

2 Spread into a greased 15-in. x 10-in. x 1-in. baking pan. Bake at 250° for 1 hour, stirring every 15 minutes. Cool completely on a w rack. Transfer to a large bowl; stir in M&l Store in an airtight container.

Yield: 11 cups.

shattered crystal ball

Taste of Home Test Kitchen

Kids love the sweet gelatin and whipped topping dessert from our home economists. Use different flavors of gelatin for color variety. The green and orange colors are perfect for Halloween.

2	packages (3 ounces *each*) lime gelatin
6	cups boiling water, *divided*
2	packages (3 ounces *each*) orange gelatin
2	envelopes unflavored gelatin
1/3	cup cold water
1-1/2	cups white grape juice
1	carton (12 ounces) frozen whipped topping, thawed

1 In a bowl, dissolve the lime gelatin in 3 c boiling water. Pour into an 8-in. square c coated with nonstick cooking spray. In ano bowl, dissolve orange gelatin in remaining k ing water. Pour into another 8-in. square c coated with nonstick cooking spray. Refrige for 4 hours or until very firm.

2 In a small saucepan, sprinkle unflavored g tin over cold water; let stand for 1 minute. grape juice. Heat over low heat, stirring u gelatin is completely dissolved. Pour in large bowl; refrigerate for 45 minutes or u slightly thickened. Fold in whipped toppin

3 Cut green gelatin into 1/2-in. cubes and ange gelatin into 1-in. cubes. Set aside 8 cubes of each color for garnish. Place 2 c whipped topping mixture in a bowl; fold in maining green cubes. Spread into a 13-in. in. x 2-in. dish coated with nonstick cook spray. Fold remaining orange cubes into maining whipped topping mixture; spread c bottom layer. Sprinkle with reserved gr and orange gelatin cubes. Refrigerate f hours or until set. Cut into squares.

Yield: 12-15 servings.

pumpkin bread

Joyce Jackson, Bridgetown, Nova Scotia

This is definitely a deliciously spicy, pumpkin-rich quick bread. I keep my freezer stocked with it.

- 2 cups sugar
- 1 cup canned pumpkin
- 2 cup *each* vegetable oil and water
- 2 eggs
- 3 cups all-purpose flour
- 1 teaspoon *each* baking soda and ground cinnamon
- 4 teaspoon salt
- 2 teaspoon *each* baking powder and ground nutmeg
- 4 teaspoon ground cloves
- 2 cup *each* chopped walnuts and raisins

In a large mixing bowl, combine sugar, pumpkin, oil, water and eggs; beat well. Combine dry ingredients; gradually add to pumpkin mixture and mix well. Stir in nuts and raisins.

2 Pour into a greased 9-in. x 5-in. x 3-in. loaf pan. Bake at 350° for 65-70 minutes or until a toothpick comes out clean. Cool in pan 10 minutes before removing to a wire rack.

Yield: 1 loaf.

x-mex dip with ooky tortilla chips

y Anne McWhirter, Pearland, Texas

e spooky ghost- or pumpkin-shaped chips, with vorful Tex-Mex dip, are perfect for Halloween.

- 0 flour tortillas (8 inches)
- 2 to 1 teaspoon seasoned salt
- 2 cans (9 ounces *each*) bean dip

- 3 medium ripe avocados, peeled
- 2 tablespoons lemon juice
- 1/2 teaspoon salt
- 1/4 teaspoon pepper
- 1 cup (8 ounces) sour cream
- 1/2 cup mayonnaise
- 1 envelope taco seasoning
- 2 cups (8 ounces) shredded cheddar cheese
- 1 cup sliced ripe olives
- 4 green onions, sliced
- 1 large tomato, seeded and chopped

1 Cut tortillas with a ghost- or pumpkin-shaped 3-1/2-in. cookie cutter. Place on baking sheets coated with nonstick cooking spray. Spritz tortillas with nonstick cooking spray; sprinkle with seasoned salt. Bake at 350° for 5-8 minutes or until edges just begin to brown. Remove to wire racks.

2 Spread bean dip onto a 12-in. serving plate. In a bowl, mash avocados with lemon juice, salt and pepper; spread over bean dip. Combine the sour cream, mayonnaise and taco seasoning; spread over avocado layer. Sprinkle with cheese, olives, onions and tomato.

Yield: about 9 cups dip and 5 dozen chips.

FUNNY BONE!
What does a mommy ghost say to her kids when they get in the car? "Fasten your sheet belts."

SWEET TREATS

What would the this spooky season be without sweets? It would be far less fun, that's for sure! Whether you're looking for a school treat or the perfect dessert for a party, you'll find the most creative recipes in these pages.

pumpkin cookie pops

Taste of Home Test Kitchen

These cookie pops from our very own home economists are a great way to liven up a Halloween party. Kids love them. Serve them standing upright in a bowl of candy (as shown at left), or place them flat on pieces of waxed paper all around your Halloween buffet.

/2	cup butter, softened
/4	cup packed brown sugar
/2	cup sugar
1	egg
1	teaspoon vanilla extract
1	cup canned pumpkin
/2	cups all-purpose flour
1	teaspoon baking powder
1	teaspoon baking soda
1	teaspoon ground cinnamon
30	Popsicle sticks
/3	cup green gumdrops, quartered lengthwise

ING:

4	cups confectioners' sugar
/4	cup water

ange and black paste *or* gel food coloring

1 In a mixing bowl, cream butter and sugars. Beat in egg and vanilla. Beat in pumpkin. Combine the flour, baking powder, baking soda and cinnamon; gradually add to creamed mixture (dough will be soft).

2 Drop by rounded tablespoonfuls 2 in. apart onto greased or parchment paper-lined baking sheets. Insert Popsicle sticks into dough. Insert a gumdrop piece into the top of each for stem. Bake at 350° for 14-16 minutes or until set and lightly browned around the edges. Remove to wire racks to cool.

3 For icing, combine confectioners' sugar and water until smooth. Remove 1/2 cup to another bowl; cover and set aside. Stir orange food coloring into remaining icing. Spread or pipe over cookies. Let stand for 30 minutes or until icing is set and dry.

4 Stir black food coloring into reserved icing. Transfer to a heavy-duty resealable plastic bag; cut a small hole in a corner of bag. Pipe icing over cookies to create jack-o'-lantern faces.

Yield: 2-1/2 dozen.

Pumpkin Primer

Pumpkins, which are actually berries, are cousins to melons, cucumbers, squash and gourds. They're not always orange, either. Some varieties are white, blue or green! All pumpkins are native to Central America. They quickly became popular in Europe when explorers "discovered" them in the New World.

ghostly pirate cake

Taste of Home Test Kitchen

This moist white cake is a snap to prepare because it starts with a mix. Have fun decorating it—we sure did!

1	package (18-1/4 ounces) white cake mix
1/2	cup butter, softened
4-1/2	cups confectioners' sugar
5	tablespoons milk
1-1/2	teaspoons vanilla extract

3	red Fruit Roll-Ups, unrolled

Shredded coconut and black food coloring

Assorted candies of your choice: Fruit by the Fo
fruit roll, M&M's, black licorice twists, carame
plain chocolate bar, dark purple Gummi Life
Saver, red-hot candy and gold candy coins

1 Prepare and bake cake according to package
rections, using two greased 9-in. round bak
pans. Cool for 10 minutes before removing fr
pans to cool completely. Cut two pieces fr
the lower edges of each cake, forming a pirat
head (save small pieces for another use).

2 For frosting, in a mixing bowl, beat butter
til creamy. Gradually beat in the confectione
sugar, milk and vanilla until smooth and flu
Place one cake on a serving platter. Spread w
1/2 cup frosting; top with second cake. Spre
top and sides with remaining frosting.

3 For pirate's bandanna, place Fruit Roll-Ups o
top edge of cake. Tint coconut with black fo
coloring; sprinkle over chin for goatee. Decor
pirate's features with assorted candies.

Yield: 10-12 servings.

bloodshot eyeballs

Taste of Home Test Kitchen

Your party guests will be surprised to find that these aren't eyeballs at all—they're peanut butter balls!

2	cups confectioners' sugar, *divided*
1/2	cup creamy peanut butter
3	tablespoons butter, softened
1/2	pound white candy coating

24	brown Reese's pieces *or* milk chocolate M&M's
1	tablespoon water
1/4	to 1/2 teaspoon red food coloring

1 In a small mixing bowl, combine 1 cup confe
tioners' sugar, peanut butter and butter. Sha
into 1-in. balls; place on a waxed paper-lin
pan. Chill for 30 minutes or until firm.

2 In a microwave-safe bowl, melt white can
coating; stir until smooth. Dip balls in coati
and place on waxed paper. Immediately pres
candy onto the top of each eyeball for pupil. L
stand for 30 minutes or until set.

3 In a small bowl, combine the water, food col
ing and remaining confectioners' suga
Transfer to a heavy-duty resealable plastic ba
cut a small hole in a corner of bag. Pipe wa
lines downward from pupil, creating the look
bloodshot eyes. Store in an airtight container

Yield: 2 dozen.

FUNNY BONE!

How do witches keep their hair in place while flying? They use scare spray.

202

carnival caramel apples

Gail Prather, Bethel, Minnesota

*With four kids, we celebrate Halloween in style
around our house. These caramel apples are
a tried-and-true favorite year after year.*

2 cup butter, cubed
2 cups packed brown sugar
1 cup light corn syrup
h salt
1 can (14 ounces) sweetened condensed milk
1 teaspoon vanilla extract
0 to 12 Popsicle sticks
0 to 12 medium tart apples, washed and
   dried
1 cup salted peanuts, chopped

In a large heavy saucepan, melt butter; add
the brown sugar, corn syrup and salt. Cook
and stir over medium heat until mixture comes
to a boil, about 10-12 minutes. Stir in milk. Cook
and stir until a candy thermometer reads 248°
(firm-ball stage). Remove from the heat; stir in
vanilla.

2 Insert Popsicle sticks into apples. Dip each apple into hot caramel mixture; turn to coat. Dip bottom of apples into peanuts. Set on greased waxed paper to cool.

Yield: 10-12 apples.

Editor's Note: We recommend that you test your candy thermometer before each use by bringing water to a boil; the thermometer should read 212°. Adjust your recipe temperature up or down based on your test.

hocolate
keleton cookies

Rupple, Keenesburg, Colorado
*these cute treats out for your next ghost and goblin
y and watch them disappear.*

1   cup butter, softened
1   cup sugar
1/2   cup packed brown sugar
1   egg
1   teaspoon vanilla extract
2-3/4 cups all-purpose flour
1/2   cup baking cocoa
1   teaspoon baking soda
1-1/2 cups confectioners' sugar
2   tablespoons milk

1 In a large mixing bowl, cream butter and sugars until light and fluffy. Beat in egg and vanilla. Combine the flour, cocoa and baking soda; gradually add to creamed mixture. Cover and refrigerate for 1-2 hours or until easy to handle.

2 On a lightly floured surface, roll the dough to 1/8-in. thickness. Cut with a floured 3-in. gingerbread boy cookie cutter. Place on greased baking sheets.

3 Bake at 375° for 7-8 minutes or until set. Cool for 1 minute before removing from pans to wire racks to cool completely.

4 For icing, in a small bowl, combine confectioners' sugar and milk until smooth. Cut a small hole in the corner of a resealable plastic bag; fill with icing. Pipe skeleton bones on cookies.

Yield: 3 dozen.

Crazy for Cupcakes!

These little cakes are taking the party world by storm, so this Halloween, don't be caught behind the curve without any on your buffet. All of these treats start with easy-to-make cake mixes and canned frosting, and the home economists in our Test Kitchen made sure that the decorations are simple, too. Get the kids in on the fun by having them add cat whiskers, creepy tombstone "fingers" or even the wart on the witch's nose!

[to]mbstone cupcakes

1   package (18-1/4 ounces) cake mix of your choice

3   cup semisweet chocolate chips

4   Milano cookies

1   can (16 ounces) vanilla frosting

2   cup chocolate wafer crumbs

1   cup chow mein noodles

4   orange gumdrops

3   green gumdrops, cut into small pieces

Prepare and bake cake mix according to package directions for cupcakes; cool completely.

For tombstones, in the microwave, melt chocolate chips. Pipe "RIP" onto cookies; place on waxed paper to dry.

Frost cupcakes; sprinkle with chocolate wafer crumbs. Carefully insert tombstones into cupcakes. Arrange chow mein noodles to resemble fingers. Use gumdrops to make pumpkins; place in front of tombstones. **Yield: 2 dozen.**

[sc]aredy-cat cupcakes

1   package (18-1/4 ounces) cake mix of your choice

1   can (16 ounces) vanilla frosting

[Ora]nge paste food coloring

1   cup chow mein noodles

2   teaspoons sugar

2   teaspoons baking cocoa

8   nacho tortilla chips, broken

[Ass]orted candies: green M&M's, miniature [sem]isweet chocolate chips, black licorice twists [and] shoestring licorice

Prepare and bake cake mix according to package directions for cupcakes; cool completely. Tint vanilla frosting orange. Using a star tip, pipe orange frosting onto cupcakes.

For whiskers, in a small bowl, combine the chow mein noodles, sugar and cocoa; set aside.

3   For cats' ears, insert nacho chips with pointed tips up. Use M&M's and miniature chocolate chips for eyes, pieces of licorice twists for noses and shoestring licorice for mouths. Arrange reserved chow mein noodles on cupcakes for whiskers. **Yield: 2 dozen.**

wicked witch cupcakes

1   package (18-1/4 ounces) cake mix of your choice

1-1/2   cups semisweet chocolate chips

1   tablespoon shortening

24   Bugles

24   chocolate wafers

1   cup chow mein noodles

2   teaspoons sugar

2   teaspoons baking cocoa

1   can (16 ounces) vanilla frosting

Green paste food coloring

1/3   cup miniature marshmallows

Miniature chocolate chips

Assorted candies: black licorice twists, black shoestring licorice and purple Nerds

1   Prepare and bake cake mix according to package directions for cupcakes; cool completely.

2   For witches' hats, in a microwave-safe bowl, melt chocolate chips and shortening; stir until smooth. Dip a Bugle in chocolate, allowing excess to drip off. Position on a chocolate wafer, forming a witch's hat. Place on waxed paper to dry. Repeat with remaining chocolate, Bugles and wafers.

3   For hair, in a small bowl, combine the chow mein noodles, sugar and cocoa; set aside. Tint frosting green; frost cupcakes. Insert brim of witches' hats into cupcakes.

4   For eyes, cut miniature marshmallows in half and pinch slightly; attach miniature chocolate chips with frosting for pupils. Place on cupcakes. Add pieces of licorice twists for noses, shoestring licorice for mouths and Nerds for warts. Arrange reserved chow mein noodles on cupcakes for hair. **Yield: 2 dozen.**

Safety First

Teach your kids these smart practices and they'll have a fun and safe Trick-or-Treat. If possible, always use sidewalks to get from house to house and cross only at street corners. Visit only houses that have a porch light on. Never go into a stranger's house. Carry a flashlight to light the way and bring a watch, too. Be cautious of animals—they're often nervous because of all the commotion. Take masks off when crossing streets and walking from house to house, or better yet, wear face paint (see ideas beginning on page 250). Say "Trick-or-Treat!" and don't forget to say "Thank you!"

Jack-o'-Lantern Origins

Today's jack-o'-lanterns are said to have their origins in Ireland, where people hollowed out turnips and beets and placed candles in them in an attempt to frighten bad spirits. Orange and black are the classic colors of Halloween. Orange represents the bounty of the fall harvest and black represents the darkness of death and the coming winter.

FROSTING:

1/4	cup butter, softened
2	cups confectioners' sugar
1-1/2	teaspoons grated orange peel
	Orange paste food coloring
2	to 4 teaspoons orange juice
1/2	cup chocolate frosting
	Black shoestring licorice
12	black gumdrops

1 In a small mixing bowl, cream butter a brown sugar until light and fluffy. Add e beat well. Beat in the applesauce, vanilla orange peel. Combine the flour, baking pow salt and baking soda; gradually add to creamed mixture. Stir in pecans.

2 Fill paper-lined muffin cups half full. Bak 350° for 20-25 minutes or until a toothp comes out clean. Cool for 10 minutes before moving from pan to a wire rack to cool c pletely.

3 For frosting, in a small mixing bowl, cream l ter and confectioners' sugar. Add orange p food coloring and enough orange juice achieve spreading consistency. Set aside cup orange frosting. Frost cupcakes.

4 Transfer chocolate frosting to a heavy-duty sealable bag; cut a small hole in a corner of l Pipe a circle of chocolate in center of each c cake. Pipe evenly spaced thin concentric cir about 1/4 in. apart. Beginning with the ce circle, gently pull a toothpick through circle ward outer edge. Wipe toothpick clean. Re to complete web pattern.

5 Cut licorice into 2-in. pieces; press eight pi into each gumdrop for legs. Place reserved ange frosting in a heavy-duty resealable k cut a small hole in a corner of the bag. Pipe e on each spider gumdrop. Position on cupca

Yield: 1 dozen.

spiderweb cupcakes

Janis Plourde, Smooth Rock Falls, Ontario
The cupcake batter and frosting contain orange flavors for a special, made-from-scratch taste.

6	tablespoons butter, softened
1	cup packed brown sugar
1	egg
1/2	cup unsweetened applesauce
1	teaspoon vanilla extract
1	teaspoon grated orange peel
1	cup all-purpose flour
1	teaspoon baking powder
1/2	teaspoon salt
1/4	teaspoon baking soda
1/2	cup chopped pecans

FUNNY BONE!
What's Dracula's favorite breed of dog? The bloodhound.

~piderweb brownies

~dy Pichon, Slidell, Louisiana
~ecorate these moist brownies for Halloween, I drizzle a chocolate spiderweb on the white icing.

4   cup butter, cubed
4   squares (1 ounce *each*) unsweetened
    chocolate
2   cups sugar
3   eggs, beaten

1   teaspoon vanilla extract
1   cup all-purpose flour
1   cup chopped pecans *or* walnuts
1   jar (7 ounces) marshmallow creme
1   square (1 ounce) semisweet chocolate

1   In a large saucepan over low heat, stir butter
    and unsweetened chocolate until melted.
    Remove from the heat; stir in sugar. Cool for 10
    minutes. Whisk in eggs and vanilla. Stir in flour
    and nuts. Pour into a greased foil-lined 13-in. x
    9-in. x 2-in. baking pan.

2   Bake at 350° for 25-30 minutes or until a tooth-
    pick inserted near the center comes out clean
    (do not overbake). Immediately drop marshmal-
    low cream by spoonfuls over hot brownies;
    spread evenly. Cool on a wire rack.

3   Lift out of the pan; remove foil. For web decora-
    tion, melt semisweet chocolate and place in a
    small resealable plastic bag. Cut a small hole in
    one corner of the bag; drizzle chocolate over top
    in a spiderweb design. Cut into bars.

Yield: 2 dozen.

~mpkin-shaped rollouts

~garet Hancock, Camp Verde, Arizona
~e cookies have a bit of orange peel added. Yum!

3   cup shortening
4   cup sugar
2   to 1 teaspoon grated orange peel
1   egg
4   teaspoons milk
2   teaspoon vanilla extract
2   cups all-purpose flour
2   teaspoons baking powder
4   teaspoon salt
~OSTING:
2   cup butter, softened
4   cups confectioners' sugar
1   teaspoon vanilla extract
2   teaspoon grated orange peel
2   to 4 tablespoons orange juice
~en and orange food coloring

~n a large mixing bowl, cream the shortening,
~sugar and orange peel until light and fluffy.
~Beat in the egg, milk and vanilla. Combine the
~flour, baking powder and salt; gradually add
~to the creamed mixture.

2   On a lightly floured surface, roll out to 1/4-in.
    thickness. Cut with 2-1/2-in. pumpkin cookie
    cutters dipped in flour. Place 1 in. apart on
    greased baking sheets. Bake at 375° for 6-8 min-
    utes or until lightly browned. Remove to wire
    racks to cool.

3   In a small mixing bowl, combine the butter,
    confectioners' sugar, vanilla, orange peel and
    enough orange juice to achieve spreading con-
    sistency. Remove 1/2 cup frosting; tint green.
    Tint remaining frosting orange. Frost cookies
    with orange frosting; add leaves and vines with
    green frosting.

Yield: about 3-1/2 dozen.

magic wands

Renee Schwebach, Dumont, Minnesota
These fun and colorful magic wands don't take a magician to make. You can change the colors for any theme party, too!

1-1/2	cups vanilla *or* white chips
1	package (10 ounces) pretzel rods

Colored candy stars *or* sprinkles

Colored sugar *or* edible glitter

1. In a microwave, melt chips; stir until smo[o]th. Dip each pretzel rod halfway into melted ch[ips]; shake off excess.

2. Sprinkle with candy stars and colored su[gar]. Place on a wire rack for 15 minutes or until [set]. Store in an airtight container.

Yield: 2 dozen.

halloween mini-cakes

Taste of Home Test Kitchen
These little cakes are sure to please everyone at your Halloween get-together.
Make a double batch, though, because these one- (or two-) bite wonders are sure to be a hit!

1	package (18-1/4 ounces) yellow cake mix
9	cups confectioners' sugar, *divided*
9	tablespoons milk, *divided*
4	tablespoons plus 1 teaspoon light corn syrup, *divided*

Orange and black paste *or* gel food coloring

1. Grease two 13-in. x 9-in. x 2-in. baking pans; line with parchment paper and set aside. Prepare cake batter according to package directions. Pour into prepared pans.

2. Bake at 350° for 20-25 minutes or until a toothpick inserted near the center comes out clean. Cool for 10 minutes. Using parchment paper, remove cakes from pans and invert onto wire racks; carefully peel off parchment paper. Cool completely. Cut one cake into pumpkin shapes and the second cake into ghost shapes using 3-in. cookie cutters dipped in confectioners' sugar. Carefully arrange individual cakes on wire racks over waxed paper.

3. For icing, in each of two large bowls, combine 4 cups confectioners' sugar, 4 tablespoons milk and 2 tablespoons corn syrup until smooth. Tint icing in one bowl orange. Place orange icing in a heavy-duty resealable plastic bag; cut a small hole in a corner of bag. Pipe over top of pumpkin shapes, allowing icing to drape over cake sides. Repeat with white icing and ghost cakes. Let stand for 30 minutes or until icing is set and dry.

4. In a small bowl, combine the remaining con[fec]tioners' sugar, milk and corn syrup. Tint bl[ack]. Pipe faces onto pumpkin and ghost cakes.

Yield: 1-1/2 dozen.

frankenstein cake

Nancy Fresler, Kinde, Michigan

Convenience items like a cake mix and canned frosting make this clever dessert a breeze to prepare. It always elicits oohs and aahs at Halloween parties.

Frankenstein Fact

Mary Shelley spent the stormy summer of 1816 with her poet husband, Percy Byshe Shelley, and their friend, Lord Byron. Both men were already established poets. To pass the time, they came up with a contest—write a ghost story. Mary's story, inspired by a dream, won the contest and became the famous novel Frankenstein.

1 package (18-1/4 ounces) chocolate cake mix

1 package (8 ounces) cream cheese, softened

2 cup sour cream

2 cup sugar

1 egg

2 teaspoon vanilla extract

1 carton (8 ounces) frozen whipped topping, thawed

s green paste food coloring

1 can (16 ounces) chocolate frosting

1 Swiss cake roll *or* Ho Ho

Prepare cake batter according to package directions. Pour into a greased and waxed paper-lined 13-in. x 9-in. x 2-in. baking pan. In a small mixing bowl, beat the cream cheese, sour cream, sugar, egg and vanilla until smooth. Drop by tablespoonfuls about 1 in. apart onto batter.

Bake at 350° for 40-45 minutes or until center is firm when lightly touched. Cool for 10 minutes before removing from pan to a wire rack to cool completely.

3 To make Frankenstein, cut a piece of cake for the head (about 10 in. x 7-3/4 in.) and neck (about 2-1/2 in. x 4-1/2 in.). Cut two pieces for ears (about 2-3/4 in. x 1/2 in.). Save remaining cake for another use. Position head, neck and ears on a covered board.

4 Place 1/4 cup whipped topping in a small bowl; tint dark green with moss green food coloring. Cut a small hole in the corner of a small plastic bag; insert round pastry tip #3 and fill with tinted topping. Set aside.

5 Tint remaining whipped topping moss green. Frost face, neck and ears, building up areas for the forehead, nose and cheeks. With reserved dark green topping, pipe mouth, stitches on neck and forehead, and eyes with pupils.

6 Cut a hole in the corner of a pastry or plastic bag; insert pastry tip #233. Fill with chocolate frosting; pipe hair 1-1/4 in. from top of head to forehead and about 4 in. down sides of head. Cut cake roll in half widthwise; place on each side of neck for bolts. Store in the refrigerator.

Yield: 12-15 servings.

FUNNY BONE!
What do polite skeletons say before eating a meal? Bone appetit!

FALL FARE

When the weather cools and the bounty of the fall harvest is upon us, we crave hearty, warming comfort foods like these. Try one on your family when the autumn winds start to blow, and you'll be sure to win compliments.

rvest vegetable bake

t Weisser, Seattle, Washington

delicious dish is packed with a large assortment of
ables. Served with a green salad, it makes an
lent entree in the autumn months.

2-1/2	to 3 pounds skinless chicken thighs
2	bay leaves
4	small red potatoes, cut into 1-inch pieces
4	small onions, quartered
4	small carrots, cut into 2-inch pieces
2	celery ribs, cut into 2-inch pieces
2	small turnips, peeled and cut into 1-inch pieces
1	medium green pepper, cut into 1-inch pieces
12	small fresh mushrooms
2	teaspoons salt
1	teaspoon dried rosemary, crushed
1/2	teaspoon pepper
1	can (14-1/2 ounces) diced tomatoes, undrained

1 Place chicken in a greased 13-in. x 9-in. x 2-in. baking dish; add bay leaves. Top with the potatoes, onions, carrots, celery, turnips, green pepper and mushrooms. Sprinkle with salt, rosemary and pepper. Pour tomatoes over all.

2 Cover and bake at 375° for 1-1/2 hours or until chicken juices run clear and vegetables are tender. Discard bay leaves before serving.

Yield: 6-8 servings.

iced pot roast

n Martin, Big Cabin, Oklahoma

pour these ingredients over your pot roast and let the slow cooker do the work. Herbs and spices give the beef
ccellent taste. I often serve this roast over noodles or with mashed potatoes, using the juices as a gravy.

	boneless beef chuck roast (2-1/2 pounds)
	medium onion, chopped
	can (14-1/2 ounces) diced tomatoes, undrained
	cup white vinegar
	tablespoons tomato puree
	teaspoons Dijon mustard
	teaspoon lemon juice
2	teaspoons poppy seeds
	garlic cloves, minced
	teaspoons sugar
	teaspoon *each* ground ginger, salt and dried rosemary (crushed)
	teaspoon *each* ground turmeric and cumin
	teaspoon crushed red pepper flakes
	teaspoon ground cloves
	bay leaf
	cooked noodles

Place roast in a 3-qt. slow cooker. In a large bowl, combine the onion, tomatoes, vinegar, tomato puree, mustard, lemon juice and seasonings; pour over roast. Cover and cook on low for 8-9 hours or until meat is tender. Discard bay leaf. Thicken cooking juices if desired. Serve over noodles.

Yield: 6-8 servings.

turkey hash

Edna Hoffman, Hebron, Indiana
This mild-tasting dish comes highly recommended by my family, and it's a good use for leftover turkey, too.

1	medium onion, chopped
1/2	cup chopped green pepper
1/2	cup chopped sweet red pepper
2	tablespoons butter
6	cups diced cooked potatoes
2	cups cubed cooked turkey
1/2	teaspoon salt, optional
1/8	teaspoon cayenne pepper
1/8	teaspoon ground nutmeg

1 In a skillet, saute onion and peppers in butter until tender. Add the potatoes, turkey, salt if desired, cayenne and nutmeg. Cook and stir over low heat for 20 minutes or until lightly browned and heated through.

Yield: 8 servings.

golden harvest cookies

Florence Pope, Denver, Colorado
Folks may be skeptical when you tell them the ingredients in these cookies. But what a tantalizing treat for the taste buds! These unique cookies are just slightly sweet and great for fall.

2/3	cup butter, softened
1/3	cup packed brown sugar
1	egg
1	teaspoon vanilla extract
3/4	cup self-rising flour
1	teaspoon ground cinnamon
1/8	teaspoon ground cloves
1-1/2	cups quick-cooking oats
1	cup shredded carrots
1	cup (4 ounces) shredded cheddar cheese
1	cup chopped pecans
1/2	cup raisins

1 In a large mixing bowl, cream butter and br॑ sugar until light and fluffy. Beat in egg vanilla. Combine the flour, cinnamon cloves; gradually add to the creamed mixt॑ Stir in remaining ingredients.

2 Drop by heaping tablespoonfuls 2 in. apart to ungreased baking sheets. Bake at 375॑ 12-14 minutes or until golden brown. Remo॑ wire racks to cool. Store in the refrigerator.

Yield: 3-1/2 dozen.

southwestern stew

Virginia Price, Cheyene, Wyoming
Slow-cooking allows the flavors in this recipe to blend beautifully. It's perfect for either before or after trick-or-treating.

2 pounds boneless pork, cut into 1/2-inch cubes
2 tablespoons vegetable oil
1 medium onion, chopped
1 can (15-1/2 ounces) yellow hominy, drained
1 can (14-1/2 ounces) diced tomatoes, undrained
1 can (4 ounces) chopped green chilies
2 cup water
1 teaspoon chili powder
1 teaspoon garlic powder
1 teaspoon ground cumin
1 teaspoon salt
1 teaspoon pepper

In a large skillet over medium-high heat, brown pork in oil. Add onion and cook for 2 minutes or until tender.

2 Transfer to a 3-qt. slow cooker; add remaining ingredients. Cover and cook on high for 2 hours. Reduce heat to low and cook 4 hours longer.

Yield: 4-6 servings.

crowd chicken casserole

Marna Dunn, Bullhead City, Arizona
If you need to feed a big group, this is the answer! It's full of the creamy, ooey-gooey goodness that will hit the spot on a cool fall day. The potato chips add a kid-friendly crunch, too.

10 cups diced cooked chicken
10 cups chopped celery
2 cups slivered almonds
2 bunches green onions with tops, sliced
2 cans (4 ounces *each*) chopped green chilies
2 cans (2-1/4 ounces *each*) sliced ripe olives, drained
5 cups (20 ounces) shredded cheddar cheese, *divided*
2 cups mayonnaise
2 cups (16 ounces) sour cream
5 cups crushed potato chips

1 In a very large bowl, combine the first six ingredients; add 2 cups cheese. In a small bowl, mix mayonnaise and sour cream; add to chicken mixture and toss to coat.

2 Transfer to two greased 3-qt. baking dishes. Sprinkle with chips and remaining cheese. Bake, uncovered, at 350° for 20-25 minutes or until heated through.

Yield: 2 casseroles (12 servings each).

cheesy tortilla soup

LaVonda Owen, Marlow, Oklahoma

My daughter came up with this dish when trying to duplicate a soup she sampled at a restaurant. I always pass on to her the rave reviews whenever this is served.

1	envelope fajita marinade mix
4	boneless skinless chicken breast halves, diced
2	tablespoons vegetable oil
1/2	cup chopped onion
1/4	cup butter
1/3	cup all-purpose flour
2	cans (14-1/2 ounces *each*) chicken broth
1/3	cup canned diced tomatoes with chilies
1	cup cubed process cheese (Velveeta)
1-1/2	cups (6 ounces) shredded Monterey Jack cheese, *divided*
1-1/2	cups half-and-half cream

Guacamole

1/2	cup shredded cheddar cheese

Tortilla chips

1 Prepare fajita mix according to package directions; add chicken and marinate as directed a large skillet, cook chicken in oil until ju run clear; set aside.

2 In a large saucepan, cook onion in butter u tender. Stir in flour until blended. Gradually in broth. Bring to a boil. Cook and stir for 2 r utes until thickened and bubbly. Add tomat process cheese and 1 cup Monterey Jack; c and stir until cheese is melted. Stir in cream chicken; heat through (do not boil). Spoon bowls. Garnish with guacamole, ched cheese and remaining Monterey Jack che add tortilla chips.

Yield: 8 servings (2 quarts).

sweet potato pineapple bake

Ruth Beers, Larkspur, Colorado

Pineapple turns this hearty casserole into a side dish with a tropical twist. It's sure to be a big hit during the holidays when served along with roasted poultry or a festive baked ham.

3	cups cooked mashed sweet potatoes
1/2	cup *each* sugar and milk
1/4	cup butter, melted
2	eggs, lightly beaten
1	teaspoon vanilla extract

Dash salt

TOPPING:

1/4	cup *each* sugar and all-purpose flour
1	can (8 ounces) crushed pineapple, undrained
1/4	cup butter, melted
2	eggs

1 In a large bowl, combine the first seven ing dients. Pour into a lightly greased 9-in. squ baking dish. Combine the topping ingredie pour over potato mixture.

2 Bake, uncovered, at 350° for 45-50 minute until a knife inserted near the center co out clean.

Yield: 8-10 servings.

ple pizza

da Mowrey, Taylors, South Carolina

*a is a favorite at our house, so when I had some
es to use up, I started searching for an apple pizza
e. I tailored this one to fit my family's tastes.*

- 3 to 3 cups all-purpose flour
- 3 tablespoons sugar
- 1 package (1/4 ounce) active dry yeast
- 2 teaspoon salt
- 2 cup water
- 4 cup milk
- 4 cup butter, cubed

PLE TOPPING:

- 4 cups sliced peeled Granny Smith apples
- 2 tablespoons butter
- 2 cup sugar
- 2 tablespoons all-purpose flour
- 1 teaspoon ground cinnamon

EESE TOPPING:

- 4 ounces cream cheese, softened
- 4 cup packed brown sugar
- 2 tablespoons caramel ice cream topping

STREUSEL:

- 2/3 cup all-purpose flour
- 1/3 cup sugar
- 1/4 cup cold butter

1 In a large mixing bowl, combine 1-1/2 cups flour, sugar, yeast and salt. In a saucepan, heat water, milk and butter to 120°-130°. Add to dry ingredients; beat for 2 minutes. Stir in enough remaining flour to form a firm dough. Turn onto a floured surface; cover and let rest for 15 minutes.

2 Meanwhile, in a large skillet, cook and stir apples in butter over medium heat for 2 minutes. Combine sugar, flour and cinnamon; stir into skillet. Cook 3 minutes longer. Reduce heat to low; cook, uncovered, for 4-6 minutes or until apples are tender, stirring frequently.

3 In a small mixing bowl, combine the cheese topping ingredients. For streusel, in a small bowl, combine flour and sugar; cut in butter until crumbly.

4 Pat dough onto a greased 14-in. pizza pan, building up edges slightly. Spread with cheese topping, then apple topping. Sprinkle with streusel. Bake at 375° for 20-25 minutes or until crust is golden brown. Serve warm or cold.

Yield: 10-12 servings.

FUNNY BONE!
Who won the skeleton beauty contest? No body.

Halloween Trivia

Here's some trivia to impress guests at your next Halloween party:

- *In 2005, Americans spent over $2.5 billion on Halloween decorations, costumes and candy. Wow!*

- *Snickers candy bars top the list of the most popular trick-or-treating candy.*

- *In one year, it is estimated that each American eats 26 pounds of candy, most of it around Halloween.*

- *The fear of Halloween is known as samhainophobia.*

- *Black cats, recognized today for being bad luck, were once thought of as the protectors of witches and guardians of their powers.*

curried lamb stew

Lorna Irving, Holberg, British Columbia
This is without a doubt the yummiest stew I've ever tasted. You can make it ahead and reheat before serving, so it's great for a get-together.

2	pounds lean lamb stew meat, cut into 3/4-inch cubes
4	teaspoons olive oil
1	medium onion, chopped
2	garlic cloves, minced
1	tablespoon curry powder
1	teaspoon salt
1/4	teaspoon pepper
1/8	teaspoon *each* ground coriander, cumin a cinnamon
1/8	teaspoon cayenne pepper
1/4	cup all-purpose flour
1-1/4	cups water
1	cup unsweetened pineapple juice
1	medium tart apple, peeled and chopped
1/4	cup tomato sauce
1/2	cup sour cream

Hot cooked noodles *or* rice, optional

1 In a Dutch oven, brown meat in oil in batche Cook onion and garlic in drippings until onio is tender. Add the curry, salt, pepper, coria der, cumin, cinnamon and cayenne; cook an stir for 2 minutes. Sprinkle with flour; coo and stir for 2-3 minutes. Stir in the wate pineapple juice, apple and tomato sauce.

2 Return meat to Dutch oven. Bring to boil. Reduc heat; cover and simmer for 1 hour or until mea is tender. Remove from the heat. Stir in sou cream. Serve with noodles or rice if desired.

Yield: 6 servings.

FUNNY BONE!
How do young ghosts get to school? They take the ghoul bus.

crunch top ham and potato casserole

Nancy Schmidt, Delhi, California

Hash browns, ham and cheese are what make this a dish that's sure to satisfy. Serve your kids this hearty casserole before they head off trick-or-treating and you'll find that they'll eat a lot less candy!

2	pounds frozen Southern-style hash brown potatoes, thawed
2	cups cubed cooked ham
2	cups (16 ounces) sour cream
1/2	cups (6 ounces) shredded cheddar cheese
1	can (10-3/4 ounces) cream of chicken soup, undiluted
1/2	cup butter, melted
1/3	cup chopped green onions
1/2	teaspoon pepper

TOPPING:

2	cups crushed cornflakes
1/4	cup melted butter

1 In a bowl, combine the first eight ingredients. Transfer to a greased 13-in. x 9-in. x 2-in. baking dish. Combine topping ingredients; sprinkle over top. Bake, uncovered, at 350° for 1 hour or until heated through.

Yield: 10 servings.

corny chili

Arlene Olson, Hoople, North Dakota

This is so delicious and simple that I had to share it. I'm sure busy moms will be just as happy as I am with the taste and time-saving convenience of this pleasant chili.

1	pound ground beef
1	small onion, chopped
1	can (16 ounces) kidney beans, rinsed and drained
2	cans (14-1/2 ounces *each*) diced tomatoes, undrained
1	can (11 ounces) whole kernel corn, drained
3/4	cup picante sauce
1	tablespoon chili powder
1/4	to 1/2 teaspoon garlic powder

Corn chips, sour cream and shredded cheddar cheese, optional

1 In a large skillet, cook beef and onion over medium heat until meat is no longer pink; drain.

2 Transfer to a 3-qt. slow cooker. Stir in the beans, tomatoes, corn, picante sauce, chili powder and garlic powder. Cover and cook on low for 3-4 hours or until heated through. Serve with corn chips, sour cream and cheese if desired.

Yield: 4-6 servings.

simple sausage ring

Jean Wilkins, Cabot, Arkansas

I received this recipe from our son, who fixed it for the family one Saturday morning. We were all pleased.

1	pound bulk pork sausage
2	tubes (12 ounces *each*) refrigerated biscuits
2	cups (8 ounces) shredded Monterey Jack cheese

1 In a skillet, cook sausage over medium heat until no longer pink; drain and set aside.

2 Flatten each biscuit to a 3-in. diameter. Press half of the biscuits onto the bottom and 2 in. up the sides of a greased 10-in. fluted tube pan. Spoon sausage over dough; sprinkle with cheese. Top with remaining biscuits.

3 Bake at 350° for 20-25 minutes or until golden brown. Let stand 10 minutes before inverting onto a serving plate.

Yield: 8-10 servings.

apple butter pumpkin pie

Edna Hoffman, Hebron, Indiana

The addition of apple butter gives this pumpkin pie a slightly fruity flavor for a special variation of the classic dessert.

3	eggs
1	cup canned pumpkin
1	cup apple butter
3/4	cup packed brown sugar
1	can (5 ounces) evaporated milk
1/3	cup milk
1	teaspoon vanilla extract
1/2	teaspoon salt
1/2	teaspoon ground cinnamon
1/8	teaspoon *each* ground ginger, cloves an nutmeg
1	unbaked pastry shell (9 inches)

Whipped cream, optional

1 In a bowl, combine first seven ingredient Whisk in the salt and spices until well blend ed. Pour into pastry shell.

2 Bake at 400° for 50-55 minutes or until a knif inserted near the center comes out clear Cover edges loosely with foil during th last 20 minutes if necessary. Cool on wir rack. Garnish with whipped cream if desirec Refrigerate leftovers.

Yield: 6-8 servings.

[ca]ramel apple crisp

[Mich]elle Brooks, Clarkston, Michigan

[Whe]n my children and I make this scrumptious layered dessert at home, we use a variety of apples to give it a nice [com]bination of flavors.

3	cups old-fashioned oats
2	cups all-purpose flour
2	cups packed brown sugar
1	teaspoon ground cinnamon
1	cup cold butter
3	cups thinly sliced peeled tart apples
1	package (14 ounces) caramels, halved
1	cup apple cider, *divided*

In a large bowl, combine the oats, flour, brown sugar and cinnamon; cut in butter until crumbly. Press half of the mixture into a greased 13-in. x 9-in. x 2-in. baking dish. Layer with half of the apples, caramels and 1 cup oat mixture. Repeat layers. Pour 1/2 cup cider over top.

Bake, uncovered, at 350° for 30 minutes. Drizzle with remaining cider; bake 15-20 minutes longer or until apples are tender.

[Yiel]d: 12-14 servings.

[g]row-together short ribs

[Son]ya Asiff, Delburne, Alberta

[This] recipe takes no time to prepare and results in [the m]ost delicious, fall-off-the-bone short ribs. [The l]onger you cook them, the better they get! [Serv]e them on a bed of rice.

1/3	cup water
1/4	cup tomato paste
3	tablespoons brown sugar
1	tablespoon prepared mustard
2	teaspoons seasoned salt
2	teaspoons cider vinegar
1	teaspoon Worcestershire sauce
1	teaspoon beef bouillon granules
2	pounds beef short ribs
1	small tomato, chopped
1	small onion, chopped
1	tablespoon cornstarch
1	tablespoon cold water

1 In a 3-qt. slow cooker, combine the first eight ingredients. Add the ribs, tomato and onion. Cover and cook on low for 4-5 hours or until meat is tender.

2 In a small bowl, combine cornstarch and cold water until smooth; gradually stir into cooking juices. Cover and cook for 10-15 minutes or until thickened.

Yield: 4-5 servings.

FUNNY BONE!
What do ghosts and goblins serve for dessert? Ice scream.

PARTIES

Want to throw a special Halloween bash this year? Whether you want to entertain the kids or adults (or both), there's a party plan for you. There are even menu suggestions, themed games and tips from the experts to make your spooky-season get-together unforgettable!

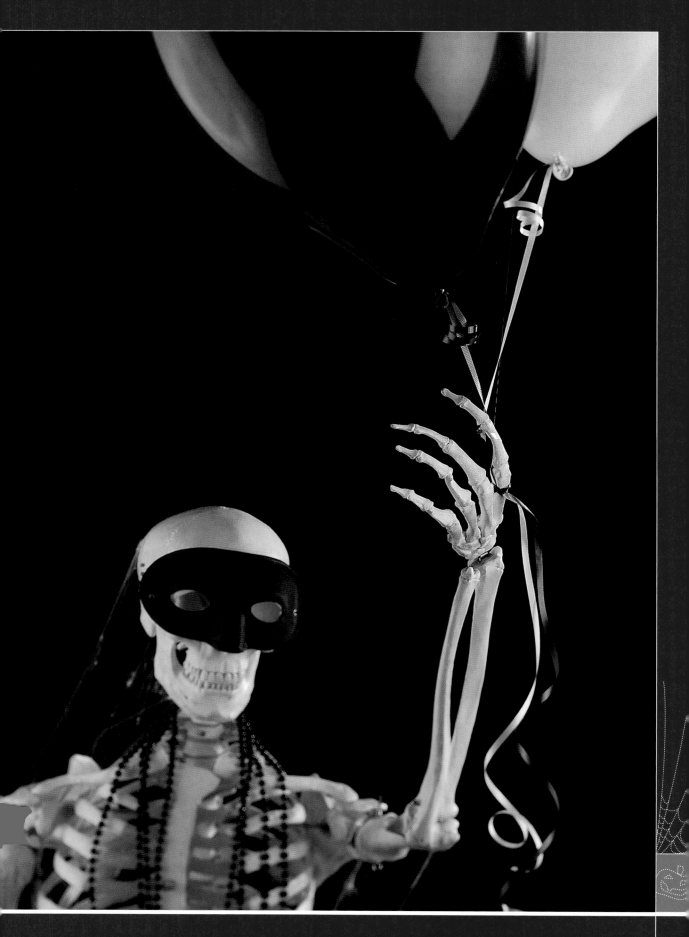

Haunted House Party

Pull out all the scary stops for kids of all ages. Turn your house into a mysterious place where anything can—and probably will—happen. This party is all about atmosphere. You don't need formal activities (kids often entertain themselves!), just a terrific environment for spooky fun.

WHAT YOU'LL NEED

For the most creative Halloween decor, look to our Crafts and Decorations chapter on pages 228-247 for lots of fun ideas, and also think in terms of the following:

Lighting:

You want things dark, but not so dark that people can't see and safety becomes an issue. Colored lights, black lights and creative use of spotlights can all be used to create the right mood.

Surprises:

Follow some of these simple tricks to create smiles and chills.

- Fake bats hanging from the ceiling
- A Frankenstein sitting at the buffet table
- Spiderwebs and black cat cutouts on walls and windows
- White sheets draped over the furniture
- Funny signs and tombstones along the walls
- Ghostly (gray, off-white and black) helium balloons with plastic spiders tied to the end of the ribbon

Space:

While people are often hesitant to dance in public, the combination of costumes, crazy lighting and surprise music may loosen up even the shyest partygoer. So have a room for dancing and a room for sitting and relaxing as well. Yes, you want fun and commotion, but also places where people can escape for a bit to enjoy food and conversation.

For great invitation and party favor ideas, see pages 234-235.

PLAN AHEAD

...tations should be both creative and de-
...ed. Is it a costume party? Will there be
...es? Will there be dancing? Is a meal being
...ed? Are children invited? Are your plans
...y enough that you should offer a warning?

...y or two before the party, have a small pre-
...y in which you, family members and a few
...ds get your space ready. Make your crafts,
...up your rooms, get food ready and test all
...effects. You can pick up inexpensive prizes
...discount store.

...a truly haunted house, you need a few actors.
...nge to have some friends or family members
...on particular roles at the party: Frankenstein
...of course, his bride), a mummy, a witch, a zom-
...nd Count Dracula are some options. Help assem-
...heir costumes, and coach them to stay in char-
...r throughout the first hour of the party. Their job:
...with guests, give simple scares, make funny
...es and set the tone for fun.

...k through sound effects well in advance of the par-
...Ds are available of nothing but eerie sounds; there
...lso many collections of Halloween songs. A quick
...ch on-line will reveal what's available. Do you want
...d effects in different parts of the house? And if you
...on having dancing, what is the best soundtrack
...our friends and family?

menu

Likely, you'll be serving food on a buffet. You want to keep it as simple and as fun as possible. Check out some of the recipes below to get the party started.

SNACKS & BEVERAGES

Hot Spiced Cider, p. 185
Hot 'n' Spicy Cranberry Dip, p. 186
Lime Fruit Slushies, p. 187
Mummy Man Cheese Spread, p. 188
Slow Cooker Mexican Dip. p. 189
Graveyard Veggie Pizza, p. 194

BUFFET MAIN DISHES & SIDES

Sweet and Sour Spareribs, p. 192
Sweet Potato Biscuits, p. 197
Turkey Hash, p. 212
Crowd Chicken Casserole, p. 213
Cheesy Tortilla Soup, p. 214

SWEET TREATS

Pumpkin Cookie Pops, p. 201
Carnival Caramel Apples, p. 203
Chocolate Skeleton Cookies, p. 203
Spiderweb Cupcakes, p. 206
Halloween Mini-cakes, p. 208
Frankenstein Cake, p. 209

SET THE MOOD

Cut a coffin shape from a piece of plywood to use as the serving
table top.

Write "Rest in Peace" on serving trays that look like cemetery slabs. Use
witch cauldrons, skulls and other Halloween containers as serving pieces.

Make a gallery of ghouls (rent or borrow mannequins from a store or stuff clothing
with newspaper): Frankenstein, Dracula, the Headless Horseman, a skeleton or a
mummy are some ideas. Keep the lights low and take guests through the gallery while
eerie music plays.

Ask guests to come as their favorite horror story character and have a prize for the
scariest costume. Of course, they have to tell the story, too!

FUNNY BONE!
What is a vampire's favorite fruit? Neck-tarines.

Scavenger Hunt

In a treasure hunt, you hide the clues or prizes for people to find. A scavenger hunt is different. Each team (usually three to five people) gets a list of objects to gather, and it is up to them to locate the iten

PLAN AHEAD

Invitees need to know exactly what they are getting into well before they arrive at the party. Will they be hiking through the woods? Driving around town? Asking store clerks or waitresses embarrassing questions? Provide the appropriate details in your invitation.

Sometimes it's fun to let neighbors and even retailers into the fun. Arrange in advance for them to hold on to items, but to not give them to the hunters unless they answer a riddle or do something silly.

✚ MAKE MEMORIES

Make it a photo or video scavenger hunt!
Instead of gathering items, require a list of digital shots such as the team singing a song to a policeman or dancing through a restaurant; a stranger spelling "pumpernickel" or putting on a wig; the team standing under a sign with the word "black" in it; and so on. Give them the assignments 48 hours in advance and make the party a viewing party with a buffet dinner.

WHAT YOU'LL NEED

Easy: a list of objects t gather. They can b themed or completel random. Make sure yo have a copy of the iter list, too. See below le for suggestions to ge you started!

Get the permission o your neighbors, particu larly if the scavenge hunt will be on foot. Le them know the types o things everyone will b searching for and discus what limits and rule you intend to share.

You'll need a clear set o rules for participant. What are the boundarie of the search? The time table? Of course, mak it clear that stealing NOT allowed under an circumstances; nor driving unsafely or run ning through anyone hedge or garden.

Don't forget food, drin prizes and a place to r lax when all the team return.

happy haunting

Here are examples of items to include in your scavenger hunt. Be careful in picking them; you want some that are easy to find and some that take ingenuity. Think through the methods people might use for finding the items, estimate the time it will take, and then add an hour to be safe. Better yet, do a dry run yourself! You don't want to find out that your hunt takes 6 hours instead of the 3 you had planned.

- ☐ AAA battery
- ☐ Acorn
- ☐ Apple
- ☐ Black fingernail polish
- ☐ Blood-red lipstick
- ☐ Broom
- ☐ Candy corn
- ☐ Golf ball
- ☐ Gourd
- ☐ Head of garlic
- ☐ Indian corn
- ☐ Lock of black, red or gray hair

- ☐ Map of the U.S.A.
- ☐ Miniature pumpkin
- ☐ Orange sock
- ☐ Pie tin
- ☐ Sewing needle
- ☐ Spider—real or fake
- ☐ Thread
- ☐ Today's newspaper
- ☐ Toothpick
- ☐ Tootsie Roll
- ☐ Whistle

PARTY IDEAS FOR BIG KIDS

BE PREPARED

...are up witch cauldrons, skulls and other Hallo-...een props as serving containers. Serve Roasted ...mpkin Seeds (p. 186) or Parmesan Party Mix ...189) in the creative containers.

...eeze fake bugs in the ice cubes used for party ...nks. Or make Magic Potion Punch (p. 181) or ...runken Apple Heads in Citrus Cider (p. 187).

...e Halloween cookie cutters, such as bats, cats or ...tches, to cut out sandwiches for the buffet. See ...aky Hand Sandwiches (p. 192).

...llect all the black plates, cups and glasses that ...u can find for the party. They'll be readily avail-...le at party stores around Halloween.

...epare all the equipment and special items need-... for the games with a few spares for emergen-...s. Make sure there are prizes!

...phasize costumes as well as games for the par-...Have prizes for the most ghoulish, the wittiest, ...e most dazzling, the best couple's costume or the ...st group costume.

ARE KIDS COMING?

If you have a party that includes both adult guests and children, consider keeping the kids busy so the adults can enjoy themselves, too. Hire a teenage babysitter or two to entertain the kids in a separate room or somewhere on the outskirts of the party. The kids can do inexpensive Halloween crafts, cut and paste construction paper jack-o'-lanterns or scarecrows, play games (see p. 227) or just color in Halloween coloring books. The adults will thank you, and the kids will have a great time, too!

MONSTER PARTY. Decorate your yard and house with signs of a monster. Create huge footprints from the street to the front door. Some doormats are shaped like footprints, and you could use them to make the monster's path or cut the prints out of foam sheets. Set a place for him at the table with a giant place mat, a straight-sided glass vase as a drinking glass and a barbecue fork, butcher knife and large serving spoon for cutlery. His plate can be a large, round tray and his soup bowl, a tureen. Pipe a loud voice down from the attic or up from the basement. Have guests dress as monsters; the scariest gets a prize.

HALLOWEEN BARN DANCE. It's the right time of year for bales of straw for seats, pumpkins and corn stalks for decorations, and country music for getting your feet going. Join with friends to rent a hall and hire a trio of musicians and a caller to get the dancing started. With a caller, even beginners can twirl like pros. Serve cider, beer and chili and have a ball. Friends can bring appetizers, too.

DAY OF THE DEAD PARTY. This November 1 Mexican holiday honors the cycle of life and death. It welcomes deceased ancestors for a yearly visit and uses skeleton-shaped foods, not to scare the living but to celebrate the dead. Serve a mole—a chicken stew with chocolate, bread of the dead shaped like a skeleton, and spicy hot chocolate with cinnamon for a drink.

HAYRIDE PARTY. An increasing number of farms have gotten into the Halloween spirit by offering hayrides, cornfield mazes, pumpkin patches, even hay-bale courses for kids to ride tricycles through. Find a farm in your area that has autumn activities and have a great day with your children and their best friends.

6 Games for BIG Kids

1 **MUMMY WRAP.** Divide guests up in pairs; give each pair a roll of toilet paper. One team member will be the wrapper, the other will be the mummy. The first team to use up its roll wins. Or you can give each team two rolls of toilet paper and after the mummy is wrapped, he or she must wrap his partner.

2 **IDENTIFY WHAT YOU FEEL.** This is a favorite game from childhood but the big kids still like it. Line up five opaque plastic dishes and cover them all with a black cloth. Let each guest stick a hand in each dish, under the cloth so that the contents can't be seen, and try to guess what it really is. You can tell the guest that the first dish holds eyeballs (really peeled grapes) and see what he or she guesses. The second dish is said to hold brains (damp coarse sponge). The third is said to hold veins (cold, cooked spaghetti). The fourth is said to hold cut-off fingers (cocktail sausages) and the fifth to hold skin (pieces of a soft flour tortilla). The person who guesses the most actual contents wins.

3 **APPLE PASS.** Divide guests into teams and line each team up. The first in line for each team is given an apple under his or her chin. Without using any hands, the apple must be passed to under the second team member's chin and from that chin to the next until all the members of the team have held the apple. If the apple drops, it must start at the beginning again. The first team to successfully pass the apple down its row of members wins.

4 **BOBBING FOR APPLES.** This is probably the oldest Halloween game on record. Fill a large tub with cold water and set it on the ground or the floor of a porch. Float some clean, stemmed apples in the tub and invite guests to try to catch an apple with their teeth—no hands allowed. Anyone who gets an apple deserves a prize.

5 **DOUGHNUT RACE.** Divide guests into teams. Hang as many doughnuts as guests from a tree limb or a clothesline by string. Without using hands, each guest must catch and eat a doughnut. The first team to finish its doughnuts wins.

6 **WHAT AM I?** Pin or tape Halloween-themed pictures on each guest's back (without the guest seeing what it is). While others can only give yes or no answers, each guest must guess what he or she is.

⑥ Games for Young Children

THE HANGING TREE. In the original game, there were 12 red apples and 1 green apple to match a poem said while spinning the children around. For a small group of children, you don't need so many. Hang the apples by long strings from a tree branch (by twisting the strings you disguise where the green apple is). For each child's turn, blindfold him or her, untwist the apples, and set the youngster toward the branch. If he or she picks the green apple, he or she wins a prize (and the apple). Put up a new green apple and give another child a turn.

PASS THE PUMPKIN. Have one fewer small pumpkins than players. Sit youngsters in a circle. Play Halloween music while they pass the pumpkins around the circle. When the music stops, the player without a pumpkin is out, but he gets to take a pumpkin with him. The rest of the players continue to play until there is a winner, who will get a prize. Make Pumpkin Cookie Pops (p. 201) to set the mood.

BALLOON SWEEP RELAY RACE. Set up a course that zigzags across the yard or playroom. Use colored rope tied to stakes (or chairs) to mark it. Divide the guests into two teams. Give each team a small broom and a blown-up balloon. Each member of a team must sweep the balloon around the course and back before the next member goes. The team to have every member finish the course first wins.

PIN THE TAIL ON THE BLACK CAT. Hang up a large picture of a black Halloween cat without its tail. Give each guest a tail with a piece of sticky tape on its base. One by one, blindfold the guests, turn them around, and then set them off toward the cat picture and see where they put the tail. The guest who gets the tail closest to its rightful place wins. A Halloween ornament (pp. 230-231) makes a perfect prize.

HALLOWEEN STORY GAME. Include the beginning of a ghost story in your party invitations and ask each child to come to the party with an ending to tell. Hear all the endings and let the guests vote for the funniest, the weirdest and the spookiest, then hand out paper and markers and ask the kids to illustrate their stories. Give prizes for the most creative illustration, too.

BUILD A SCARECROW. Divide the guests into teams. Give each team a pile of old clothes (including hats), pillowcases for heads, newspapers for stuffing, ropes for tying, and markers for making faces. Give each team 15 minutes or 20 minutes to make a scarecrow. Give prizes for the silliest and the scariest and hang them outside or let the kids take them home as a special party favor.

PREPARE FOR A KIDS PARTY

- Send invitations that are colorful and enticing for the kids, but that also give thorough details to the parents. Make it clear if it is to be a costume party; whether kids need sneakers; whether a full meal, snacks or cake will be served; and if kids need to bring anything, like a gift or a trick-or-treat bag.

- Figure out a short parade route for the guests when all have arrived so that they—and you—can appreciate their costumes.

- Plan the games for outdoors if the weather is nice, but have a backup plan for the playroom or some other part of the house if the weather fades.

- To keep things happy, try to keep the number of guests fewer than the years in your child's age.

- Substitute craft projects for some of the games, such as painting small pumpkins with acrylics or decorating inexpensive masks with feathers, sequins, glitter and other notions.

- Have a teacher or performer come in costume and read a short ghost story. Check your local library for likely candidates.

- Don't plan to do everything yourself. Enlist a spouse or family friend or hire some older children to help.

Crafts & Decor

Here, you'll find new takes on the classic Halloween crafts, like far-out jack-o'-lanterns and unique candy wrappers, but you'll also find creative twists on the traditional, like Halloween ornaments. Enjoy this spooky season making these simple, attractive, BOO-rific crafts.

Halloween Ornaments

Christmas isn't the only holiday you can use ornaments! Hang these from your mantel, in front of a window, or even from a coffee-mug rack!

BASIC SUPPLIES

Cardboard form *or* circle cut out from thick cardboard

Pencil

White paper

Scissors

White glue

Large needle *or* compass point

Liquid beads (beads floating in a glue-like gel medium) *or* microbeads (tiny plastic beads) and tacky glue in colors of your choice, see options for individual ornaments

Glittery string or thread

Jack-o'-Lantern Ornament

EXTRA SUPPLIES:

Black craft paint

Orange liquid beads or microbeads

Small, star-shaped stickers
(we used glow-in-the-dark ones)

1 To make a form, cut a circle shape out of th cardboard. Paint it black.

2 Using a pencil, draw a pumpkin face onto a p of paper at a size that will fit your ornament fo Cut it out and glue it to the form.

3 Use a large needle or compass point to pu small hole at the top of the form. Thread the tery string through the hole, estimate how m room you'll need for hanging and tie ends secure knot or bow.

4 If using liquid beads, apply them to the pump Use different colors to depict the carved a of the pumpkin.

5 If using microbeads, coat the pumpkin area tacky glue and pour orange microbeads onto glue. Carefully apply tacky glue to carved ar Slowly add dark microbeads to these ar taking care to avoid dropping beads orange sections. Gently tap off exc beads after the glue has dried.

6 Add stickers to the border if des We used glow-in-the-dark stic for extra fun!

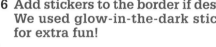

~~S~~pooky Witch Ornament

~~EXT~~RA SUPPLIES:

- ~~colo~~red construction paper of your choice
- ~~liq~~uid beads or microbeads in colors ~~of y~~our choice

~~1~~ Follow step #1 from Pumpkin Ornament.

~~2~~ Photocopy a drawing of a witch, ghost, ~~s~~kull-and-crossbones or any other Halloween image on colored paper at a size that will fit your ornament. (We

copied our pumpkin carving template for the witch from page 242.) Cut it out. Glue it to the form.

3 Follow step #3 from Pumpkin Ornament.

4 If using liquid beads, apply them to the background around image. If using microbeads, coat the background area with tacky glue and pour microbeads onto the glue. Gently tap off excess beads after the glue has dried.

~~S~~pider Ornament

~~EXT~~RA SUPPLIES:

- ~~ora~~nge and black craft paint
- ~~2~~ oval-shaped gemstones
- ~~whi~~te glossy or 3-D paint
- ~~ora~~nge glitter glue

~~1~~ Follow steps #1 and #3 from ~~P~~umpkin Ornament, but do ~~n~~ot paint black.

~~2~~ Paint the entire surface of ~~c~~ardboard form with orange ~~p~~aint. When it's dry, use a ~~p~~encil to draw the spider and ~~i~~ts web.

~~3~~ Use black paint to fill in the spider and ~~its~~ legs. When it's dry, add tacky glue to the back ~~of~~ gemstones and position them on the spider.

~~4~~ Trace over the webbing lines with white paint. ~~A~~dd dots of glitter glue to intersections of the ~~w~~ebbing and to spider legs.

~~B~~at Ornament

~~EXT~~RA SUPPLIES:

- ~~rou~~nd gemstone
- ~~liqu~~id beads or microbeads in colors of your choice
- ~~pale~~tte knife or flexible plastic knife
- ~~seq~~uins in colors of your choice
- ~~ora~~nge and white craft paint
- ~~glit~~ter glue in colors of your choice

~~1~~ Follow steps #1 and #3 from Pumpkin Ornament, but do not paint black.

~~2~~ Using a pencil, draw an outline of a bat and ~~a~~ moon (the same size as gemstone).

~~3~~ If using liquid beads, apply them directly to the

background areas using a palette or plastic knife. If using microbeads, coat background area with tacky glue and pour microbeads onto the glue. Gently tap off excess beads after a few minutes.

4 Fill in the bat shape with tacky glue. Stack sequins into glue, beginning at the bottom of the wing and working upward.

5 Add two orange dots with orange paint for eyes. Allow to dry.

6 Glue gemstone into moon outline.

7 Use a dry brush and white paint to lightly apply highlights to ridges of the wings. Outline the bat figure and moon with glitter glue. Let dry.

Paper-Wrapped Vase

Top off your spooky decor with a few of these fun vases. They're easy to make, and you probably have the materials on hand.

1	12-inch x 12-inch piece of scrapbook *or* parchment paper
1	cylinder vase

Halloween stamps *or* motifs

Double-stick tape

Ribbon

Tea light *or* plumber's candle

Shallow bowl

Colored popcorn *or* Indian corn

1 Trim a 12-inch x 12-inch piece of scrapbook or parchment paper as needed to fit the outside of a clear glass cylinder vase.

2 Stamp or paste Halloween motifs around the top edge of the parchment paper as shown in photo.

3 Wrap the paper around a clear glass cylinder vase with the design at the top and secure it with double-stick tape.

4 Tie a coordinating narrow ribbon around the vase below stamped area.

5 Place a tea light or plumber's candle inside the vase.

6 Stand the vase in a shallow bowl filled with colored popcorn or Indian corn.

Halloween Movie Night

Grab the kids, turn off the lights, get into the Halloween spirit, but (thankfully) don't scare them out of their wits! Here is a collection of recommended Halloween and fantasy movies that will enhance the mood of the spooky season but won't give the kids nightmares.

For very young children:

• *Bedknobs and Broomsticks (1971—an oldie but a goodie)*

• *It's the Great Pumpkin, Charlie Brown (1966—the classic Halloween story)*

• *Mickey's House of Villains (2002)*

• *Pooh's Heffalump Halloween Movie (2005)*

For school-age children:

• *Scary Godmother Halloween Spooktacular (2003)*

• *The Corpse Bride (2005)*

• *The Nightmare Before Christmas (1993)*

• *The Simpson Trick or Treehouse (2000)*

• *Worst Witch: A Mean Halloween (2001)*

String of Paper Lanterns

re up some ambience at your next Halloween
y with these lanterns. You can use any stamp
gn you'd like. Leave them up all season—
're so cute and fun!

- hment paper
- orative edge scissors
- ight-edge scissors
- inch round paper punch
- oween stamps *or* motifs
- g of orange mini-lights
- ble-stick tape

For each lantern, trace pattern at right onto
parchment paper.

Use decorative-edge scissors and straight-edge
scissors to cut out lantern from parchment paper as shown.

Use a 1/4-inch round paper punch or a straight-
edge scissors to cut out a small circle where
shown on pattern.

Stamp a Halloween design onto the cutout.

Wrap paper lantern around an orange mini-
light, overlapping the straight edges. Use double-stick tape to hold the overlapped edges
together.

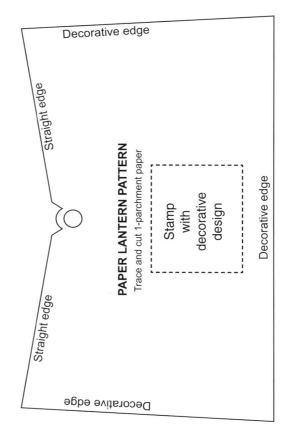

PAPER LANTERN PATTERN
Trace and cut 1-parchment paper

Decorative edge

Straight edge

Stamp with decorative design

Decorative edge

Straight edge

Decorative edge

Halloween Party Invitations

Here at Taste of Home, we all like to get in on crafting fun. Our dedicated Vice President, Executive Editor/Special Interest Publications, Heidi Reuter Lloyd, shares some of her creative, spooky-season party invitations, candy wrappers and scrapbook ideas on the next few pages.

Purchase a set of invitation stamps that contains a "You're Invited" stamp plus a second stamp that includes the date, time, place and occasion. You can use your computer instead of stamps to write the words. A black cat or bat stamp can be substituted for the spider. A patterned ribbon is an inexpensive way to add fun to the card.

9	sheets of 8-1/2 x 11-inch orange cardstock
18	pieces of 2-1/2 x 2-1/2-inch white cardstock
18	pieces of 2-3/4 x 2-3/4-inch black cardstock
1	spider stamp
1	black dye-based ink pad
1	set of invitation stamps
6-1/2	feet of thin decorative black ribbon, cut into 18 segments, 4-1/4 inches long *each*

Double-sided tape *or* Mono-Adhesive

1 Cut each piece of orange cardstock in half lengthwise, creating 18 pieces of 8-1/2 x 5-1/2 inches.

2 Fold each piece in half.

3 Stamp one spider on each piece of white cardstock.

4 Adhere white cardstock to black cardstock.

5 Adhere black cardstock to front of card.

6 Stamp "You're Invited" below spider.

7 Adhere black ribbon below "You're Invited" stamp.

8 Stamp inside of card with a single stamp that includes a line for the date, time, place and occasion.

Images copyright Stampin' Up!

pider-Wrapped Candy

*e easy treats are fun to hand out at classroom
ies or to trick-or-treaters. For the simplest
on, do black stamping on white paper (shown
w left). To dress them up with color, use magic
kers to fill in the spider's eyes and body, then
e eye-catching borders with contrasting
loween colors.*

-)   **mini chocolate bars, such as Hershey Nuggets**
- 2   **sheets of 30 plain white 1 x 2-5/8-inch address labels**
-)   **clear 2 x 3-3/4-inch plastic craft bags**
- te cardstock cut into 30 pieces of 7/8 x 2-1/4 inches
- k cardstock cut into 30 pieces of 1/2 x 4-1/4 inches
- small spider rubber stamp
- large spider rubber stamp
- black dye-based ink pad
- ble-sided tape *or* Mono-Adhesive
- ler
- w, orange, purple and green markers, ptional

With black ink, stamp small spiders lengthwise
on white labels.

Remove outer wrapper from candy bars and
replace with stamped labels.

Place two candy bars in each mini bag.

With black ink, stamp 3 large spiders on each
piece of white cardstock.

Fold each piece of black cardstock in half.

Center white cardstock on black and adhere,
with fold at top.

Place black cardstock around plastic bag and
staple at bottom to hold.

If desired, use markers to color in spiders and/or
add colored borders to edge of white cardstock.

es copyright Stampin' Up!

Halloween Scrapbook Pag

To make a scrapbook page quickly, buy a group of Halloween images and a phrase or two at a craft store. Although this design features a stamped spider and bat, you could easily use another image or two from the self-adhesive Halloween grouping instead.

2	sheets of 8-1/2 x 11-inch orange cardstock
1	sheet of 8-1/2 x 11-inch white cardstock
1	scrap piece of black cardstock
8	black self-adhesive photo corners
2	Halloween snapshots
1	set of Halloween self-adhesive words & images

Spider and bat stamps, optional

1	black dye-based ink pad, optional

8-1/2 inch segment of decorative black ribbon

Double-sided tape *or* Mono-Adhesive

1 Tear white cardstock across top quarter for ragged-edge effect. Adhere smaller white piece to orange cardstock. Save larger white piece for another use.

2 Choose a headline from self-adhesive Ha ween grouping and place on page.

3 Using a computer, write a caption and pri on orange cardstock. Trim around the capt forming a rectangle.

4 Cut a piece of black cardstock that is 1/4-i bigger than the caption rectangle on all sid

5 Adhere caption to black cardstock.

6 Adhere decorative ribbon to bottom quarte page.

7 Position photos on page. Adhere photo cor where needed.

8 Adhere caption rectangle to page.

9 Add art elements from Halloween groupin stamp spider and bat.

Images copyright Stampin' Up!

10 Candle Safety Tips

Never leave a burning candle unattended or even out of your line of sight.

Never place a burning candle on or near anything that can catch fire or where it can be knocked over.

Keep burning candles out of the reach of children and pets.

Use sturdy fireproof holders and containers made specifically for candles.

Trim the wick to 1/4 inch before each use. Extinguish and trim a flickering or high-flaming candle.

Burn candles in a well-ventilated room but away from drafts, vents and fans.

Don't touch or move a burning candle.

Stop using a candle when 2 inches of wax remains (1/2 inch in a container).

Keep matches, wick trimmings and debris out of the candle wax.

Never use a candle as a night-light.

FUNNY BONE!
What does a ghost get when he falls and scrapes his knee? A boo-boo.

Autumn Wreath

If you thought wreaths were only for winter holidays, think again. You can make a wreath that celebra~~ almost any holiday or season, and Halloween is no exception. And if you don't care for elaborate decorations, don't have the time to make them or don't have the space to display them, hanging a Halloween-themed wreath on the door is a subtle and elegant way to pay tribute to the holiday. In the wreath design here, various brightly colored items stand out in contrast to the traditional leaves and nu~~ of autumn. You can find the supplies you need to make a wreath at your local craft store.

rying the leaves

dry the oak, bay and other leaves following
e steps:

ort the leaves into small bunches and remove
ny excess foliage from the lower stems.

n a dry, warm, dark and airy place, either stand
he branches upright in an empty container or
ecure the ends of the stems with string and
uspend them upside down. Let them dry for a
veek or so; the time will depend on the size and
noisture content of the individual pieces.

Making the wreath

1 Attach a length of wire across the back of the wreath base so that you can hang the wreath on a hook like a picture.

2 Start by filling in the background. Push small branches of salal leaves into the base. Intersperse them with oak and bay leaves. Make sure that the top and sides are covered and that the base is concealed. Allow some branches to hang into the center of the circle and some to overhang the outside edge. Once you are happy with the arrangement, glue the leaves into place using the hot glue gun.

3 Glue small groups of pinecones and Halloween items randomly around the wreath. If some of the Halloween items are too awkwardly shaped to glue, secure them with wire in the next step. Make sure that some of the groups are toward the inner side, some are on top, and some are toward the outer edge. Be sure to glue the pinecones and Halloween items to the base, not to the leaves. Turn the wreath as you work to ensure a balanced result.

4 Place groups of wired nuts close to the cones and fix them in place by pushing the wires through the vine base and twisting the wire around the vine at the back. Arrange the poppy seed heads, fanning them out around the cone groups, and when you are pleased with the result, glue them into place. Let the glue dry and hang on your door.

*To wire a nut, stand the nut on end in play clay and drill a small hole using a drill with a fine bit. Push a short length of thin wire through the hole.

FUNNY BONE!
What do you get when you divide the circumference of a jack-o'-lantern by its diameter? Pumpkin pi.

10 Tips for Perfect Jack-o'-Lanterns

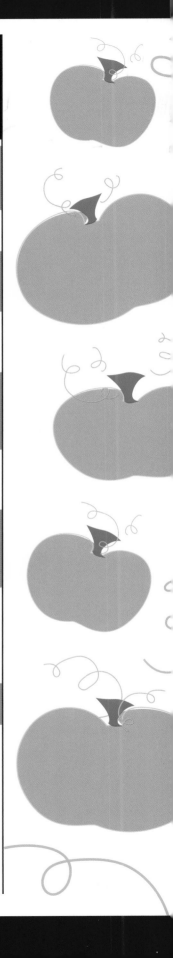

1 Never carry your pumpkin by the stem. It's part of the visual allure, and if it snaps, it can accelerate the pumpkin's rotting. Always carry the pumpkin from the bottom.

2 Store your uncut pumpkin in a cool, dry place. Once pumpkins ripen, they will deteriorate fast—heat and light speed up the process.

3 Wash the exterior of the pumpkin before carving. Use a solution of 1 gallon water and 1 teaspoon chlorine bleach. This will help prevent mold.

4 Draw your pattern on paper or use a pumpkin-carving template. (See pages 241-245 for ideas.) This is easier and cleaner than drawing right on the pumpkin and makes revisions a snap.

5 To transfer a template to the pumpkin, enlarge it, cut it out and adhere it to the pumpkin with masking tape. Then either use pin-pricks to mark the shapes and lines on the pumpkin or use a craft or utility knife and cut through the design to score it on the surface.

6 Don't just think of face designs. Moons, stars, cats and witches are all fun and easy to do. You can even use a drill to make patterned light holes.

7 Consider buying a pumpkin-carving kit. Often they can be found for just a few dollars. Kits usually contain small scoops and serrated saws that aren't commonly found in the typical toolbox. They're great for detailed carving work.

8 When cutting out your shapes, always use a sawing motion. Go slowly and gently. A small serrated saw is best for the detail work. Never try to forcefully cut your pumpkin with a straight-edge razor—you'll damage the pumpkin, hurt the knife and possibly cut yourself!

9 The more pumpkins in your display, the better. Four or five small pumpkins have much more visual impact than one large one.

10 If scraping out a pumpkin is too much hassle for you, consider buying a hollow acrylic or craft pumpkin. These are becoming increasingly popular, thanks to their realistic appearance and their ease in carving. Yes, you carve these soft plastic pumpkins just like a real one; most are made to be about 1/4 inch thick with inside colors that match a real pumpkin. And they last forever, meaning instant jack-o'-lanterns for next year!

Wicked Pumpkin Carving Templates

next page for templates.

1 Boo!

2 Flying Witch

3 Starry Night

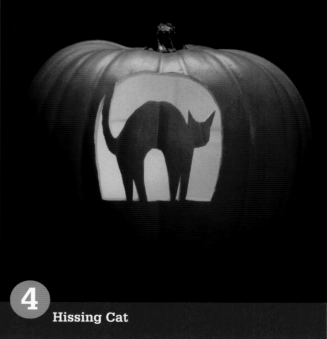

4 Hissing Cat

FUNNY BONE!
Where do fashionable ghosts shop for their clothes? BOO-tiques.

CRAFTS & DECOR

Enlarge any of these templates on a photocopier to the desired size, then follow the tips on page 240 for fantastic results!

1 Boo! Template

2 Flying Witch Template

3 Starry Night Template

4 Hissing Cat Template

Wicked Pumpkin Carving Templates

...ext page for templates.

5 Who, Me?

6 Lopsided Grin

7 Cat's Whiskers

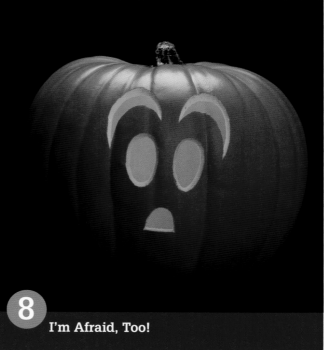

8 I'm Afraid, Too!

FUNNY BONE!
What do mummy children call their parents? Mummy and Deady.

5 Who, Me? Template

6 Lopsided Grin Template

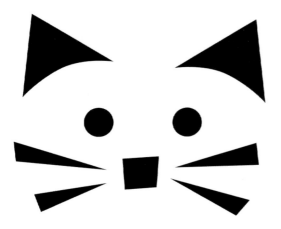

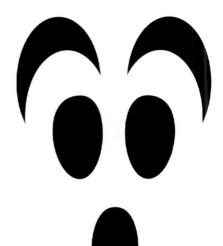

7 Cat's Whiskers Template

8 I'm Afraid, Too! Template

More Pumpkin Design Tricks

Think about light:

art of the art of great pumpkin carv-
g is thinking about shadows. Small
esigns in the back of the pumpkin
an cast a wonderful shadow on a wall
r door behind the pumpkin. Just re-
ember to keep the design small, be-
ause the light that emerges gets mag-
fied. If you are going to do this, be sure
 scrape the inside of the back of your
umpkin to slightly under 1 inch in thick-
ess.

The mouth:

hen you are working on the mouth, you
an make more realistic teeth by only
eeling off the outer skin of the pumpkin
ithin the mouth and leaving the pale
esh beneath. You can then carve lines
etween individual teeth. The candle-
ght will shine through the fleshy
eth, but you can also make an open-
g between upper and lower teeth for
ore light to come through.

Adding pieces:

ou can use the pieces of pumpkin that you
ave carved out to fashion ears and fit them
to slits that you have cut. Or you can use
orks for ears (make holes and wedge them
). You can carve hair at the top of the
umpkin by scraping straight or curling
nes all around the cap. Use a chisel or a
noleum cutter for this. Try a carrot for a
ose or maybe a radish.

Finishing touches:

hen you are finished, use a paper towel to
b petroleum jelly over all the cut surfaces,
side and outside the pumpkin. This will
elp preserve it for several days.

Create a Walkway

*Why not light the path to your front
door with a line of small pumpkins?
Pick small pumpkins and prepare
them as you would a jack-o'-lantern,
except make the opening in the bottom
instead of the top so that you can insert lightbulbs from underneath. Then
run an outdoor string of lights (such as
Christmas lights), and place several
bulbs in each of the pumpkins. As long
as you use approved outdoor lighting,
they will be beautiful and safe.*

Pumpkin Carving Fiesta

On the weekend before Halloween, invite friends and family to a BYOP (bring your own pumpkin) carving party. Dazzle your friends with a well-equipped outdoor workshop (or garage) for the task, with loads of space for people to work and all the tools you'll need. Add in fun music and finger foods appropriate for the messy fun, and it'll be like having two Halloweens in one week!

WHAT YOU'LL NEED

Several sturdy tables each covered with newspapers or disposable plastic cloths

Pumpkin cleaning gear (paper towels, spray bottles of water, small container of baby wipes)

Old T-shirts, dress shirts, or smocks

One pumpkin-carving kit for every three people:

Sharp kitchen knife

Large, strong tablespoon or ice-cream scoop

Sharp-tip marker (non-permanent)

Electric screwdriver or drill with varying bit sizes

Thin-blade serrated saws

Bucket for seeds

Decorating supplies for kids: paints, stickers, etc.

BYOP! (Bring Your Own Pumpkin)

best place for your party is outdoors among
changing leaves and cool breezes of autumn.
have a backup plan for indoors, just in case
ain. Wherever you are, be prepared for a
s! If you can, collect all pumpkin waste for
posting (or pumpkin seed roasting); also
garbage cans around for the soiled news-
rs and paper towels.

t crowd your artists. You'll probably want
nore than three pumpkins being worked
t any given table. So be sure to have am-
olding tables, picnic tables and makeshift
es (plywood on top of sawhorses, for exam-
so everyone has a space to work.

music ready for outdoors. A boom box
ing a collection of Halloween music will
perfect ambience.

diversions ready for the kids. It can take more
an hour to carve a pumpkin, and kids often get
y before the work is complete. Have some mini-
pkins available for painting, face-painting kits,
ecrow-building supplies and party games ready.

Decorate!

Decorate! Help create a
Halloween mood by decorating your workshop with hay
bales, finished jack-o'-lanterns,
gourd displays and more.

ADD TO THE FUN

Want to give your guests extra creative opportunities? Put out a
bowl of precut vegetables and toothpicks. Let them add pieces to their
pumpkins—carrot antennae, broccoli ears, green bean whiskers and so on.

Make it a contest. When the carving is complete, line up the finished jack-o'-
lanterns and either let people cast votes or have a "distinguished panel" make the deci-
sions. Whatever the method, be sure to give out lots of prizes, including silly ones like
"most crooked smile" and "pumpkin you'd least like to meet in a dark alley."

Make it a costume-making party instead. Like a pumpkin carving party, you want to provide your guests all the things they might need for a costume—old clothes, fabrics, scissors, construction paper, decorating supplies, lots of paper for stuffing things, wooden
dowels—the list goes on. Or make it a scavenger costume party—once everyone arrives,
give each person 1 hour and a budget of $20 to jump in the car, find or buy materials and
return to make a costume. Don't forget your camera!

FUNNY BONE!
What is a witch's favorite subject in school? Spelling.

FACE PAINT & COSTUMES

Need some fresh, easy and inexpensive costume ideas? All you need is right here! Learn face-painting techniques from a professional makeup artist, then fashion a no-sew costume and your kids will haunt the streets in style. The best part—you'll save time and money when you follow our expert advice.

crappy the
scarecrow, p. 255

Face Painting
MADE EASY

What makeup professionals know is no longer a secret: You can buy an inexpensive kit of safe, washable face paints and turn your Halloween child into whatever she or he fancies in a matter of minutes!

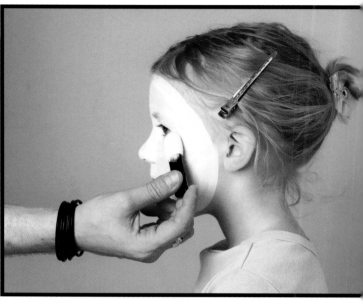

That's what we learned when we invited Broadway and television makeup artist Joel Mendenhall and his assistant Sadiya Sellers to our studios, along with some willing and curious children. We gave Mendenhall strict instructions: Spend less than $10 for makeup supplies per child (with all materials coming from an everyday drugstore), and take 20 minutes or less to apply the makeup.

The results were stunning. We learned that even the most basic and inexpensive face-painting kit allows you to create professional-level mustaches and beards, animal noses and whiskers, quizzical eyebrows and a scarecrow's face. You can paint on a pirate's bandanna that won't come off during the evening's activities. You can paint a panting puppy's tongue under a painted puppy nose.

Fairy princesses can be made more glamorous with fanciful painted eye treatments and glitter, rem cent of New Orleans Mardi Gras masks (see p. 2 A clown is so adorable after a few simple app tion steps (see p. 251 and p. 254).

There's more to Halloween face painting than jus and surprise. There's safety, too. Masks severel strict vision, leading to accidents. There's also an er benefit—with a well-painted face, the rest of costume can be much less elaborate, saving time expense.

If you finish off the makeup job with a dusting of p der, it will be less likely to rub off on clothes and holstery. And at the end of the evening, removing paint is simple: just start the cleanup process commercial pre-moistened towelettes or a washrag with baby shampoo, and follow up wi scrubbing with soap and water.

GETTING STARTED

Buy a face-painting kit (from a craft or discount store) that contains the colors you want and has instructions for completing the design that you have in mind. Although most kits contain safe, washable paints, you might want to do an allergy test on your child. Dab some paint in the crook of the youngster's arm at the elbow. If no rash appears after 12 hours, you can proceed.

Sit your child in a chair that is high enough that you can work on the face without bending over. Tie the hair away from the face. Most kits come with applicators, but you may find that you are more comfortable working with your own. Soft sponges, like stipple sponges from an art store, are good for applying base paints.

Thin paintbrushes or makeup sticks or crayons from the kit are good for making lines. Your own powder puff is best for finishing off the face painting. You can use baby powder to set the paints and brush off the excess with a cosmetic brush.

A BASIC KIT

- **Foundtion makeup (often white, sometimes in a tube)**
- **Four or more colore makeups**
- **Black makeup penc**
- **Paint sticks or crayo in various colors**
- **Application sponge**
- **Application brushes**
- **Step-by-step instruc tions with pictures**

FACE PAINTING 101

RT FRESH: *Begin with a clean face. Pin a towel d the child's neck just in case the makeup drips.*

APPLY THE BASE: *Use a sponge and only dilute the paint if it is too thick to spread.*

THE DETAILS: *Apply second and third colors. blue goes around the eye in an inverted teardrop and red defines a large mouth.*

EMPHASIZE: *Outlining the new color areas with black makes them stand out. Use a paintbrush or makeup stick.*

ESSORIZE: *Props complete the image: a curly green fake red ball nose and an outrageous oversized bow e added.*

JOIN THE FUN: *The youngster from Step 1 is now a bona fide clown, ready for a night of trick-or-treating.*

PRINCESS GRACIE, A GOOD FAIRY

All the colors of her costume—lavender, pink, blue and white—are used in the enchanting design around her eyes. Paintbrushes and makeup sticks were the primary tools, starting with a pink line that defines her eyes and then spreads out toward her temples. Her cheeks and temples were painted lavender with a pad applicator. Blue squiggles were applied next with a paintbrush or makeup stick, which also made the white lines and white dots. Gossamer wings, a beribboned net skirt and a jewel-studded wand complete her costume.

THE MASKED GREEN GO-GETTER, SUPERHERO

The green mask that won't blow away in flight (and is much safer than a plastic one) was speedily applied with a sponge and outlined with a paintbrush. The eyebrows were made with a small pad applicator. A swishing cape attached behind his shoulders allows him to take off quickly.

NICKO,
THE CLOWN

Here is a very quick but lively clown
makeup that doesn't use a base
paint. His eyes are enlarged with
white sponge-applied face paint,
black paintbrush or makeup stick
outlining, and green highlighter
lines (also applied with a
paintbrush or makeup stick).
A big red mouth applied
with a pad applicator is
outlined in white and
black, and black-
rimmed white dimples
dot both ends.
A polka-dot hat,
a big bow tie and
curly green hair
complete the
silliness.

is happy face would hardly scare away a wren,
t it will delight the hosts of Halloween parties.
r makeup starts with a yellow sponge-applied
se. Black paintbrush or makeup stick lines,
ghlighted with white paintbrush lines sew
her mouth, make patches on her forehead
d cheeks and extend her eyes. A straw-
led hat and a straw-stuffed flannel
irt are the perfect accessories.

Costumes!
low-sew, no-sew

"What are you going to be for Halloween?" It's the question that animates kids' conversations each and every October. Look no further for the answers!

When children's imaginations run too wild, it makes life tough for Mom and Dad. Do you rent, buy or spend weeks making an outfit from scratch? Isn't there a compromise that will thrill your child and be easy for you as well?

Absolutely! We asked Catherine Alston, a theatrical costume designer in Vermont, to create easy-to-make costume designs that would please children of all ages and be a relief for parents as well. She certainly delivered!

Catherine showed us that you can quickly improvise any number of wonderful costumes with a little fabric, some common accessories, a hot glue gun, some staples, or if you have a sewing machine, a few stitches.

In the pages ahead, we'll show you how to pull off five quick, inexpensive Halloween transformations.

The ideas will likely get your own imagination go so that when your daughter wants to be an astro or your son wants to be Julius Caesar, you will k just what to do.

The tricks are simple. For example, start with a or scheme that will determine the base garments you need. For example, witches usually wear b turtlenecks and black tights—unless they c from The Wizard of Oz and need colorful tights.

Once you determine the base clothing you n think about the other pieces of the costume. Ca hats, tails, ears and stripes are easily created easy-to-find materials. Chances are, you can ma terrific costume in just 90 minutes! You'll save a tune, thrill your child, amuse other kids and gro ups and feel great that you made it yourself.

Popular Costumes

According to the National Retail Federation, the top five children's costumes in 2006 were: princess, pirate, witch, Spiderman and Superman. The top five for adults were: witch, pirate, vampire, cat and clown. Although traditional costumes never go out of style, current movie characters are often a popular choice, too.

WHAT YOU'LL NEEI

Here are nine items tha are most often needed make a costume:

- Base garments
- Cutting wheel and self-healing mat
- Fabrics
- Hot glue gun
- Needle and thread
- Patterns
- Scissors
- Sewing machine
- Staples

GETTING READY

Once you have an idea for a costume, you might want to check a party store for components you will not have to make: a witch's hat, for example, or a knight's sword. Fabric and craft stores, particularly around Halloween, offer wide assortments of costume materials that won't ravel—like fake furs, felts and fleeces—and endless trimmings that can be sewn or glued on.

The first step in making a costume is to gather the various pieces together and check that you have everything you are going to need. Be sure the basic garments on which you plan to build are clean and pressed.

If you are making one of the costumes in this chapter, read the directions carefully. Check that your tools are ready: extra sticks for the hot glue gun, extra staples for the stapler, the correct color thread for your needles or sewing machine, and so on.

classic witch

You and your child can put together this smashing version of the classic costume in no time.

1	round black tablecloth, 84-inch diameter
1	yard elastic cord
1	yard 1/4-inch black elastic
1	roll electrical tape
1	black turtleneck
1	pair black tights
1	witch hat

1. Fold tablecloth in half, then in quarters, and finally in eighths, giving you a narrow cone of fabric. Measure 4 inches down from the peak and cut the peak off. Discard this fabric. Now measure 10 inches down from the cut and cut again (this will be the cape). The remaining 28 inches of fabric will make the skirt.

2. Open the cape and skirt pieces to semicircles and punch holes 1 inch apart on the inside edges of each. Thread the elastic cord through the holes. Gather the cape and tie it at the neck (see photo below). Shred the ends of the cape.

3. To make the skirt, thread 1/4-inch elastic through the waist holes and gather to fit the youngster's waist. Tie the ends. Shred the bottom. Add reflective tape detailing for nighttime safety.

4. Dress the child in the turtleneck and tights under the costume and add the hat.

snuggly lion

This furry lion costume feels soft and snuggly because it uses a thin, very soft type of fleece available at most fabric stores.

1/2	yard (18 x 60 inches) lightweight brown-and-tan-patterned fleece
1	yellow sleeper
1	yellow baby cap with ties
1	square (12 inches) brown felt
1	square (12 inches) tan felt
1	square (12 inches) yellow felt

1. To make the lion's mane, cut the fleece into three pieces, each 6 x 60 inches. Layer the pieces on top of each other and stitch or staple them together down the center of the 60-inch length. On both sides of the three-layer strip, make cuts at 1/2-inch intervals almost to (but not through) the 60-inch stitch line (see photo at right). Measure the neck of the sleeper and cut a piece of the three-layered, clipped mane to match. Attach this strip to the neck of the sleeper along the stitch line (see photo on p. 259, top). Use the remaining mane strips to trim the cap in three rows. Save an inch of the mane strips to finish off the end of the tail. Fold back and fluff the fleece strips.

2. Cut two outer ear pieces from the brown felt and two inner ear pieces from the tan felt, using the photo at right as a guide. Glue inner ear pieces to outer ear pieces and attach to cap with a glue gun, staple, or needle and thread.

3. Make the tail by cutting a 2 x 12-inch strip of yellow felt. Fold the strip in half lengthwise and staple or stitch together. Invert and attach fleece tassel to one end (see photo at right). Attach the other end to the back of the sleeper.

4. Dress baby in sleeper and cap.

lion's mane

lion's ear

lion's tail

Kids' Costumes

Most adult and older kids' costumes have intricate ʍ and accessories that make them unique, but toddle costumes need to be simpler. Using a sleeper as the and adding soft fleece not only makes this costume and comfortable, it keeps the baby warm and cozy

attach mane to
neck of sleeper

attach flowers
to headband

bouquet of flowers

Turn your tiny trick-or-treater into a bouquet of flowers, and no one will be able to resist!

1	bunch fabric flowers from a craft store

Soft headband

12	yellow felt circles, ½-inch diameter (optional)
1	yard green yarn
1	yellow shirt
1	pair yellow pants
6	fabric leaves from a craft store

1. Remove as much plastic from flowers and leaf stems as possible to make them lie flat. Attach flowers to headband with stitching or hot glue until headband is covered (see photo on p. 260, top). Glue yellow felt circles to center of flowers if desired.

2. Cut 18 inches of yarn and place it on the front of the shirt in a flower stem pattern (see top photo on this page). Sew or glue it in place. Use the remaining yarn to continue the pattern down one pant leg, matching the overlap (see photo at left). Sew or glue in place.

3. Attach leaves along the stem.

4. Dress child in shirt, pants and headband.

er stem
ern on shirt

er stem
ern on pants

easy ladybug

Ladybugs are the one crawly creature most kids find fun, cute and friendly. Any child will feel the same wearing this simple, comfortable costume.

2	pieces (12 x 18 inches) stiff red felt
1	piece (12 x 18 inches) black felt
2	hook-and-loop stick-on buttons
2	large black chenille pipe cleaners
1	regular black pipe cleaner
1	square (12 inches) stick-on black felt
1	black headband
1	black turtleneck top
1	pair black leggings

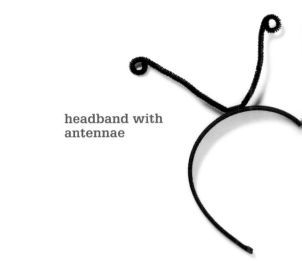

headband with antennae

1. To make the ladybug's wings, draw a semicircle on each piece of stiff red felt. You can attach a 12-inch piece of string to a pencil and, holding the string end midway on the 18-inch side of the felt, draw a semicircle by swinging the pencil in an arc. Curve the top of each wing as shown at right.

2. To make the yoke, fold the black felt piece in half lengthwise. At the center of the folded edge, cut a 5-inch, curved neck opening. Curve the outer edges of the yoke and cut the center open as shown in the photo at right.

3. Attach the top of the wings to the back of the yoke with glue or needle and thread. Add hook-and-loop buttons to either side of the yoke opening. Sew or glue the large chenille pipe cleaners to the outside joints between the yoke and the wings: these are the bug's extra legs.

4. Use a glass to trace 7 black dots on the stick-on black felt. Cut out the dots and stick them to the ladybug wings as shown at right.

5. Glue the center of the regular black pipe cleaner to the center of the headband. Reinforce it with a strip of black stick-on felt. Curl ends of pipe cleaner to complete the antennae.

6. Dress the child in the black turtleneck, leggings, wings with yoke and headband.

yoke with wings attached

ass
astplate)

isse
igh)

greave
(shin)

lmet

helmet

silver knight

You'll need to visit a hardware store, a sports store and a party shop for the components of this costume unless, of course, you have items around the house that will do.

1	gray hooded sweatshirt
1	roll of silver insulation
2	foam kneepads with elastic holders
6	yards elastic cord
1	pair gray sweatpants
1	roll clear tape, 2 inches wide
4	black shoelaces, 27 inches each
1	paper paint bucket, 5-quart size
1	plastic or cardboard shield
1	plastic sword

1. To make the armor, start with the leg pieces. You need to cut out of the insulation two cuisse pieces to cover the thighs and two greave pieces to cover the shins. The kneepads will cover the knees. Measure your child's legs and cut pieces in the shapes shown at left.

2. Punch holes in the insulation pieces as shown in the photo on the facing page. Punch two holes in top of each kneepad and two holes at the bottom. Thread a 30-inch elastic cord through top of each cuisse piece and each greave piece. Tread a 24-inch elastic cord through one bottom and one top kneehole on the left side and then repeat on the right side. Use these cords to attach kneepads to cuisse and greave pieces as shown on facing page. Fit these pieces on the youngster over the sweatpants. Tighten the knee elastic and tie it off.

3. To make the breastplate, or cuirass, cut a piece of silver insulation 16 x 36 inches according to the photo above left. Fold under side edges 1 inch and tape down with clear tape. Curve bottom ends and tape down with clear tape. Cut center back opening and neck opening. Punch four holes on each side of back opening. Thread laces as shown in photo above left and tie. Glue shield to center of front.

4. To make helmet, trace sides and top of bucket on paper to make a pattern. Add 1 inch on each edge, cut out pattern, and use to cut out silver insulation. Cut face opening in bucket, according to photo at left. Carefully glue silver insulation all around bucket. Cut face opening in insulation, leaving 1 inch extra to fold back and glue. Turn under top and bottom edges of silver insulation and glue down. Glue round insulation piece to top.

5. Dress the child in the sweatshirt, cuirass, helmet, shield and sword.

making a mask

Here's basic wisdom for fun and effective mask making.

1. Get a mask that—like a good pair of sunglasses—fits comfortably, can be worn for an extended length of time and complements your facial shape. If you are going to decorate the mask, make sure it has a surface that is easy to work with. Some masks are easy to draw on but don't hold glue well; others are the opposite.

2. Make sure there are extra-large holes for your eyes. They generally look better than smaller eye holes and are much easier to see through.

3. Be creative! Be prepared for the mask to take on its own life as you progress.

4. If you're a beginner, don't try to create a symmetrical design because it can be very hard to achieve. Asymmetrical designs are often more alluring and individualistic.

5. Less is more. Once the glue is pouring, it's easy to get crazy with glitter, stars and pompons. Then suddenly you're not a mysterious baroness but a circus clown!

6. If you paint your mask, shade it by making recessed areas darker and protruding areas lighter. This will immediately distinguish your mask from others.

7. Think about fun add-ons. Consider using feathers, fabrics, stones, ribbons, chain, beads and more. Add details that make the mask your own.

8. Reinforce the band that holds the mask to your face so you are assured it will withstand several hours of wearing. And just in case, keep extra elastic bands in your pocket or purse in case the mask band snaps.

9. Like any craft, you can take mask making to highly advanced levels. If you find that a craft-store mask is too simple for you, then explore the many books that teach the art of mask making for Mardi Gras or for specific cultures or religions. You may find yourself involved in a whole new hobby!

Mask-Making Lore

The wearing of masks dates back to primitive people, who most likely made and wore them to imitate game animals to improve hunts. Back then, masks weren't costumes or art, but functional objects that brought food, fertility or healing. Later on, the Greeks introduced theatrical masks for their plays, and the Halloween and Mardi Gras parties in New Orleans made the decoration of "false faces" both popular and fun! Today, masks are a central part of Halloween traditions all over the globe.

ative Ideas for Mask Making

put whatever you want on your mask, and you'll find that the more personalized it is, the more you'll like
can add traditional decor, such as glitter, feathers and pompons (see the examples below), but you can also
ividual flair, too. Add extra googly eyes, letters, stick-on metallic shapes, even small photos. Just remember
the design simple—the goal is to express yourself and have fun in the process!

FUNNY BONE!
What is a baby ghost's favorite game? Peek-a-BOO!

bewitching bashes 267